Tastes of the Empire

Tastes of the Empire
Foreign Foods in Seventeenth Century England

JILLIAN AZEVEDO

McFarland & Company, Inc., Publishers
Jefferson, North Carolina

ISBN (print) 978-1-4766-6862-8
ISBN (ebook) 978-1-4766-3117-2

LIBRARY OF CONGRESS CATALOGUING DATA ARE AVAILABLE

BRITISH LIBRARY CATALOGUING DATA ARE AVAILABLE

© 2017 Jillian Azevedo. All rights reserved

No part of this book may be reproduced or transmitted in any form or by any means, electronic or mechanical, including photocopying or recording, or by any information storage and retrieval system, without permission in writing from the publisher.

Front cover illustrations © 2017 iStock

Printed in the United States of America

*McFarland & Company, Inc., Publishers
Box 611, Jefferson, North Carolina 28640
www.mcfarlandpub.com*

In Memoriam
John J. Azevedo, Jr.
(1933–2016)

Acknowledgments

My fascination with the history of food and what it could reveal about a society began during my graduate studies at UC Riverside where this project first began as my dissertation. I am especially thankful to my advisor, Thomas Cogswell, along with my two other dissertation committee members, Jonathan Eacott and Christine Ward Gailey, for their invaluable guidance and advice. I am confident that this book would not have taken its current shape if it were not for their counsel and feedback. I am eternally grateful for the support and encouragement that I received from V.P. Franklin while working at *The Journal of African American History* as well. His wisdom and advice served as points of inspiration when I needed it most.

I cannot thank enough those who have taken time out of their busy schedules to offer advice, read passages, or function as sounding boards as I work through a research or writing dilemma. Justin Reed, Stephanie Wilms Simpson, and Ea Madrigal, in particular, have been consistent sources of assistance throughout this project. I'll be forever grateful for the countless hours they've each spent discussing various aspects of this book over lunch, drinks, or even baseball games.

I gratefully salute my colleagues at the University Writing Program at UC Davis; even as we were just getting to know one another, many of them encouraged me to undertake this book project, although it felt like a daunting task at the time. Working alongside of them has truly been a privilege and I know my writing, and therefore this book, has greatly benefited because of it.

Ultimately, I am indebted to my family who has offered their unwavering love and encouragement through all my academic and professional endeavors. Words cannot explain how invaluable the support of my parents, Mike and Leslie Azevedo, and grandparents, John and Geri Azevedo and Burns and Esther Baker, have been. I would not be the woman, the scholar, or the author that I am today without them.

Table of Contents

Preface   1
Introduction   7

1. Culinary Travels: William Dampier
   and Travel Narratives   19
2. "Let the skie raine Potatoes": Foreign Foods
   in English Plays   49
3. "The Queens Closet Opened"   72
4. Foreign Additives in Domestic Remedies   95
5. Vices and Virtues: Tobacco, Chocolate, Coffee,
   and Tea in Print   122

Conclusion   152
Appendix: English Plays Featuring Foreign Foods   161
Chapter Notes   178
Bibliography   196
Index   213

Preface

Several genres of historical research have touched on foreign foods in early modern England and the implications that can be drawn from their consumption. As of yet, however, none have come together in an effort to understand what a study of foreign foods in seventeenth century texts and culture can tell us. Studies of medieval and modern English cookery books and the non–European goods they call for have been completed, yet they ignore the period when transoceanic trade routes where first emerging and foreign foods were made more accessible. This is not surprising, though, as Katharina Vester contends that just "thirty years ago, food and its discourses were mostly neglected by academe.... Food belonged to the private sphere and therefore was not of obvious scholarly interest; it was a topic slightly too mundane, too feminine, and (within the context of affluent societies) insufficiently political. But recent scholarship has enthusiastically endorsed the importance of food as a lens for approaching the past, or a gateway to studying culture."[1]

Within this recent scholarship, a great deal of work has been done on European medieval cuisine including the foreign spices that were popular during the time. These texts offer a survey of the period being analyzed, describing the common elements of European diet, as well as European endeavors to gain access to the spice trade. These include Ken Albala's *Cooking in Europe, 1250–1650* as well as his *The Banquet: Dining in the Great Courts of Late Renaissance Europe* and *Eating Right in the Renaissance*, Paul Freedman's *Out of the East: Spices and the Medieval Imagination*, Jack Turner's *Spice: The History of Temptation*, John Keay's *The Spice Route: A History*, Andrew Dalby's *Dangerous Tastes: The Story of Spices*, and Michael Krondl's *The Taste of Conquest*. Such studies provide excellent background information regarding the

Preface

state of the European diet prior to the early modern period and especially the way that foreign foods such as spices were consumed prior to transoceanic trade routes.

Other authors have chosen to look specifically at England, restricting their study to either specific periods or regions. Kate Colquhoun's *Taste: The Story of Britain Through its Cooking,* L.A. Clarkson and E. Margaret Crawford's *Feast and Famine,* Joan Thirsk's *Food in Early Modern England,* Annette Hope's *Londoners' Larder,* Maguelonne Toussaint-Samat *A History of Food,* and Joan Fitzpatrick's *Food in Shakespeare* are all texts that explore the emergence and popularity of certain foods in differing aspects of English culture. While such studies prove insightful, they do not explore the relationship between foreign foods and seventeenth century English consumers.

Still others have written histories of food items, illustrating the importance that particular products have had for prolonged periods of time. Sidney W. Mintz's *Sweetness and Power,* Brian Cowan's *The Social Life of Coffee,* Gary Y. Okihiro's *Pineapple Culture,* Sandra Sherman's "The Pineapple in England," William Gervase Clarence-Smith's *Cocoa and Chocolate,* Mark McWilliams' "The American Pumpkin," and Andrew F. Smith's "The Fall and Rise of the Edible Turkey" all focus on the history of one particular food item. While such studies do provide a better understanding of the food in question, they lack any explanation of the integration of foreign foods into English culture.

Endeavoring to illustrate this importance, some scholars have examined the relationship between foods and their introduction into foreign societies, especially those that were part of the Columbian Exchange. First discussed by Alfred W. Crosby, the notion of the Columbian Exchange is that during an age of Old World exploration and colonization of the Americas, an exchange of cultural commodities was taking place between the two entities.[2] While Crosby and other scholars have chosen to concentrate on many aspects of this exchange, including food items as well as diseases, people, animals, textiles, and ideas, some have chosen to look at only certain aspects. Reay Tannahill and Linda Civitello, for example, chose to narrow their scope to identify the role that food products have had in the relationship between the Old World and the New. The problem that seems apparent in the majority of texts concentrating on the Columbian Exchange, though,

Preface

is that they overwhelmingly focus on the influence the exchange had on the Americas. While it is commonly acknowledged that Europeans gained material and knowledge from this trans-Atlantic relationship, little work has been done to analyze the affect that, for example, American foods had on the Europeans who consumed them.

The few works that have endeavored to explore the connection between foreign foods and their English consumers have come to the conclusion that this relationship was not fully developed or even relevant until the modern era. In an article on imperial foods, Troy Bickham argues that foods from the empire did not become popular until the eighteenth century, citing, amongst other things, the price of sugar, the amount of food imported by the English, the emergence of pictorial advertisements, and the notion that English cookery books did not become popular until after the 1730s.[3] Carole Shammas also indicates that the English did not begin consuming imperial foods, or at least not a rate that could be considered important, until the 1700s, again citing foreign trade statistics and comparing them to those of the seventeenth century to show how much importation had expanded.[4] While foreign foods certainly did grow in popularity in the eighteenth century, they were by no means absent in English culture prior to that. By ignoring the importance of foreign foods before the mid 1700s, scholars such as Bickham and Shammas are only able to provide a partial picture of the ways in which foods were able to influence English perception of their expanding empire.

This is a sentiment that Ken Albala hints at in several of his works, though one he never fully explores. Although the majority of Albala's works stays rooted in medieval or Renaissance culinary culture, he notes that cookery books can be clearly driven by religious, cultural, or political agendas. Speaking briefly of the colonial cookery books of British India, he states, "one might argue that all exotic cookbooks appeal to those for whom strange new tastes are a substitute for real foreign travel and real colonization. They are a way of appropriating the other by consuming their cultural products…. They aim toward people who generally don't have the wherewithal to go half way around the world to be served a meal."[5] This appropriation of the cultural products of those who have been colonized is happening at around the same time that he contends early modern European countries were forging

Preface

distinct identities, partly through "codifying what might be called a national cuisine."[6] Thus, Albala touches on the idea that foods foreign to England from other areas of the British Empire are an element of the forging of a new imperial identity occurring during the seventeenth century.

Although focused more on slavery than food products, Susan Dwyer Amussen's *Caribbean Exchanges* comes closest to understanding the effect that foreign objects and people had on the English during the seventeenth century. While Amussen does examine the influence the English had on their Caribbean territories, she also spends equal, if not more, time illustrating the affect that New World people and objects had on English society. Using the Helyar family as an example of men who developed Caribbean plantations while their family remained in England, Amussen illustrates that the English not only took many of their traditions and products to the Caribbean, but that the men who communicated with and traveled back home took products and even people from the Caribbean with them to England. As Amussen brilliantly illustrates, this allowed for a sharing of foods, peoples, material objects, and also encouraged the English to view themselves as members of a larger Empire, not just an island state. In crafting her study this way, Amussen does not fall into the problem that so many other scholars writing about the Columbian Exchange have, as she analyzes the impact of foreign goods in both New World and Old World societies. Unlike Bickham and Shammas, she sees the importance of examining the period before the eighteenth century, even though many of the topics she addresses certainly did become more prevalent during that period.[7]

Another important aspect of Amussen's text is that she includes the idea that English women were actors in the development of a larger empire, especially during the seventeenth century. Describing the use of black servants in portraits of noble women, Amussen depicts the way women were capable of bringing colonial objects to the forefront of society's thoughts. She states that, "in contrast to the dramatic depictions of the colonies, most of which kept slavery firmly offstage, these paintings placed slaves clearly in view."[8] The black children in these portraits are certainly included as objects of display, such as a piece of jewelry might be, but their inclusion is important when endeavoring

Preface

to understand women and their role in empire building. Although English women were not exploring or conquering new lands for the crown, and often times not even living in settler colonies in the new territories, they actively adopted elements of the empire into their daily life, as these portraits illustrate. Thus, when provided the opportunity, seventeenth century English women were engaging in empire building activities.

This is apparent in an examination of contemporary cookery books, written for and occasionally by women, and the foreign foods included in them. As Gilly Lehman argues in her *The British Housewife*, sixteenth and seventeenth century women were at the center of any culinary activity that took place in their home and their family's diet. Because of this, the inclusion of foreign foods in cookery books demonstrates that women were eager to engage with foreign products that were made available in the domestic marketplace because of England's growing empire.

This relationship stretches into cookbook recipes that were meant to instruct women how to concoct homemade medicinal remedies rather than just dishes for a meal. As Andrew Wear argues in his *Knowledge and Practice in English Medicine*, there was a link in early modern England between cooking food and making medicine that "placed medicine squarely in the realm of the kitchen and women's work."[9] This is, at least in part, due to the fact that humor theory, which dictated early modern English medicinal practices, also played a role in the preparation of foods, linking cooking and doctoring together. He further goes on to contend that although many of the remedies offered to lay women were based on those used by contemporary doctors or prescribed by ancient Latin texts, they were reinvented to fit into the household economy.[10] Because of the adaption that recipes would often undergo before they were published in cookery books for housewives, new ingredients, including foreign foods, were often added in an effort to modernize them.

Looking specifically at medicinal recipes and the way they evolved throughout the early modern period, Jennifer K. Stine contends that though medical remedies did undergo revisions, they most commonly did not rely on foreign ingredients. She states that, "while an intrepid few Englishmen and women looked outward to continental Europe, the Far East, and the New World for new medicines, many more searched locally."[11] Although the majority of the ingredients that medicinal recipes called for did come from the British Isles, even Stine herself notes that foreign products such as sugar, guaiacum, tobacco, coca, ipecacuanha, plantains, nutmeg, cinnamon, pepper, ginger, and cloves were being used in medicines throughout the early modern period.[12]

It becomes clear, then, that whether the female head of the household was doing the cooking herself or delegating it to an employed servant, she was responsible for the preparation of food for the family meals. Therefore, the mistress of the house would be in contact with the ingredients that cookery books called for, including foreign foods that were being integrated into English cuisines and medicinal recipes. Early modern English cookery books, and English gender and class norms provide the image that English women were using cookery books calling for foreign products; but no comprehensive study on this has been conducted.

With an increasing number of cookery books being published in the seventeenth century corresponding with the increasing availability of foreign products, it is important to understand what impact these foods had on the society consuming them. This is even truer when the various elements of popular culture that reference foreign foods are considered as well. Together, cookery books and medical texts as well as travel narratives, plays, and tracts and treatises extolling the virtues of foreign products indicate that foreign foods were being consumed at an unprecedented rate in seventeenth century England and cannot and should not be ignored.

Introduction

Like many of the cookery books published in the seventeenth century, *The Queens Closet Opened*, published in 1661, contains recipes for food dishes as well as home remedies for a variety of ailments. One such recipe for a cure, entitled "A green oyntment good for Bruises, Swellings, and Wrenches in Man, Horse, or othr Beast." advises the reader to:

> Take six pound of May Butter unsalted, Oyl Olive one quarter, Barrows-grease four pound, Rosin, and Turpentine, of each one pound, Frankincense half a pound: then take these following-Hearbs, of each one handful: Balm, Smallege, Lovage, Red Sage, Lavender, Cotton, Marjoram, Rosemary, Mallows, Cammomile, Plaintain, Alheal, Chickweed, Rue, Parsley, Comfrey, Laurel leaves, Birch leaves, Longwort, English Tobacco, Groundswel, Woundwort, Agrimony, Briony, Carduus Benedictus, Betony, Adders Tongue, Saint Johns-wort, pick all these, wash them clean, and strain the water clean of them... For a man [to use] it must be well chafed in the Palme of the hand three or four times. If you use it for a Horse, put to it Brimstone finely beaten, and work it altogether, as aforesaid.[1]

The fermentation of this mixture may seem to be the most fascinating part, as the recipe later calls for the ointment to be set in "a Horse Dunghil one and twenty days." Yet even more interesting is the diversity of the ingredients used. Although many of the ingredients, like betony, birch leaves, and St. John's wort, are indigenous to Europe, what stands out are those that came from abroad. After all, the frankincense, cotton, plantains, and tobacco called for in this medicinal recipe were the products of English interaction with the Americas, Africa, and Asia.

This integration of foreign goods into seventeenth century English recipes goes beyond the initial excitement of experimenting with foreign food items and illustrates a theme that was apparent in other

Introduction

aspects of English culture as well. Foods from Asia, Africa, and the Americas were being displayed, discussed, imagined, and commented on in contemporary books, broadsides, tracts, and even plays. While some foods were more apparent than others, it is obvious that the English were imagining and employing the dietary resources gained from their interactions with foreign lands.

Not only did the incorporation of foreign foods revolutionize English popular culture, but it also provided women a way to actively engage with England's growing seventeenth century empire without leaving their homes. The fact that the English were reaping the benefits of the new territories their country acquired indicates that they were becoming aware that their state, once restricted to the British Isles, was expanding into an overseas empire; an empire that could offer them new practical as well as luxury goods.

English Food Culture Before 1600

To understand the role foreign foods played in seventeenth century England, it's first important to understand what English men and women were consuming leading up to this period. Prior to the 1600s, the English diet relied heavily on breads and meat dishes. Barley bread had long been the staple for most English men and women, except in the north where oat bread was preferred. By the end of the fifteenth century, the elite were consuming wheat bread as barley bread had been stigmatized as bread for the poorer classes. The most popular form of meat in the medieval period was mutton followed by beef, pork, and poultry. In some regions of England, the consumption of goat meat was not uncommon either. Fish was also an important component of their diet, especially considering rules for fasting that existed in pre–Reformation England. Dairy products, such as cow's milk, curds, and whey, were considered to be lower class foods; in upper-class households, ewe's milk replaced cow's milk, and cheese was occasionally eaten. Herbs and native greenery became important ingredients, as the keeping of gardens became important amongst all classes.[2]

Spices played an important role in English food culture as well and were arguably the most sought after foreign food products before

Introduction

the seventeenth century. Spices proved popular for many reasons, including the social distinction that came with being able to afford them. Many scholars have claimed that since meat, game, and fish were consumed at all levels of society, spices were used to improve the taste of meat in an effort to differentiate the upper class cuisine from that of lower classes. This contradicts the long held notion that spices were used with meats in medieval Europe to act as a preservative. Referring to this "false idea," Paul Freedman contends that it "constitutes something of an urban legend, a story so instinctively attractive that mere fact seems unable to wipe it out. Actually, spices don't do much to preserve meat compared with salting, smoking, pickling, or air curing. The bad taste of spoilt meat, in any event, [would not] be substantially allayed by spices, or anything else."[3] Instead, spices were paired with meats to satisfy the fashionable desire for acidic or bitter meat sauces as well as to signify wealth.

Overland trade routes from Asia allowed Europeans access to spices throughout the medieval period, yet the cost to transport these items prohibited them from being affordable to any but the elite. As Erik Gilbert and Jonathan T. Reynolds contend, "for European noblemen, the consumption of spice was one way of showing wealth."[4] For those in England who could afford it, Asian spices such as pepper, saffron, ginger, nutmeg, cinnamon, and cloves were very popular. Spices were not used sparingly by the upper class, despite costs. As Ken Albala has argued, spices, and especially sugar, were used in large quantities throughout the sixteenth century, as one would not want to seem as if they were "tightfisted." He concludes that this "not only proclaims the lengths a person [would] go to flavor food but [that food] is also the most conspicuous form of consumption."[5] Because of this, spices were quite popular with the upper class and proved to be a lucrative business to those who imported and sold them.

The disdain for the "speciarius," an urban spice seller, and the wealth he accumulated is prevalent in contemporary print culture as well.[6] In *Piers Plowman,* William Langland portrays vendors of spices in a less than flattering light, contending that they make their fortune from a trade based on the gluttonous desires of others.[7] The gluttonous aspect of the sale and consumption of spices during this period is a common theme in contemporary print. With spices being an expensive

Introduction

commodity in medieval England, it was not uncommon for religiously minded authors to accuse those consuming them of committing one of the seven deadly sins. This, however, did nothing to curb the consumption of spices amongst those who could afford them.

Another aspect of the popularity of spices is the credibility given to Galenic medical treatises and especially humoral theories. As Freedman notes, "the importance of spices in the diet, according to theories of health in the Middle Ages, was their role in harmonizing the body's primary fluids, or humors, liquids that caused moods and affected character, and whose imbalance was a major cause of disease."[8] Because spices were viewed as having hot and dry properties, they were paired with meats and fishes, many of which were believed to have moist and cold properties.[9] In fact, these theories were so influential that the English continued to rely heavily on spices until the seventeenth century when "the humoral theory and Galenic medicine in general were challenged first by Paracelsian and then by Helmontian medicine, both of [which were] based on chemical principles."[10] This allowed for a healthy shift away from spices, causing a change in taste preferences to occur.[11]

The new medical theories of the late seventeenth century corresponded with new culinary desires to emphasize the flavor of a dish's main ingredient. As Albala has noted, "distinction of taste no longer depended on the quantity of food served or the exotic seasoning but on meticulous preparation, careful blending of flavoring and reduction, and, more importantly, the invention of new techniques such as roux-thickened stocks, butter-based sauces, and a preference for salty flavors rather than spiced ones."[12] While spices never went out of use, their popularity and specialness dwindled. Instead, fruit garnishes began to play an increasing role in meals, especially adding to the esthetic appeal of the plate if they were foreign fruits. Sugar and aromatic perfumes, both of which became more attainable through transoceanic trade routes, were also increasingly popular in seventeenth century food culture.

It was the original desire for spices, however, that brought about oceanic explorations, which made these foreign fruits, sugar, and aromatics more easily accessible to Europeans. Christopher Columbus set out in 1492 in search of spices, endeavoring to find a westward passage

Introduction

to India where they were available in abundance. Although he did not find India, the lands of the New World offered a variety of new foods, such as turkeys, pineapples, potatoes, and pumpkins, as well as some of the spices that Europe had long been importing from the east, including cinnamon, nutmeg, and sugar. Only a few years later in 1497, the Portuguese explorer Vasco da Gama sailed around the African Cape of Good Hope to India where he was able to buy a cargo of pepper to take back to Europe.[13] Both these voyages, and the future trade networks that developed from them, revolutionized the way that Europeans consumed foreign foods and drugs. Since maritime trade proved much more cost effective than overland routes, foods that previously only the elite could afford became more accessible during the seventeenth century to a wider array of people.

English Trade Endeavors

Although the Spanish and the Portuguese were the first to fund explorations that revolutionized transoceanic trade and colonization, other European entities including the English and the Dutch were not far behind. One outstanding difference between European colonizers was the manner in which they regarded agriculture. Despite the fact that transoceanic trade began with hopes of procuring spices, the Spanish and Portuguese quickly became preoccupied with the precious metals that could be obtained, especially in the New World. As Anthony Pagden argues, this preoccupation with gold and silver, along with other precious metals, caused them to neglect the development of agriculture and trade in their foreign possessions. By the beginning of the seventeenth century it had become apparent to the English, as well as other foreign powers, that their future fortunes lay in trade.[14] Susan Dwyer Amussen argues that the primary goal of English colonies was to produce products that the English could either consume themselves or trade on the European market.[15] Because of this, the empire that the English constructed was very different than that of the Spanish and Portuguese and almost entirely centered on trade.

Beginning in 1496, England's Henry VII granted John Cabot and his group of merchants a charter to sail north, east, or west, allowing

Introduction

them to land along the inhospitable shores of what is now Nova Scotia. Less than one hundred years later, Elizabeth I granted Sir Walter Raleigh permission to establish the historically ill-fated Roanoke Island colony, the first English colony in the New World. Following this, in 1609, the English royal charter for the Virginia Company established a claim for all of North America.[16] Only ten years later, enslaved Africans were first imported into Virginia to serve as the agricultural labor force, making it clear that agricultural developments were a prime goal in North America. In the late 1620s, Charles I gave the first proprietary patents for the islands of the Caribbean from St. Eustatius to Barbados. The English further strengthened their presence in the Caribbean by defeating the Spanish in Jamaica and taking control of the island from them.[17]

From these New World colonies, the English were able to gain foods that were both familiar and unheard of to Europeans. New World products such as maize, green beans, a variety of squashes, tomatoes, potatoes, nasturtium, Jamaica spice, vanilla, cochineal, grapefruits, pineapples, hazelnuts, peanuts, turkeys and chocolate were native to various regions in North and South America but foreign to the rest of the world.[18] While new foods from the Americas did help to enhance European culinary culture, the most significant New World food product was unarguably sugar.

Sugar was present in Europe centuries before Christopher Columbus landed in the New World. Prior to the sixteenth century, sugar was mainly imported from India, as well as from Cyprus, Crete, Madeira, and the Canary Islands in Europe.[19] However, because of overland transportation costs and the insufficient quantities of sugar being produced compared to its demand, sugar prices remained high and mostly consumed by the elite. Sugar cultivation thrived in the Americas, though, and could be produced cheaply due to slaves imported from Africa. Amussen contends that in 1660, the English imported approximately 8,000 tons of sugar, primarily from Barbados, and by 1700 that number had jumped to approximately 23,500 tons.[20]

With this surge in sugar production and more effective trade routes, the way that the English consumed the product was revolutionized. No longer a luxury item, sugar became affordable to those farther down the social ladder and became a staple in seventeenth

Introduction

century diets. Other spices that could be produced in the Americas followed a similar pattern as well. The prices of black pepper, cinnamon, ginger, and saffron were all brought down due to more effective trade routes and additional areas of production outside of Asia.[21] Thus, sweet and spicy cuisine was no longer a privilege only the rich could afford.

Early modern English trade expanded beyond the Americas as well. Elizabeth I granted royal charters to the Levant Company in 1581 and the East India Company in 1600.[22] In the fifteenth and sixteenth centuries, Europeans were regularly importing goods from the Levant such as pepper, ginger, cloves, nutmeg, cumin, galangal, almonds, and even cotton.[23] In the seventeenth century, coffee was added to that list and was integrated into English culture. As Brian Cowan has noted, coffee was an unknown product prior to the fifteenth century when it was adopted into drinking practices of peoples around the Red Sea Basin. It then spread to the Ottoman Empire in the sixteenth century, where English travelers and merchants began to observe and comment upon the Turkish practice of drinking coffee.[24] This quickly led to the importation of coffee to the British Isles and, along with the importation of chocolate and tea, led to what many historians have dubbed the "hot beverage revolution" of the seventeenth century.

Even bigger than coffee and the Levant Company, however, was the British East India Company. In the fifteenth and sixteenth centuries, the Portuguese controlled the Asian "spice islands." To maximize their profits, they enforced strict monopolies, making it impossible for other European countries to trade directly with the islands. In an effort to break into the spice trade, Elizabeth I founded the East India Company (EIC) and granted it "the sole power to trade east of the Cape of Good Hope to the Straights of Magellan."[25] The Dutch likewise established an East India Company, Vereenigde Oost-Indische Compagnie (VOC), in 1602. While the EIC and VOC were often at odds with one another, they were both successful at chipping away at the Portuguese spice monopoly and taking control for themselves.

Never neglecting an opportunity, the English began to move into Africa during the 1640s after the Dutch had broken the Portuguese monopoly along the western coast of the continent. Twenty years later, after the British Civil War and Interregnum, Charles II granted the

Introduction

Royal African Company, led by the Duke of York, a royal charter.[26] Unlike European trade with the Americas, Asia, or the Ottoman Empire, exports from Africa were much less diverse. Enslaved Africans, gold, and ivory were the leading European exports during the seventeenth century, with other products such as hides and malaguetta pepper only making up a small percentage of miscellaneous exports.[27] Such exportations did benefit other European trade networks. Without enslaved Africans, American sugar production, on a large scale, would not have been possible. The gold exported from Africa was used to trade for spices in many Asian ports.[28] But while African foodstuffs may not have been popular in early modern Europe, the plants that could be used for medicinal purposes certainly were. The publication of Dutch manuscripts revealing what the Dutch West India Company, Geoctroyeerde Westindische Compagnie (GWIC), was trading in has helped historians discern popular products for European trade networks in Africa. In these manuscripts, pages are devoted to the plasters, ointments, syrups, purgatives and waters that can be made from a variety of different African plants. There is further evidence that Europeans exported these plants out of Africa, although again not at the levels of slaves or gold.[29]

Intellectual Consumption

With all of these foreign trade networks in place, it is clear that by the early seventeenth-century the English, like their European counterparts, were becoming increasingly able to consume products from outside of Europe. While there were other foreign objects being incorporated into seventeenth century English culture, for example furs or textiles, the consumption of foreign foods proves especially intriguing. Commenting on the culture of English consumption in general, Joyce Appleby states that due to the disappearance of threats of famine, a population boom, and world commerce, "English men and women in the middle of the seventeenth century ... crossed a barrier which divided them from their own past and from every other contemporary society."[30] This was especially true when considering foreign foods, since the consumption of food products in general is essential to daily life. As Sidney Mintz notes, "our tastes and habits in other spheres of

Introduction

consumption—dress, say, or music—while also important to us and to our self-conceptions, do not approach food in significance."[31] The consumption of foreign foods, therefore, plays a more integral role in the consumer's life than that of a foreign hat or dress.

Looking at seventeenth century culture and the way that foreign foods and drugs were integrated into it, it is clear the English were considering and envisioning these products even before they had access to them. This is important, as it would take some foods longer than others to reach English domestic markets; American fruits, for example, were notoriously hard to grow in England and could not withstand a transoceanic voyage. Their inclusion in texts and plays, however, indicates the English were eager to consume them in mind, even when it may not have been possible to consume them in body.

The most common usage of foreign foods in print is in travel narratives that discuss foreign lands. Such printed matter tries to captivate the reader's imagination, describing voyages to far away places and the people and foods encountered there. For example, in *A New Voyage Round the World*, published in 1697, William Dampier describes the abundance of tortoises, yams, potatoes, sugar, cocoa, avocados, guavas, plantains, and pineapples that are available to the English in the Caribbean.[32] As Chapter 1 highlights, the inclusion of foreign foods in print culture, especially when referenced with the lands they originated from, illustrates that the English were becoming aware of their growing Empire and conceptualizing and imagining the goods that they could consume from these areas.

Foods native to Africa, America, and Asia were also frequently referenced in seventeenth century English plays, the subject of Chapter 2, and often commented on their physical appearance as well as their taste and believed powers. Contemporary physicians believed that certain foods would encourage or cause different moods, an idea that playwrights often incorporated into their work. The appearance, taste, and smell of these foods were also popularly referenced. In Francis Beaumont's *The knight of burning pestle*, the Old Merchant is seen singing "Nose, Nose, jolly red Nose, and who gave thee this jolly red Nose? Nutmegs and Ginger, Cinamon and Cloves, And they gave me this jolly red Nose."[33] In this reference to spices, it is clear contemporary playwrights expected their audience to understand the smell or invested

Introduction

powers of the food. This demonstrates not only that foreign foods were part of seventeenth century popular imagination, but also that the English were fairly familiar with the products being discussed.

Together, the travel narratives and plays discussed in the first two chapters of this text illustrate that as early as the seventeenth century, the English were reaping the benefits of transoceanic trade networks. The usage of foreign foods in contemporary print speaks to the idea that the English were consuming these products in mind if not in body. Whether they had affordable access to the foreign foods being referenced almost becomes irrelevant, for it is clear that these foods were being conceptualized and imagined, even if never eaten. Therefore, foreign foods impacted the way the English imagined and thought of contemporary culinary culture.

Physical Consumption

Cookery books and medical treatises, discussed in Chapters 3 and 4, respectfully, in both printed and manuscript form, illustrate that foreign foods were being physically consumed within the domestic sphere under female supervision. While the foreign foods and printed cookery books may have been bought from a public vendor, both the food and the text were consumed at home in the kitchen, the epitome of seventeenth century domestic space. This demonstrates that there were gender and class components involved in the building of a larger British identity, at least when it came to the physical consumption of these foods. Since cooking and doctoring fell under female control in the seventeenth century household, it was the mistress of the house who would have introduced ingredients to her family. And, as these contemporary texts illustrate, several foreign foods were incorporated into English culinary culture. Sugar and spices were being featured in recipes at an unprecedented rate, and American products like tortoises, turkeys, potatoes, and, plantains were called for more and more as the period progressed. What appears, then, is an interesting connection between the English, the foreign foods they were physically consuming, and the mothers and wives in charge of their family's diet that were causing this consumption to happen.

Introduction

Thus, English women were provided a domestic outlet to act as members of the growing British Empire by incorporating foreign foods into their household cuisine and pharmacopeia. It was not just the elite women making use of these foreign foods either. Unlike other places in Europe, certain foreign foods can be found in recipes that clearly were not produced with an elite audience in mind. This illustrates that for the first time exotic foods were not being used to reinforce class divisions in England.[34] This connection between seventeenth century gender, class, and foreign foods, however, is one that has gone largely unnoticed.

Texts referring to the consumption of tobacco, chocolate, coffee, and tea demonstrate that the seventeenth century English consumed foreign products in the public sphere as well, and serves as the subject of Chapter 5. First introduced to England in the sixteenth century, tobacco's popularity amongst the English soared in the seventeenth century. While some authors took to print to extol the virtues of smoking tobacco, others, including King James I, endeavored to vilify the product for its foreignness and discouraged its consumption. Chocolate, coffee, and tea would gain similar popularity in the later seventeenth century as well and were featured as the subject of several texts wishing to advise the public about them, especially since chocolate- and coffee-houses had become popular in urban centers. The information these texts offer about tobacco, chocolate, coffee, and tea, where they can be bought, their cost, and who is consuming them, prove that these four foreign products had become completely entrenched in seventeenth century English culture and were being physically consumed on a regular basis.

Taken together, consumption of foreign foods, both physical and intellectual, indicate that the English were engaging with extra-European products at an increasing rate. This in itself is important, as it indicates the English were eager to learn about and incorporate foreign foods into their daily lives. When ingesting them was not yet possible, they were still connecting with the products through the travel narratives they read or the plays they saw. Whether being consumed in body or in mind, foreign foods were becoming an integral part of seventeenth century English life.

1

Culinary Travels
William Dampier and Travel Narratives

A true man of the English empire, William Dampier circumnavigated the globe three times before his death in 1715, alternating between sailor, buccaneer, explorer, and privateer. Despite these accomplishments, it was Dampier's knack of bringing aspects of the empire back to the English people that brought him fame and fortune. Capitalizing on the growing interest in the lands and people that lay outside of Europe, he first achieved financial success with Prince Giolo, whom he purchased in the Philippines and brought back to England with him.[1] A London advertisement from 1692 describes Giolo, the "famous painted Prince," in great detail, closing with information about where and how to see the tattooed royal. It states "he will be exposed to publick view every day at his lodgings … where he will continue for some time, if his health will permit. But if any Persons of Quality, Gentlemen, or Ladies, do desire to see this noble Person, at their own Houses, or any other convenient place, in or about this City of London, they are desired to send timely notice, and he will be ready to wait upon them in a Coach or Chair."[2] Giolo proved to be profitable for Dampier, as one shilling, six pennies were charged to Londoners who wished to view the subjugated Prince. Smallpox brought an end to this arrangement, however, when Giolo was stricken with the disease and ultimately died while in Oxford in 1693.[3]

Upon Giolo's death, Dampier embarked on another global voyage. When he returned to England years later, he turned his travel journals into a narrative recounting what he had seen and the people he had met. The text, entitled *A New Voyage Round the World*, was, as Joel Baer argues, "a great success, not principally as a tale of buccaneering but as an objective and useful account of lands unknown—and a revelation of Spain's wealth and weakness; seven printings in English and translations into Dutch, French, and German appeared during [Dampier's] lifetime."[4] Its success was certainly due in part to the level of detail that he provided his readers. Dampier explains in his preface that "in the Description of Places, their Product, &c I have endeavoured to give what satisfaction I could to my Country men; tho possibly describing several things that may have been much better accounted for by others: Choosing to be more particular than might be needful, with respect to the intelligent Reader, rather than to omit what I thought might tend to the Information of Persons no less sensible and inquisitive, tho not so Learned or Experienced."[5] There was a wide audience that admired this attention to detail too. Mariners and explorers lauded the text for the advice given about how to survive abroad and sales indicate that Dampier's "Land Readers" found it fascinating as well.[6] It is because of this that the text achieved great success and was republished in 1698, 1699, 1703, and 1717.

Dampier's text offered readers a truly global perspective, setting it apart from contemporary travel narratives that tended to focus on either the East or West Indies. Following the same course that Dampier traveled, the text begins in Central America and the Caribbean islands, briefly veers south towards Peru, and then moves across the Pacific Ocean to Guam, the Philippines, islands along the Chinese coast, and finally Sumatra. As Susan Amussen notes, leading up to the seventeenth century, English travelers, like Dampier, "began to publish accounts of journeys, peoples, and places in Africa and the New World, based on the very real voyages that were taking place at the time.... These works were very popular at the start of the seventeenth century ... [and] included more complex portrayals of the rest of the world, with cultures having both positive and negative characteristics and familiar and unfamiliar aspects."[7] Like his fellow travel writers, Dampier was able to captivate the literate portion of the English population interested in empire building endeavors. Although the vast majority of the readership would never travel to the East or West Indies, they were still intrigued by these lands and their natural resources, including their foods.

1. Culinary Travels

Travel writers consistently commented on products native to foreign lands, featuring information on a given food's appearance, size, taste, texture, and manner in which it should be prepared. The inclusion of such details has two implications. When reading about a food that has already been integrated into English culture, it is possible the author was offering suggestions on alternative ways to consume it. In doing this, though, the author illustrates that some form of consumption was already occurring. Conversely, an author could be endeavoring to provide his reader with insight about a food he is sure the reader would never have encountered. In this scenario, the author's attention to detail would seem to indicate how interested in foreign or exotic foods he expected his readers to be. Whether introducing readers to new foods or new information about foods that had already been transported to England, the desire to learn about foreign foods and the various ways they could be incorporated into English culture is clear.

It is the details that writers like Dampier included in their texts that make seventeenth century travel narratives so interesting. They demonstrate the process of a foreign food's discovery, beginning with the explorer's initial experience with the product in a far away region and then related back to people in England, with the expectation that this information will spark curiosity and desire for consumption in those who never left home. For the modern reader, these texts also illustrate a familiarity with foreign foods that had already been incorporated into English culture, proving these products were not just being talked about but eaten as well. Because of this, travel narratives definitively prove that intellectual consumption of foreign foods was regularly occurring and growing in frequency in seventeenth century England. For some foods, the texts also illustrate that physical consumption was actively taking place as well.

British North America

Leaving England in 1681, Dampier traveled west to Central America and the Caribbean islands. Although neglected by Dampier, many seventeenth century travel narratives were published about the eastern coast of North America. Such westward exploration was popular during the period; the majority of contemporary travel narratives were concerned with some aspect of the "New World." It is true that these western regions were "newer" to Europeans than the lands that lay to the east. Yet this burst in western travel narratives was related to the development of English colonies there. Unlike other regions of the Americas farther south, the lands in British North America, including New England and Virginia, remained un-colonized by Europeans prior to English exploration. It is for this reason that many contemporary travel writers were still endeavoring to explain to their readers the foods they encountered in this corner of the world. While John Smith, John Josselyn, and Nathaniel Crouch published some of the more detailed accounts of the foods they encountered, other authors recounted what they ate while in the area, too.

John Smith, one of the more famous English explorers of the early seventeenth century, was himself author of several travel narratives. His texts proved extremely popular with contemporary audiences, causing them to be republished many times over. One such republication of his *A Map of Virginia* explains on the front piece that although authored by Smith, the 1612 edition was edited by Thomas Abbay and bound and sold with W.S.'s *The Proceeding of the English Colonie in Virginia*.[8] Abbay provides interesting insight into the audience that he expected would read the text. In the Introduction, he states that:

> if [this book] be disliked of men, then I would recommend it to women, for being dearly bought, and farre sought, it should be good for Ladies. When all men reiected Christopher Collumbus: that ever renowned Queene Izabell of Spaine, could pawne her Iewels to supply his wants; who all the wise (as they thought themselves) of that age commented. I need not say what was his worthiness, her nobleness, and their ignorance, that so scornfully did spit at his wants, seeing the whole world is enriched with his golden fortunes. Cannot his successfull example moue the incredulous of this time, to consider, to conceaue, & apprehend Virginia, which might be, or breed, us a second India? hath not England an Izabell, as well as Spaine, nor yet a Collumbus as well as Genua? yes surely it hath, whose desires are no lesse then was worthy Collumbus, their certainties more, their experience no way wanting, only there wants but an Izabell, so it were not from Spaine.[9]

Abbay's juxtaposition of the founding of the Spanish Empire in the New World with England's involvement in Virginia is striking. He clearly understands that if England is to achieve global financial success

1. Culinary Travels

like Spain, the English must take every opportunity to build colonies in lands that could prove profitable.

Another interesting aspect of Abbay's Introduction is his acknowledgment that women comprise a significant portion of his text's audience. As he explains, female support is vital to the building of an English Empire. The implication that England had its own Isabella is an obvious reference to Queen Elizabeth, a monarch who supported English trade and exploration in the New World. Despite the notion that empire building was an arena reserved for men, Abbay's Introduction demonstrates that female support was necessary when empire building was at hand.

Smith's *A Map of Virginia* also proves interesting as it describes and discusses some foods using their Powhatan name; only a few of the foods he encounters, like sassafras and turkeys, are referred to by their English name. For example, he explains that "in the watry valleys groweth a berry which they call Ocoughtanamnis very much like vnto Capers. These they dry in summer. When they will eat them they boile them neare halfe a day; for otherwise they differ not much from poyson."[10] In another instance, he states "the cheife roote they haue for foode is called Tockawhoughe, It groweth like a flagge in low muddy freshes. In one day a Savage will gather sufficient for a weeke.... Raw it is no better then poision, & being roasted, exceot it be tender and the heat abated, or sliced and dried in the sub, mixed with sorrel and meale or suck like, it will prickle and torment the throat extreamely, and yet in sommer they vse this ordinarily for bread."[11] From this, it appears Smith used the Powhatan name when there was no English alternative to use. He did endeavor to compare the food in question to a known equivalent however, using capers and potatoes as points of reference for his readers. This, perhaps, also explains why he spent more time explaining these foods, for he knew they were entirely foreign to his audience. Thus, Smith's text illustrates how foods were first introduced to the English and the details that were considered pertinent regarding a new food.

Also fascinating is Smith's 1630 *True Travels, Adventvres, and Observations of Captaine Iohn Smith* as it includes narratives from both Smith and other men that he traveled with. The front piece explains that with Smith, the text was "written by actual Authors, whose names you shall find along the History."[12] Based on the narrative, it seems that men who spent time with Smith in North America, and could therefore speak to their experiences there, assisted in penning the text. Their names are included at the end of each individual chapter.

Thomas Simons, Rowland Gascocke, and Nicholas Burgh are credited with writing a chapter about their time on St. Christopher, entitled "The beginning and proceedings of the new plantation of St. Christopher by Captaine Warner."[13] According to the chapter, it appears the new plantation grew tobacco, as the production and sale of each tobacco harvest and the merchants they were in contact with take up the majority of their writing. However, the reader does learn that while living there, the authors "lived upon Cassado bread, Potatoes, Plantines, Pines, Turtles, Guanes, and fishplentie."[14] They go on to further explain tortoises, relating that they are plentiful from May to September as "they come out of the sea to lay their eggs in the sand, and are hatched as the other; they will lay half a pecke at a time, and neere a bushell ere they have done; and are round as Tenis-balls: this fish is like veale in taste, the fat of a brownish colour, very good and wholsome."[15] Clearly, they did not imagine their English audience had consumed a tortoise before, or even was familiar with one for that matter.

Simons, Gascocke, and Burgh also describe the other foods they ate on St. Christophers. Of cassado they explain that it "is a root planted in the ground, of a wonderfull increase, and will make very good white bread, but the Iuyce ranke poison, yet boyled, better than wine." They note that the island is full of potatoes, cabbages, radishes, maize, plantains, apples, prickle-pears, and pineapples "so bigge as Hartichocke."[16] They write there is also pepper on the island, and contended that it is quite better than that from East India.

It is within this discussion of foods that the authors include a description of annatto: a small tree whose seeds can be used for dyes. Interestingly enough, this plant would become very important to eighteenth century cheese-makers in Cheshire who used it to give their naturally pale white cheese an orange color. While there were other dyes that could achieve the same effect, annatto was preferred because it did not add any additional flavor to the cheese.[17] Like many of the

1. Culinary Travels

foreign foods that travel authors wrote about, annatto would end up revolutionizing English food culture.

Another American food that would revolutionize English culture was the turkey. Many travel authors, including Smith, provided their readers with little information on the bird, though. For example, in Smith's 1616 *A Description of New England*, he writes that turkeys could be found frequently in New England, yet does not provide any further information about the bird. Other texts written throughout the seventeenth century, including *A Treatise of Nevv England*, *A Description of the Province of New Albion*, *A Perfect Description of Virginia*, *A True and Faithful Account of the Four Chiefest Plantations of the English in America*, and *Good Order Established in Pennsilvania & New-Jersey in America*, also speak to the high volume of turkeys in North America and their frequent consumption. The lack of information about the turkey itself, how it acted or what it looked like, for example, speaks to the idea that the English already knew of it. This makes sense, though, since turkeys were first introduced to England in the early sixteenth century.

The only seventeenth century text that provides more information about turkeys is John Josselyn's *New-Englands Rarities Discovered*, published in 1675. His insight into the bird proves that a strong tradition of turkey consumption in England had already been established. He notes that New England turkeys are "blacker than ours" and "some English bring up great stores of the wild [turkey], which remain about their Houses as tame as ours in England."[18] Josselyn's reference to "our turkeys" proves they had already been integrated into English culture by the time he was writing.

In addition to his commentary on turkeys, Josselyn's text endeavors to illustrate the medicinal benefits of New England's foods. Written after he had returned to England from living with his brother in Maine for eight and a half years, the text is formatted almost like an encyclopedia of things that could be found in the area.[19] Josselyn writes on the title page that not only will his book focus on the various animals and plants he saw, but also "the Physical and Chyrurgical Remedies wherewith the Natives constantly use to Cure their Distempers, Wounds, and Sores."[20] Josselyn expected his readers would be eager to learn how Native Americans used the foods he was encountering and whether they were able to cure ailments or help restore a balance to the body's humors. This indicates that he anticipated his readers would have access to these products in the domestic market at some point in the near future.

Josselyn, for example, chose to concentrate on the curative properties of the watermelon instead of discussing its taste or the manner that Native Americans ate it as other contemporary travel writers did. He explains that a watermelon is "a large Fruit, but nothing near so big as a Pompion, colour, smoother, and of a sad Grass green rounder, or more rightly Sap-green; with some yellowness admixt when ripe; the seeds are black, the flesh or pulpe exceeding juicy.... It is often given to those sick of Feavers, and other hot Diseases with good success."[21] Because Josselyn explains that watermelons are good for "hot diseases," it seems that watermelons were thought to help rebalance humors by introducing coldness to an over-hot body; this knowledge would have been especially intriguing to contemporary readers who looked to humor theories to treat their ailments.

Of sassafras, Josselyn divulges a bit more information about its curative properties. Noting that it is often referred to as "Ague Tree," he says that the chips of the roots can be boiled and drank to reduce a fever and that the bark works well as an ointment against bruises and "dry blows." He also notes that the bark of the root of the plant can be used in place of cinnamon. Because of its overall effectiveness, he poses to the reader that perhaps sassafras was one of the key ingredients of a cure that had already made its way to England. He asks "may not this be the Bark the Jesuits Powder was made of, that was so Famous not long since in England, for Auges?"[22] Even if it is not the same bark, Josselyn's suggestion that it has a similar curative property would certainly entice English consumers.

Josselyn also offers interesting insight into tobacco consumption amongst Native Americans; yet, contrary to the assessment of Smith and other authors, he claims that there was not an abundance of tobacco in British North America. Smith, Christopher Levett, Sir William Alexander, the anonymous author of *A Perfect Description of Virginia*, and Samuel Clarke claimed in their respective texts that copious amounts of tobacco was available in the region, to the point that tobacco could be purchased rather cheaply.[23] Josselyn, however, states

1. Culinary Travels

that the "Indians make use of a small kind with short round leaves called Pooke." With it, he notes, Native Americans make "a strong decoction of Tobacco they Cure Burns and Scalds [with], boiling it in Water from a Quart to a Pint, then wash the Sore there with, and strew on the powder of dryed Tobacco."[24] While other contemporary travel writers note that Native Americans smoked tobacco, or, according to John Brereton, drank it, Josselyn concentrates on how it could be used medicinally.[25] This would suggest that, as far as Josselyn was concerned, the English were familiar with smoking tobacco, but were still unaware of the medical usages of it at the time he was writing.

Like Josselyn, it was not at all uncommon for contemporary travel writers to focus on the medicinal benefits a food had to offer. This was especially true considering the tenets of humor theory that the English still strongly believed in. However, not all travel authors relayed such details. Nathaniel Crouch's *The English Empire in America*, published in 1685 and written under the pseudonym R.B., for example, described the foreign foods he encountered yet did not provide information on their medicinal properties.[26] For Crouch, he seems to have been more focused on conveying what life in British North America was like, offering information on the environment of the area as well as how English colonists and the Indians lived.

Crouch begins his text by positioning a rather detailed map of British North America adjacent to the cover piece (Figure 1.1). The map endeavors to list many of the places that the text addresses and depicts various Indians, animals, and vegetation throughout the area. While many of the animals are hard to identify, with the exception of one large deer, it is clear Crouch is trying to convey the vast resources that the area had to offer. While Indians and colonists are shown clashing in Virginia, the overall impression is of a large, peaceful, and prosperous land.

Crouch begins his text describing the voyage he endured getting there. He relates that "hence by August 24 we discover Flores, and Corvo, two of the Azores or Tercera Islands: and Sept. 9 having first suffered a terrible Storm upon the English Coast, which carried away all our Sails, and indgered the loss of all we had got; yet at last by the mercy of God, and favour of a good Wingd, they arrived safely at Plymouth."[27] Not only does Crouch recount to his readers his journey to

Figure 1.1

1. Culinary Travels

the New World, but he articulates it in a manner that makes Plymouth sound like a mecca.

Crouch offers interesting insights about his experience in British North America, too; his text, for example, provides one of the more thorough accounts of rum. He explains that New England's Indian population was introduced to rum, also known as rumbullion or Kill-devil, by English and French men. He states that the "cursed liquor" is "stronger than Spirit of Wine, drawn from the dross of Sugar and Sugar Canes, which they love dearer than their lives, wherewith if they had it, they would be perpetually drunk, though it hath killed many of them, especially old Women."[28] While we know that Crouch and his English peers must have had access to rum, since the English were partly responsible for introducing it to the Indians, he provides no insight into English consumption habits of it.

Crouch also provides a plethora of information on Indian corn, or maize. A staple of the Native American diet, he notes that there are "divers ways [it can be] prepared; sometimes Roasted in the Ashes, sometimes beaten and Boyled in Water, which they call Homine; they also make cakes, not unpleasant to eat."[29] His assessment that corn cakes were not unpleasant further supports his contention that English planters frequently consumed them as well, explaining they found them "wholesome and good in use."[30] Travel narratives throughout the period, including *A Relation or Journall of the Beginning and Proceedings of the English Plantation settled at Plimouth in New England, New Englands Plantation, A Treatise of New England, A Perfect Description of New England, Good Order Established in Pennsylvania & New-Jersey*, and *Massachusetts*, echo the idea that Indian corn was a mainstay in the English colonist's diet as well. Together, the authors show the value of Indian corn, illustrating it was a food conducive to English tastes.

Based on the writings of contemporary authors who traveled to British North America, the modern reader is able to see how writers first introduced their respective audiences to the new foods they were encountering. Although some of these foods, like potatoes and turkeys, had already reached England, others were still entirely foreign to them. Not only does this provide insight into how the English learned of new American foods, but it also illustrates how these foreign foods were used to entice the English and encourage them to want to build an American empire.

West Indies

While the English may have had a monopoly on exploration and expansion in New England, the same did not hold true for many of the other regions of the New World. Although the seventeenth century saw the English establishing colonies in the Caribbean Sea, the area was first publicized and explored by the Spanish. Because of this, some of the products the West Indies had to offer had already reached England through Spain. Thus, the narratives from travel writers who ventured there often contained information on foods the English already knew of as well as products that were still entirely foreign to them. Therefore, the information they chose to include or leave out of their texts points to English familiarity, or the lack thereof, with the food in question.

Because of Spain's success in the Caribbean, there were texts that became available to the English public during the seventeenth century that were actually translations of older Spanish texts. Pietro Martire d'Anghiera's *De Orbe Novo*, for example, was translated and sold under various English titles from 1555 to 1628.[31] Despite this, English consumers were still eager to learn of the rich lands Spain had acquired. Full of information about rivers of gold and cannibalistic Natives, d'Anghiera does offer a few insights into the foods being discovered as well. He recounts that Columbus stated that Hispaniola had "no trees knowne unto them" and explained that because of the climate, these trees produced fruit all year long.[32] He also recounts how some of these foods were brought back to Spain's King Ferdinand, although their quality after the voyage was questionable. He explains that while a great quantity of fruit was brought for Ferdinand to try, "only one remained vncorrupted, the other being putrified by reason of the long voyage."[33] The uncorrupted fruit seems to have been a pineapple, although the mushy fruit that d'Anghiera describes the King eating points to it being a rather spoilt pineapple. Not only does this highlight the eagerness of Europeans to consume foreign foods, but it also

1. Culinary Travels

illustrates the struggle that would last for years to transport fruits across the Atlantic.

While such Spanish accounts remained popular during the seventeenth century, the narratives of Englishmen offered a more up-to-date account of the Caribbean. Our own William Dampier's text is a prime example of this, as he writes that his experiences in the Caribbean began in 1681 and his text was first published only sixteen years later. Dampier begins his narrative of the Caribbean at "Blewfields River," undertaking the first of several discussions on tortoises. He explains how he went with "Mosquito men" out in canoes to capture tortoises, noting that because a tortoise has better eyesight than hearing, the Mosquito men would essentially sneak up behind one and use a spear-like tool to penetrate the shell so it could not escape.[34] While Dampier goes into great detail about the method and tools used in capturing a tortoise, something the average Englishman had surely never done, he never states why the natives would want to do this. Obviously, he felt that by the time his text was published in 1697, sixty-seven years after Simons, Gascocke, and Burgh felt it necessary to describe what the animal looked and tasted like in their text, it was commonly understood that tortoises were feasted upon in the New World.

This assumption on Dampier's part was surely influenced by the texts of other travel authors before him and their descriptions of tortoises as well. Sir Francis Drake's 1652 *Sir Francis Drake Revived*, for example, details the vast quantities of tortoises available in the Americas. He states that once his ship had returned to Cape St. Anthony, his crew made efforts to replenish the ship's food supplies. To do this, they gathered turtle eggs on the shore by day and "took two hundred and fifty Turtles by night."[35] Charles-Cesar Rochefort includes similar information in his 1687 text, explaining that "sea-men" who travel to the Cayman Islands "may every night in less than three hours turn forty or fifty of them, the least whereof weighs a hundred and fifty pounds, and the ordinary ones two hundred pound; nay some of them will have two great pails full of egges in their bellies."[36] Although lacking details on the number of tortoises that could be caught in the Caribbean, Richard Blome states that tortoise-shells are in abundance there, going on to contend that they are much esteemed in England "for several curious works." He does add, though, "their flesh are excellent meats."[37]

Tastes of the Empire

That such other travel authors had focused on the large volume of tortoises available explains why Dampier did not feel the need to dedicate more time on the subject as he felt the English public already knew this information.

Just as with the tortoise, Dampier does not provide his reader with any real kind of information about potatoes or yams; he does, however, repeatedly list them amongst foods that he and his companions ate. Travel authors before him, though, provided much more insight to both, but especially the potato. Richard Ligon's 1657 *A True and Exact History of the Island of Barbados*, for example, states that in Barbados, potatoes are used as a source of bread. He explains that "at the time we first came, there was little else used, at many a good Planters Tables in the Island."[38] William Hughes agrees that potatoes are plentiful in the Caribbean, adding in his 1672 *American Physitian* that there was more than one type of the tuber to be had. He states that the potatoes he encountered while in the Caribbean were much better than the "Spanish Potatoes [that were] brought into England." He explains that American potatoes "breed very good nourishment; they corroborate or strengthen exceedingly; they chear the heart; and are provocative of bodily lust."[39] He goes on to say they are especially useful to natives, as he claims that they are prone to be weakened by heat and need something nourishing and easily digestible. Clearly, he wanted readers to understand there was a wider world of potatoes than they had been exposed to. His comments also illustrate that by the time his text was published, potatoes were already available to consumers in England.

Like Hughes, John Poyntz explains in his 1695 text *The Present Prospect of the Famous and Fertile Island of Tobago* that there are various types of potatoes, two of which were needed to make the island's most popular liquor. After stating the island has white, yellow, and red potatoes, he writes "now of the Yellow sort more ingenious, with a Tincture of the Red, make a pleasant Liquor, which when sweetened with Sugar they bottle it up, and after twenty four hours its ready for drinking: This is the Liquor known only by the name Mobby, and is the universal drink in the Island of Tobado and Barbadoes."[40] While Poyntz was correct about the popularity of mobbie, sweet potatoes were actually used to make the alcoholic beverage, not potatoes. Regarding mobbie, Amy Stewart has explained that it is a "fermented

1. Culinary Travels

drink of sweet potatoes, water, lemon juice, and sugar" originating from Barbados.[41]

Seventeenth century travel writers reference yams far less frequently than potatoes, yet their juxtaposition with potatoes when they are mentioned is elucidating. Dampier himself references potatoes and yams together six times in his text.[42] Writing some twenty years before Dampier, Hughes is the only author to provide insight into the yam, portraying it as an inferior cousin to the potato. He explains that yams "do nourish very well, but not so much as the Potatoes do; neither are they so delightful in taste" but they "are ordered and dressed the way potatoes are."[43] Although Hughes' discussion of yams does come right after his description of potatoes, it is apparent from his description of yams that he expects his readers to have eaten a potato for themselves. He states that yams are similar in taste to potatoes, yet never describes to his reader how potatoes taste. This must indicate that potatoes, at least those imported from Spain, had already been established in England, otherwise such a comparison would have fallen flat.

While contemporary travel authors may have chosen not to bore their readers detailing foods they already knew of, they were happy to provide extensive information when introducing entirely new foods. Dampier was no exception to this. While in the Bay of Panama on the island "Chepelio," he writes of encountering a delicate fruit called the "Avogato-Pear," presumably what modern readers would identify as an avocado. Because he is confident he is introducing his readers to this fruit for the first time, he explains what the "avogato-pear" tree looked and felt like, the shape and size of its leaves, and the size and color of the fruit it produced. Of the "avogato pear" itself, he explains that beneath the skin it is green and similar in consistency to butter and "hath no taste of it self, and therefore 'tis usually mixt with Sugar and lime-juice, and beaten together in a Plate, and this is an excellent dish." He continues by saying that "the ordinary way to eat it [is] with a little Salt and rosted Plantain, and thus a man that's hungry, may make a good meal of it." To conclude his discussion of the "avogato-pear," Dampier notes that the fruit is said to cause lust in those who consume it, which accounts for why it is so popular amongst Spaniards.[44]

Similar to the "avogato-pear," Dampier provides a plethora of details about the "Guava-Fruit" he encountered in the town of "Ria

Tastes of the Empire

Lexa." Again he explains what the "guava-fruit" tree looked and felt like, the size and shape of the leaves and branches, and the nature of the fruit itself. On this he notes the rareness of the fruit, explaining that "it may be eaten while it is green, which is a thing very rare in the Indies: for most Fruit, in both the East or West Indies, is full of clammy, white, unsavory juice, before it is ripe, though pleasant enough afterwards." Despite this uniqueness, though, he states the "guava-fruit" can be baked like a pear, either coddled or in a pie, and, depending on when it is eaten, can either be a binding or loosening agent.[45]

Dampier details other fruits he encountered in the Americas as well. He, like other contemporary travel writers before him, appears to have been quite taken by plantains, which Dampier describes as an "extraordinary sweet" fruit.[46] Sir Francis Drake's text *The World Encompassed*, first published in 1628, offers insight into the variety and beauty of the fruit trees Englishmen encountered in the Caribbean. Speaking of plantain trees, he writes "all of the trees were ever laden with fruit, some ready to be eaten, others coming forward, other over ripe. Neither can this seem strange, though about the middest of winter with us, for that the Sun doth never withdraw himself farther off from them, but that with his lively heat he quickneth and strengthen the power of the soile and plants."[47] Published almost thirty years later, Ligon's text provides drawings of a plantain tree "blossomed" (Figure 1.2) and its close cousin, the banana. Although Ligon writes that plantains are never especially tasty, he states that the English prefer to eat them when they are yellow and ripe, whereas the "Negres chuse to have it green, for they eat it boyl'd, and it is the only food they live upon."[48] He counters that the banana, although not as beautiful, is much more satisfying. Along with an image of "the bonano [tree] with the fruit ripe," (Figure 1.3) he explains "the fruit is of a sweeter taste then the Plantain; and for that reason the Negroes will not meddle with them ... but we find them as good to stew, or preserve as the Plantine, and will look and taste more like Quince."[49] While not providing his opinion on bananas, John Poyntz supports Ligon's observations of plantains in his 1695 text, stating, "planton of all Fruits the Negroes love best, and is a nourishing sovereign wholsom Food."[50] While the appeal of plantains varied from author to author, plantains were clearly part of the diet of any Englishmen in the Caribbean.

Although Dampier only mentions pineapples in a list of foods he

1. Culinary Travels

Figure 1.2

encountered in Ria Lexa, authors before him devoted more time to the majestic fruit. In his 1651 *A Description of the New World*, George Gardyner describes pineapples as "an excellent fruit" that those in Santo Domingo can enjoy "all the year long."[51] Ligon also elucidates readers about the pineapple, or, as he calls it, "The Queen Fruit" (Figure 1.4). He exclaims that "nothing of rare taste can be thought on that is not

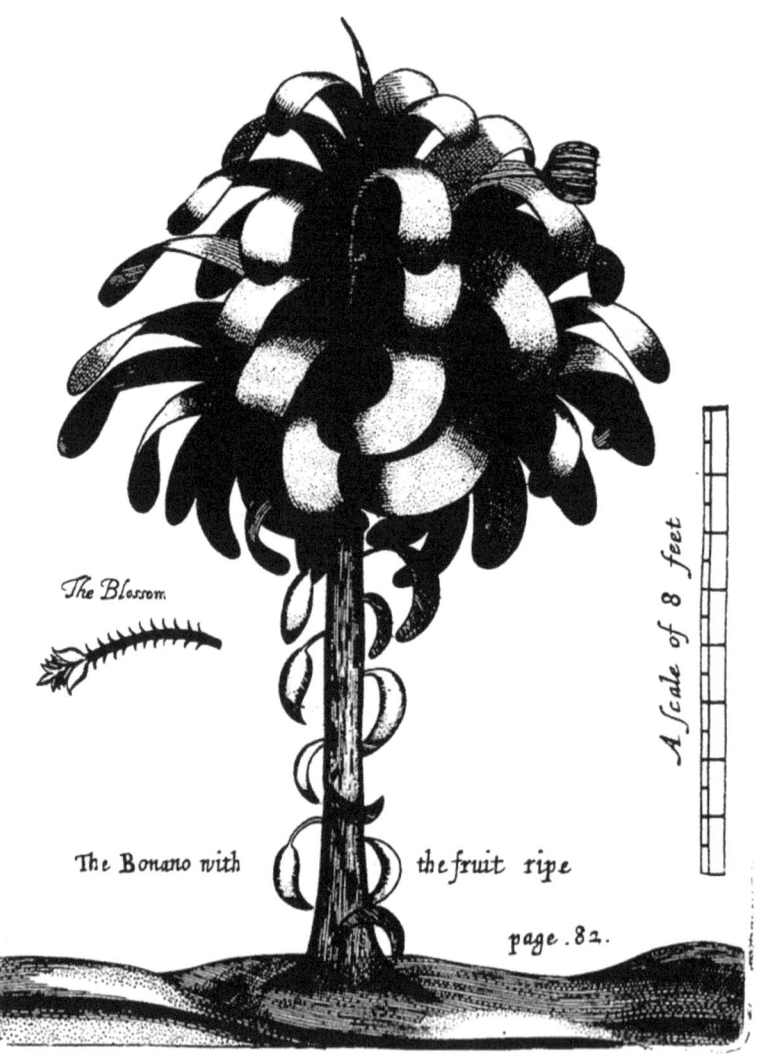

Figure 1.3

there; nor is it imaginable, that so full a Harmony of tastes can be raised, out of so many parts, and all distinguishable."[52] Poyntz again echoes Ligon's sentiments, writing that "the Pine-Apple I must confess is a Fruit of that Excellency, that I want Rhetorick and Oratory to express

1. Culinary Travels

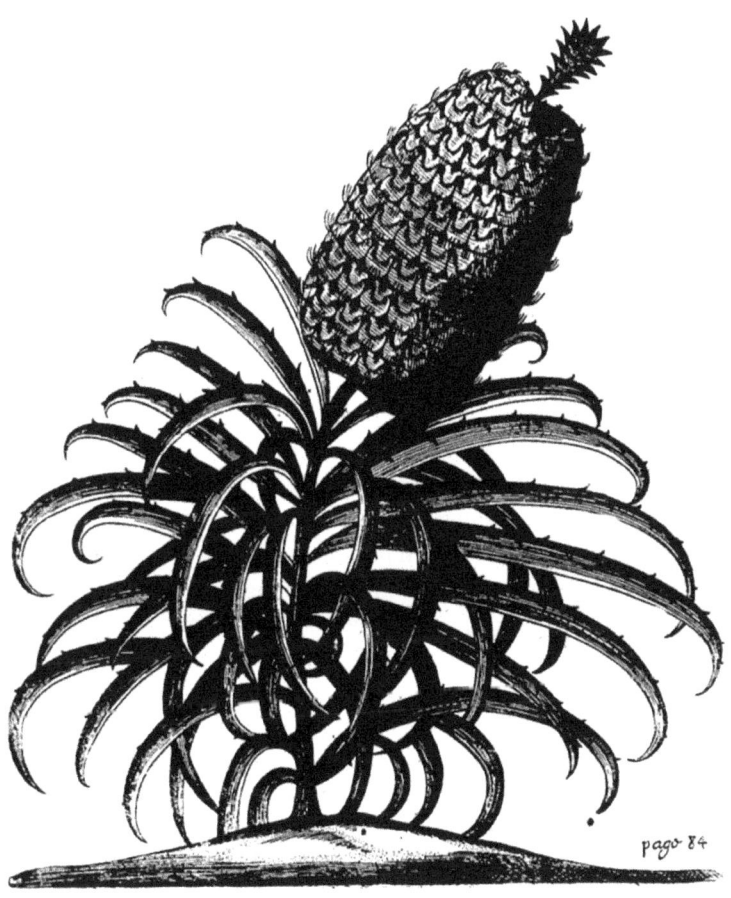

Figure 1.4

it. Some bears a Crown, and is the King of Fruits; but to them with three crowns the Idolatrous pray their Superstitions: The fruit of it self is of Fruit most delicious, and the Liquor botled up makes an admirable drink."[53] More than any other foreign food, pineapples impressed the Englishmen who encountered them, so much so that the fruit was verbosely lauded in print.

Tastes of the Empire

Although Dampier authored what is perhaps the most complete account of foods in the Americas, he deferred to his predecessors on some subjects. For example, because Ligon's text had became the authority on Caribbean sugar production, Dampier informed his readers that he abstained from any lengthy discussion of sugar because Ligon had covered the subject so well. While other seventeenth century authors, including Thomas Gage, Drake, Samuel Clarke, Blome, Thomas Dalby, and anonymous merchants, endeavored to explain to English readers the vast quantities and profits of sugar production in the Caribbean, none were able to do so quite like Ligon.[54] Perhaps this is because Ligon was interested in sugar from the English planter's point of view, detailing the growth and production of sugar in "sugar works" along with the profits such production secured. Included in this discussion are the different types of sugar that could be produced and his opinion of them, an opinion he was able to form first-hand after spending three years in Barbados. What is missing from his thorough discussion of sugar, however, is its dependence on slave labor. While Ligon is more sympathetic to the slave experience than some of his contemporaries, his time as a Barbadian plantation manager or overseer surely shaped the tone he wrote in when addressing such matters.[55]

Ligon begins by noting that planters first brought sugar "plants" to Barbados from Brazil. He explains that the first crops were not successful and it was only through trial and error by planters and advice from Brazilian visitors that any kind of decent sugar crop could be harvested. When Ligon arrived in 1647, he said there were many sugar works on the island "but yet the Sugars they made, were but bare Muscavadoes, and few of them Merchantable commodities; so moist, and full of molosses, and so ill cur'd, as they were hardly worth the bringing home for England. But about the time I left the island, which was in 1650, they were much better'd; for then they had the skill to know when the Canes were ripe."[56] Ligon makes clear that Barbadian sugar was near useless unless it was white "lump sugar," the term Ligon says the English used to describe their desired sugar, which he claims can on average be sold in London for twelve pence per pound.[57] Considering that sugar was the largest crop in seventeenth century Barbados, there was clearly a large demand for it in England; a demand that those in Barbados were expected to satisfy.

1. Culinary Travels

But Ligon notes that "lump sugar" was not the only sugar product produced on the island. Besides the molasses that was made as the sugar cane was boiled down in a cistern, Ligon explains that, when distilled, the skimmings from the cistern will make "the strongest Spirits that men can drink."[58] According to him, the liquor is so potent that a jar of it ignited when it was taken too close to a candle, killing the slave who was carrying it. Despite this, it was consumed and sold quite regularly in Barbados. Ligon states that it was a commodity, explaining "some they sell to Ships, and is transported into foraign parts, and drunk by the way. Some they sell to such Planters, as have no Sugar-works of their owne, yet drink excessively of it." From this, he estimates planters with sugar works make "30 [pounds] sterling, besides what is drunk by their servants and slaves."[59] The liquor being discussed is never identified, but it seems plausible it could be rum since it is distilled from sugarcane byproducts. Since the liquor is never named, though, and Ligon spends a fair amount of time describing the effects of it, it is unclear whether this is a product that ever found its way to English consumers.

It is amidst this discussion that Ligon mentions, in only small detail, the slaves needed to produce a sugar crop. Referring to them as "Negres," Ligon explains that the aforementioned spirit has "the vertue to cure many [negres]; for when they are ill, with taking cold, (which often they are) and very well they may, having nothing under them in the night but a board, upon which they lie, nor anything to cover them: And though the daies be hot, the nights are cold, and the change cannot but work upon their bodies, though they be hardy people."[60] While this no where near touches on the horrible conditions slaves endured working to harvest sugar, Ligon concludes by stating that "as this drink is of great use, to cure and refresh the poor Negres, whom we ought to have a speciall care of, by the labour of whose hands, our profit is brought in; so it is helpful to our Christian Servants too; for when their spirits are exhausted, by their hard labour and sweating in the sun, ten hours every day ... and much weakened in their vigor every way, a dram or two of this Spirit, is a great comfort and refreshing to them."[61] Although remaining naïve that liquor could in any way comfort slaves, Ligon's comments do seem to foreshadow the abolitionist movement that would take hold in England in the eighteenth century and spawn a sugar boycott.

Tastes of the Empire

Just as Ligon published the authoritative text on sugar, Thomas Gage and William Hughes's respective texts provide extensive information on cocoa and the making of chocolate. Dampier and other authors like Jose de Acosta, Drake, Blome, Phillip Ayers, Alexandre Olivier, and Dalby discussed the prevalence of cocoa trees in the New World and how cocoa was made into chocolate.[62] None surpassed Gage's *The English American his Travail by Sea and Land*, published in 1648, or Hughes's *American Physitian*, published in 1672, in their level of detail, though.

The first to write at any length on chocolate, Thomas Gage spent much of the 1620s travelling Central America and the Philippines on a Catholic mission, returning to England in 1637 and penning his travel narrative some ten years later. He opens his five-page chapter on chocolate by acknowledging that "chocolate [is] being this day used not onely over all the West-India's but also in Spain, Italy, and Flanders, with approbation of many learned Doctors in Physick."[63] While Gage seems impressed by the variety of people engaging with chocolate, noticeably missing from his description is England. The only conclusion to draw is that the English were not yet consuming chocolate like some of their other European counterparts at the time of Gage's writing.

Gage describes that chocolate could be made a variety of ways, but recounts for his reader the ingredients necessary for it from a recipe he received from one Antonio Colmento. The recipe reads, "to every hundred cocoa's, two cods of Chile, called long red Pepper, one handfull of Anniseed and Orejuela's, and two of the flowers called Mechasuchil, or Bainilla, or instead of this six roses of Alexandria, beat to powder, two drams cinnamon, of Almonds and Hazel-nuts, of each one dozen; of white Sugar halfe a pound, of Achiotte, enough to give it the colour. This author thought neither Clove, nor Musk, nor any sweet water fit."[64] He further explains that to make the drink, a tablet of chocolate first must be formed that can then be taken and, along with other ingredients, mixed with water.[65] Referring to the health benefits of chocolate, Gage states that for twelve years he drank between four and five cups of chocolate a day and lived "without any obstructions, or oppilations, not knowing what either augue or fever was."[66]

Speaking less from personal experience and more as a horticulturalist, Hughes featured a fifty-five-page discourse on the "cacao-nut-tree"

1. Culinary Travels

and the chocolate it produced at the end of his *American Physitian*. He explains that the "cacao-nut-tree" grows throughout the Americas, but is especially prevalent in "Nicaragua, New Spain, Mexico, Cuba, Hispaniola, &c. and in Jamaica."[67] He relates that the Native women there believe that if they eat the cocoa dry without beating or grinding it first, they will "become Leucophlegmatical," although he notes that he thinks them mistaken in this. In his estimation, the natural "ruddy" complexion of the women of the area makes it seem that their appearance changes after eating the dry cocoa. He supports this by noting it is "doubtless women in England might eat a long time these same Cacao's, before they would finde any alteration or change thereby in themselves."[68]

Having assured the English that eating dry chocolate would not over whiten their skin, Hughes moves to advice regarding where the English could obtain the best chocolate domestically. He writes that he is "perswaded there is no better Chocolate to be had in England, then that which Mariners and Sea-men bring; which is made up in the Country where the Cacao's naturally grown." He explains that the best chocolate he ever consumed was made into a paste in Jamaica and that "it maybe had often here in England, neat and good, of Merchants and Sea-men that travel to those parts and bring it over."[69] While he does not explain why domestically produced chocolate could not equal in quality chocolate imported from the Americas, he does express his distaste for chocolate made in Europe when discussing drinking chocolate.

Writing of chocolate the beverage, Hughes notes that at the time of his writing in 1672, it is "a drink in great request, and well known to most parts of Christendome," yet he is not pleased with the quality and authenticity of the chocolate being served.[70] He writes that "what we now use in England, is but a compound of Spices, Milk, Eggs, Sugar, &c. and perhaps there is in it a fourth or sixth part of the chiefest ingredient, the Cacao; whereby the intention of what it should be, and the property thereof from it naturally is in it self, is quite changed."[71] He counters this with how the "Native Indians" consume the beverage, explaining they "seldom or never use any Compounds; desiring rather to preserve their health, then to gratifie and please their Palats."[72] Because of the vast difference between the two, he contends "it is the adulteration of this Nectar which undeservedly makes it ill thought of."[73] Thus, he recommends that all who wish to consume chocolate for their health should prepare it themselves or purchase it from seamen or merchants to ensure authenticity. Not only did he advise contemporary readers about the merits of chocolate and how they can obtain an unadulterated version of it, he illustrates to modern readers the extent to which chocolate had been integrated into seventeenth century English life.

Another food that both Hughes and Gage discuss in relation to chocolate is the "chili," also known as the "red pepper" or "bastard pepper." "Bastard pepper," Hughes explains, being the name English planters used for it. He reasons this is because chili peppers are very much alike in appearance and taste to East India pepper, which they are accustomed to. Just like East India pepper, Hughes states that chili peppers are hot and dry in temperature and are good "to eat with Pease, and the like, to expel the windiness thereof, and is used in Chocolate."[74] By comparing the Caribbean "chili" to East India pepper, Hughes is able to accurately relate the nature of the "chili" without boring his readers with excessive details about it. Such a comparison also functions to highlight an existing English familiarity with East India pepper.

Like Dampier, contemporary travel writers who visited the West Indies illustrate that, while there were still a few entirely foreign foods that they could inform their audience about, most of the foods they came across in the Caribbean had already reached England. Some, like sugar and potatoes, had been integrated into English culture and physically consumed regularly. Others, like plantains and pineapples, may have been difficult to obtain because of difficulties in transportation, yet were frequently discussed and therefore consumed in mind if not in body. Either way, the eagerness of travel writers to provide readers with information regarding foreign foods and the speed at which these foods were being consumed proves impressive.

East Indies and Persia

From the West Indies, Dampier briefly veered south before continuing west across the Pacific Ocean to the East Indies. This was

1. Culinary Travels

familiar territory for English explorers; eastward adventures, first by land and later by sea, were something Europeans had long known of. Assumedly, because of this, Dampier and his contemporaries found it unnecessary to provide lengthy descriptions of the foods they encountered, for many had already made their way back to England. Although there were a handful of foods that the authors still provided specifics about, the overall lack of details would seem to indicate that such foods had already been integrated into English culture.

Dampier's text was no exception to this, either. While on islands in the River of Cambodia, he described that he tasted delicious and juicy mangoes, although different in size and shape than those from Fort St. George in India. Although Dampier does not provide information regarding Indian mangos, W. Glanius, whose travel log was published some fifteen years before Dampier's, does describe the fruit and trees they grew on. He explains that mangos "grow on trees not much unlike our Nute Trees, but they have not so many leaves: They are of the bigness of a Peach, but longer and something bending like a Crescent of a light green, drawing a little towards red. It has a great shell, that encloses an Almond of greater length than breadth, and eaten raw is very distastful, but roasted on the coals is not unpleasant: 'tis useful in Physick against the Worms and Diarrhea."[75]

While Glanius discusses the medicinal effects of mangos, Dampier devotes time to a discussion of the pickling of young mangoes, which he states he had never seen before his time in Cambodia. He explains that young mangoes could be pickled in salt, vinegar, and cloves of garlic and made an excellent sauce termed "mango achar." He explains, "in the East Indies, especially at Siam and Pegu, there are several sorts of Achar, as from the young tops of Bamboes, &c. Bambo-Achar and Mango-Achar are the most used."[76] Dampier's desire to educate his contemporary English readers about this mango sauce works to illustrate another point for modern readers. He describes the mangoes he encountered and used to make the sauce as different from those from Fort St. George, seeming to suggest that his readers would have been familiar with Indian mangoes. It is unclear whether Dampier believes Indian mangoes could be used to make the mango-achar he describes, but what is clear is the notion that the English had already heard of, if not personally encountered, a mango from some region of the world.

Tastes of the Empire

Dampier deals with tea in a similar fashion while writing of his time in China. He explains that there was an abundance of tea in the country and men and women of all rank frequently drank it. Comparing it to tea he had consumed from other places, he states "the tea at Tonquenn or Cochinchina seems not so good, or of so pleasant and bitter, or of so fine a colour, or such virtue as this in China; for I have drank of it in these countries."[77] Here again, though, the details he provides about tea suggest that he is writing under the assumption that his readers already have a basic understanding of what pleasant tea would taste like, what color it should be. Although he does provide insight into the different types of tea that he encounters, just as he attested to coming across a new variety of mango, the basic assumption that the English already had knowledge of these products proves they were already consuming them on some level. This is supported by the fact that some ten years prior to the publication of Dampier's text, Nathaniel Crouch lists tea as a product being exported to England from the East Indies in his *A View of the English Acquisitions in Guinea and the East-Indies.*[78]

While Dampier does not generally provide his reader with information regarding the exportation of products as Crouch did, he does provide a glimpse into the mighty spice trade that consumed much of the East Indies. Speaking of the Dutch monopoly of cloves in particular, he relates that one Raja Lant told him "that if the English would settle [in and around the Island of Banda], they could order matters so in a little time, as to send a Ship-load of Cloves from thence every year." He further explains this is because there are so many trees on the island that the cloves fall from the trees and rot on the ground.[79] Dampier similarly makes note that there is plenty of nutmeg to be had in the East Indies, as well.[80]

Dampier was not the only travel writer to comment on the spice trade, nor was he the first. Even in the beginning half of the seventeenth century, texts like *An Historicall and True Discourse of a Voyage Made by the Admirall Cornelis Matelife the Yonger into the East Indies*, *An Exact and Cvriovs Svrvey of all the East Indies*, and *News From the East-Indies* recounted to English readers the large volume of spices being sent from the region to Europe.[81] Richard Boothby's 1646 *A Briefe Discovery or Description of the Most Famous Island of Madagascar or*

1. Culinary Travels

St. Lavrence in Asia is framed around the profits he earned buying and selling goods as a merchant in the East Indies; he likewise illustrates that spices were the chief commodities of the area. He lists "sticklack" pepper, cloves, mace, nutmeg, long-pepper, cubebs, cardamom, green ginger, dry ginger, preserved ginger, sugar and sugar candy among the products that he bought and was able to later sell with large profit margins.[82] Again, his description proves that a plethora of spices were being consumed regularly and the demand for them was high, allowing merchants such as Boothby to make a small fortune selling them. Following Boothby's lead, authors including Edward Terry and Josiah Child echo the same point.[83]

Publications of travel writers seeking to enlighten readers on the spice trade spiked in the 1690s, when Dampier's own text was released. George White commented that the East India Company was supplying the world with mace and nutmeg from the Spice Islands in his 1691 text.[84] Looking at other European powers, the anonymously published *The East-India Trade* of 1693 describes the various Dutch and Portuguese settlements in East India and the spices that were moved through them. It explains that China has a plethora of goods Europeans desire, including gold that the King of Spain wished to get his hands on. As for foods, it states China is rich with "sugar pouder and Candy, Green ginger, China Rubarbe, Musk, Pearls, [and] Cinamon."[85] The author seems to feel the commodities China has to offer are important, as he explains that trade there is "not so difficult as Portingalls and Hollanders would perwade the World for their own advantage."[86] Clearly, this author felt the Portuguese and Dutch were willing to do anything necessary to keep control of the spice trade.

The East-India Trade concludes by listing all "the commodities which usually are brought home into Europe" from the East Indies. Within this diverse list, salt, spices, pepper, cloves, nutmegs, mace, ginger, cinnamon, sugar, powder candy, musk, amber-grease, galangal, long pepper, dried Salmon, tobacco, turtle shells, and coconut shells are featured alongside cloth, skins, rugs, and dishes.[87] The extensive nature of this list, taking up almost a page and half, illustrates the eagerness of Europeans to consume objects foreign to them.

Looking particularly at spices, this enthusiasm was also touched on by Abraham Du Quesne, Gabriel Dellon, and John Fryer in their respective late 1690s texts.[88] Fryer provides his readers with intriguing insight into pepper, explaining "the best Pepper in the World is of the growth of Sunda, known in England by Carwar Pepper."[89] This illuminates two important points; firstly, even the best variety of pepper had already been integrated into English culture as suggested by the English name Fryer provides. Secondly, pepper consumption in England had reached a point where patrons were not just looking for pepper, but for the best pepper. The exoticism of the product had worn off so that the consumption of pepper was not impressive in and of itself.

Just as spices were the most prevalent food discussed in the East Indies, coffee seemed to monopolize any discussion of food products in the "near east," also referred to as Persia. This is one part of the world where Dampier's travels did not take him, however; instead, from the East Indies he sailed south around the Cape of Good Hope and back to England. Still, Persia and the Arabian peninsula continued to remain a popular subject amongst seventeenth century travel writers, despite the fact that European merchants had long visited the region as they searched for products brought west from the Silk Road. Perhaps this was in part due to newer products like coffee that were just beginning to reach English consumers.

While featuring information about the "Arabian Deserta," Pietro della Valle's 1665 text explains that coffee is often consumed by natives whose strict religious codes keep them away from wine. della Valle writes that it is "made by a black seed boyled in water, which turns it almost into the same colour, but doth very little alter the tast of the water; it is very good to help digestion, to quicken the spirits, and to cleanse the blood."[90]

Published some eight years after della Valle's text, John Ogilby also argues in his *Asia* that drinking coffee is a fixture of Persian culture. He states that "the Persians generally with their Tobacco drink Coffee, made from the Arabian Caowa, or Persian Cahwee, which they dry and pulverize, and after decot, as we now use, and have learn'd from them."[91] Interestingly enough, Ogilby provides no description of what coffee looks and tastes like, but instead indicates that he sees coffee prepared in Persia as the English have learned to prepare it. This suggests that between the two publications, the consumption of coffee had been popularized in England. Further supporting this idea are Jean-Baptiste

1. Culinary Travels

Tavernier and Sir John Chardin's respective 1680s text which mention coffee drinking in Persia, but provide no details about it.[92]

Curiously, in the same section that they write of coffee, Ogilby, Tavernier, and Chardin also write of the Persian consumption of tobacco. Intriguing, though, is the type of tobacco that Ogilby notes that Persians desired. He states that "they are great Takers of Tobacco, insomuch that People of all sorts and Degrees Smoak it in their temples and other publick Places; They have it from Bagdad or Babylon, and Curdistan, but so ill prepar'd, that they desire our European Tobacco, which they call Ingles Tambacu, because we bring the greatest quantities thither."[93] Although this does not directly speak to English consumption of tobacco, it seems safe to assume that if English merchants could bring great quantities of tobacco to Persia, they were certainly doing the same in their own domestic markets.

While contemporary travel narratives illustrate the process and speed at which New World foods were integrated into English culture, products from the East Indies, Persia, and Arabia demonstrate that this integration was not merely an obsession with the new and exotic. Many of the foods being referenced by travel writers were known of in England long before New World exploration began. Although navigational advancements did make these products cheaper and more readily available, their newness and exoticism had certainly diminished enough to prove interest in them was not simply a fad. Foreign foods from this region prove that the English had a real desire to discover the products that lie beyond their boarders and incorporate them into their own culinary culture.

Conclusion

The seventeenth century was full of English travel writers recounting the new, odd, and even exotic things they saw on their adventures. Few would achieve the literary success that Dampier obtained with his *A New Voyage Round the World*, yet they all succeeded in illustrating to their English audience what the world beyond Europe had to offer. As Joel Baer argued, "none of [Dampier's] voyages made him rich, yet by recreating a new world of natural wonders, fetched from afar but bearing the sense of reality, he became the most important explorer before Cook to sustain the nation's interest."[94] The foreign foods that Dampier and his contemporaries wrote of offered real evidence of how a larger English Empire could benefit those at home; more than gold or silver, these foods suggested that daily life could be improved from products brought home from abroad.

Travel narratives also prove that foreign food consumption was already occurring in seventeenth century England. While some of the foods, especially Caribbean fruits, were more difficult to get to an English market than others, it remains apparent that travel writers envisioned their readers had been exposed to knowledge of them, proving they were consuming such foods in mind if not in body. Because of this, they continued to describe in detail the new foods they encountered, understanding that their readers would want to mentally consume them as well. For other foods like sugar, tobacco, chocolate, and potatoes, the manner that travel narratives describe and discuss them in proves that actual physical consumption was occurring. Taken together, it is clear that foreign food consumption was transforming seventeenth century English culinary culture.

2

"Let the skie raine Potatoes"
Foreign Foods in English Plays

In *The Merry Wives of Windsor,* William Shakespeare crafts a comedic tale around the ever-popular Falstaff and his endeavors to woo two married women. The final scene features Falstaff, describing himself as a "Windsor stag," anxious to rendezvous with the married Mistress Ford, likening their meeting to the many paramours that Jove had with mortals. Upon seeing her, Falstaff exclaims: "My Doe, with the blacke Scut? Let the skie raine Potatoes: let it thunder, to the tune of Greene sleeues, haile-kissing Comfits, and snow Eringoes: Let there come a tempest of prouocation, I will shelter mee heere."[1] While the image of potatoes, comfits, and eryngoes falling from the sky may seem odd, Shakespeare is playing on the contemporary notion that each of these foods was a well-known aphrodisiac. Further, it is interesting that Shakespeare includes the potato in this list at all; they were only introduced to Europeans less than fifty years earlier by Spanish explorers who encountered them in Peru.[2] Whereas a storm of potatoes may have signified to Shakespeare's contemporaries an amorous mood, to modern readers it illustrates the speed at which the foreign potato had been integrated into English imaginations.

Shakespeare was not the only playwright to comment on the lustiness of potatoes, either. George Chapman's 1608 *Byron's Conspiracie,* for example, attributed the tricks that men carry out on others, due to their excess desires, to their eating of potatoes.[3] In the same manner, in 1637 James Shirley features Penelope making note of the "lustie-pie of Aarticchoke and Potato" that a "handsome gentleman" was eating in *The Gamester.*[4] Thomas D'Urfey even used the potato in his 1698 *The Campaigners* to explain that it was potato-inspired lust that influenced the tenacity of Hannibal's army, with Min Heer Tomas stating that they "ate nothing but Potatoes."[5] Although clearly impossible, the idea that such an army would have been encouraged by the nature of the potato provides insight into contemporary ideas about it.

Seventeenth century English plays featured a myriad of other foreign foods as well. Still subscribing to Galen's humor theories, contemporary physicians believed that certain foods would have different effects on the body. This is an idea that playwrights often incorporated into their work as Shakespeare, Chapman, and D'Urfey did. The appearance, taste, or smell of a foreign food was also commonly discussed, as was the social implications that came along with the consumption of certain products. This makes sense, as Katharine Eisaman Maus and David Bevington have pointed out that the English Renaissance theater had a profound "engagement with the pleasures of consumption."[6] While physical consumption of these foods is often difficult to establish, the inclusion of foreign foods in contemporary plays proves that the English were consuming these products in mind if not in body. As playgoers, they were exposed to conversations surrounding foreign foods and invited to think of and imagine them themselves. Whether they had affordable access to the products almost becomes irrelevant, for it is clear that foreign foods were being conceptualized and thought of, even if never eaten.

Through an examination of contemporary published plays and the foreign foods discussed within them, it becomes apparent that the English were incorporating and quickly adopting the foreign foods they were encountering while expanding their empire. Foreign foods were mentioned more than one thousand times in approximately five hundred published plays in the seventeenth century.[7] Clearly, contemporary playgoers would have been immersed in foreign foods whenever at the theater.

While other forms of popular culture speak to the idea that foreign foods were being consumed in mind if not in body, contemporary plays uniquely prove that consumption was occurring at all levels of society. Playgoing transcended social class, gender, and literacy divides, and was an activity available to all. Whether a food was being discussed in relation to its taste, smell, size, bodily effect, or some class distinction associated with it, the audience was taking part in intellectual consumption of the product. Thus, foreign foods in contemporary plays illustrate that the average seventeenth century English man and woman, rich or poor, literate or illiterate, were familiar with foreign foods and how they could be used, even if they were not eating them themselves.

Seventeenth Century Play Culture

To understand the significance of foreign foods in contemporary plays, a brief survey of the developing play culture of the period is important. Despite the tumultuous political climate during the Civil War and Interregnum of the 1640s–50s that closed the theaters for an unprecedented period of time, play going was an important facet of seventeenth century English life. Because plays were performed for men and women at all levels of society, any mention of foreign foods in them proves extremely valuable. Such references are, perhaps, the most telling example of universal mental consumption, as they demonstrate a familiarity with the products that is not restricted to a certain social class or gender.

Although play going was a staple in contemporary English life during the seventeenth century, it was actually a fairly new phenomenon. Maus and Bevington note, "England had long enjoyed a lively tradition of dramatic performance, but in medieval England no single population center was large enough to support a professional acting company on an ongoing basis."[8] It was not until the sixteenth century when wealth and power were concentrated in London that a strong theater presence was able to develop there.[9] And a strong theater culture certainly did grow; Andrew Gurr estimates that between 1580–1640, an average of twenty five thousand people would frequent some sort of theater each week, which totals to about fifty million visits in those sixty years.[10] Thus, by the dawn of the seventeenth century, playgoing had become an established activity that transcended socioeconomic and even gender boundaries.

Contemporary playgoers either frequented an amphitheater or playhouse when they went to see a play in London. Amphitheaters, such as the Rose, the Swan, the Globe, the Fortune, the Hope, Red Bull, and the Boar's Head were located in the city's suburbs and could hold thousands of people at a time. The Globe, for example, is believed to have been able to accommodate more than three thousand people at once. Such a large crowd required a variety of viewing arrangements that coincided with a person's social class. At the most basic level, a playgoer could pay a penny to stand in the yard, an area open to the elements and immediately surrounding the stage. Most playgoers, however, paid an extra penny to have a seat under the roof in the amphitheater's gallery. Spectators willing to pay even more found themselves with more private boxes and cushioned seats. Andrew Gurr has explained that this set up perfectly replicated contemporary society, featuring "the lowest in the yard below [the stage] to the lords' room on the stage balcony above the actors, placed at the middle level between the stage as earth and the stage cover as the heavens."[11]

Playhouses, like Backfriars, the Cockpit, Salisbury Court, the Curtain, and the Theater, were quite different, though. Probably because many of these playhouses were within London's city walls, they were much smaller than amphitheaters. Contemporary accounts seem to indicate that Blackfriars could hold fewer than one thousand people at once, while the Cockpit was thought to provide "seating at 18 inches per bottom for fewer than 700 people."[12] Performances at playhouses were more expensive, too. Since there was not a section for patrons willing to stand, the cheapest seats went for sixpence and were furthest from the stage in the uppermost gallery; the most expensive seats were in boxes and stalls close to the stage. This highlights one of the biggest differences between contemporary amphitheaters and playhouses, for in a playhouse close proximity to the stage indicated wealth whereas the reverse was true in an amphitheater.[13]

While play going as a whole transcended social class, the differences between amphitheater and playhouse demonstrate that the clientele each facility would have attracted was different. This could easily be attributed to admission price, for apprentices and serving men would have likely been unable to afford a performance in a playhouse. Certainly, an indoor playhouse would have been the more attractive choice to merchants and wealthy citizens who could afford it, though. Although this division would seem to indicate that two distinct play going cultures emerged, Gurr argues quite the opposite. He contends

2. "Let the skie raine Potatoes"

that because plays originally performed in amphitheaters could be later performed in playhouses, and vice versa, a subculture specific to amphitheaters or playhouses did not develop. Instead, he says this "division was more of social class than audience taste. That in turn implies that the price of admission had more effect than any class loyalty shown for the specific repertoires."[14]

Similarly, Maus and Bevington contend that there was little difference between a performance at an amphitheater and a playhouse. They argue:

> it would be a mistake to stress too greatly the differences between the public-theater plays and the private-theater plays. A number of playwrights, including Jonson, Middleton, and Beaumont, wrote successfully for both public and private theaters. The King's Men performed much of the same repertory at their two theaters. Webster's *The Duchess of Malfi* and Jonson's *The Alchemist*, for instance, both of which were probably first performed in the private Blackfriars Theater, also received performances at the Globe amphitheater. Fletcher's and Shakespeare's plays were also popular in both venues. Courtly and bourgeois drama drew on each other, and English drama was richer for it.[15]

This echoes Gurr's opinion that the division between public amphitheater and private playhouse had more to do with social class than anything else. Clearly, playwrights were not crafting plays with specific audiences in mind.

If anything, plays seem to have been crafted and performed for the masses. John Brewer contends that dramatists and actors unsurprisingly "recognized the power of the public, especially in the cheaper galleries, to shape theatrical taste and interpret theatrical performance."[16] This idea fits with Gurr's regarding the socioeconomic status of contemporary playgoers, as according to him the middle segment of society made up the "great bulk" of theater audiences.[17] He argues that "all of the distinct classes in [society's] middle stratum" were playgoers, including urban artisans, citizen merchants and manufacturers, schoolmasters, scriveners, and the clergy.[18] Because plays were being seen by the masses, the foreign foods they were mentioning were being consumed, at least intellectually, by the average English person as well.

Another important facet of the seventeenth century theater audience was the presence of women from all classes. In explaining the relevance of female playgoers, Gurr notes that, "women from every section of society went to plays, from Queen Henrietta Maria to the most harlotry of vagrants" to the extent that playwrights such as John Fletcher began to write specifically with the female audience in mind.[19] While prostitutes did frequent plays, Gurr argues that this was comparable to any public area and their presence should in no way demonstrate the theater as a singularly male space. In fact, he posits the idea that perhaps prostitutes frequented theaters to market themselves and be spectators at the same time, bolstering the idea that the theater transcended social status.[20] Whether a queen, a whore, or an average English woman, that plays offered females a space to interact with foreign foods is quite fascinating. It demonstrates that they were part of the public that was actively engaging in intellectual consumption of these foods.

The presence of prostitutes and other undesirable figures at amphitheaters and playhouses helps to explain the sinful reputation they obtained. As Brewer explains, "the association of theater with brothel was reinforced by the proximity of almost every London theater to bagnios and houses of ill fame. Which came first—playhouses or whorehouses—is a moot point, but the connection was firmly established by the seventeenth century."[21] This connection was viewed as dangerous to some contemporary English men and women, as at the theater "players and spectators colluded in pleasurable deception."[22] The hazards of such deception speak to the notion that playhouses and plays were able to influence the mind and imagination of the audience.

Added to this danger was the prejudice towards plays that Protestants had long harbored. Brewer notes "hostility to the stage was deeply embedded in the English Protestant consciousness. The stage was viewed as a place for trickery and deceit, full of illusions and magic similar to those that the Roman Catholic Church had used to bamboozle ignorant observers into becoming credulous believers. For many Protestants, especially clerics, it was a cardinal principle that playgoing and going to mass were both forms of idolatry."[23] It was amidst such fears that Parliament decided to order the closure of all amphitheaters and plays in September 1642. The closure of these establishments was not unprecedented; Parliament had ordered them closed before in an effort to combat the plague and other epidemics. This closure, however, was, as Gurr puts it, Parliament's attempt to "batten down the hatches in a time of political storm."[24]

2. *"Let the skie raine Potatoes"*

It was not until Charles II took the throne in 1660 that amphitheaters and playhouses reopened and English drama was able to return to what it was before. While Charles is said to have loved the theater, he saw the benefits of regulating playwrights and actors, ensuring that all remained loyal. Looking at the Restoration theater, Brewer explains that "it was regulated in two ways: the right to perform was restricted to those to whom the crown granted patents or licenses, and the content of the performance was subject to the approval of a royal servant, the Master of the Revels."[25] A system that would remain in place for over a century, Charles's method of censorship ensured that plays continued to entertain the masses without inciting any treasonous ideas.

Thus, the authority that contemporaries believed actors, plays, and playwrights had over the public, coupled with the diverse body of playgoers attending the various theaters, demonstrates that the inclusion of foreign foods in seventeenth century English drama is vital when endeavoring to understand their consumption. While plays certainly do not indicate that these foods were actually being eaten, they illustrate that English men and women were actively thinking of them, and therefore consuming them in mind if not in body. Plays also demonstrate the kind of information about a given product that had entered popular thought; was the food's color or smell its most striking characteristic or was it the notion that it could cure the body of a particular ailment? Such information proves that foreign food consumption, in body or in mind, was not restricted to upper class men and women, but an activity that the masses participated in.

Familiarity with Foreign Foods

The most significant examples of foreign foods in plays are those that suggest the average English man or woman had personally interacted with them. Plays that discuss the size, smell, or color of a particular foreign food, for example, can only lead modern readers to conclude that the audience had some experience with them. This might be one of the most important signs that certain foods were widely available in the domestic marketplace, as it seems anyone who would know of the appearance of a food would have seen it at some point. Because of this availability, it seems fair to conclude that the average seventeenth century English person was physically encountering some of the foreign foods introduced to England.

Pumpkins serve as a prime example of this, as their large size seems to have served as the basis for many insults in contemporary English plays. In Thomas D'Urfey's *A Fool's Perferment*, for example, a character accuses another of being "as puft out [as] a pumpkin."[26] Similarly, in *The Life and Death of Doctor Faustus*, William Mountfort describes a peck of prescribed pills as being "as big as a Pumpkin," and in *Belphegor: or The Marriage of the Devil*, John Wilson describes the devil as having "eyes as big as Pumpkins."[27] The large and rotund size of pumpkins was clearly common knowledge, and all together, pumpkins were included in six different contemporary plays (see Appendix). Because of this, it seems only logical that the average English person would have had some personal experience with the squash. This is supported by the fact that the English began to grow pumpkins domestically as early as the mid sixteenth century.[28]

Apart from comments about their lustiness, the physical size and shape of potatoes were also mentioned. In John Dryden's *Troilus and Cressida*, a character is accused of having "a fat rump, and potato fingers," providing the audience with an amusing description of fat fingers.[29] Also using the potato for an insult, in the comedy *Greenwich-Park*, Mountfort relies on the starchy nature of the tuber to describe a "Drugster" as having "no more Moisture than a Potato."[30] While instances like these illustrate that the English were familiar with the physical properties of potatoes, more striking is the linkage that appears between the Irish and potatoes at this early date. In Joseph Harris' *Love's a Lottery, and a Woman the Prize*, for example, an "eminent" London merchant "dealt and traded for.... Irish Potatoes."[31] While this demonstrates nothing about English consumption, it seems reasonable to conclude that if the Irish were growing potatoes and the English were importing them, potatoes had become somewhat common in contemporary culture.[32] This is supported by the fact that potatoes were mentioned in thirty-five separate seventeenth century English plays (see Appendix).

A familiarity with the diverse spices being used in England is evident in plays as well. Various references to cinnamon were made in

2. *"Let the skie raine Potatoes"*

fifteen contemporary dramas (see Appendix). Common amongst these was the color of cinnamon, as its hue was used to describe the brownness of something. It is in this fashion that cinnamon is discussed in *The Committee: A Comedy*. Here Sir Robert Howard features Colonel Careless telling Mrs. Day that, although in disguise, he knows her "as well as if [she] were in [her] Sabbath-dayes Cinamon Waistcot," clearly comparing the color of Mrs. Days' waistcoat with the color of the spice.[33] Similarly, in Sir William D'Avenant's *The Distresses*, Androlio states that he knows Orco by his "Aggot eyes, and [his] Cinnamon face."[34] One must assume that the English masses knew what color cinnamon was, otherwise, such comparisons would have fallen flat.

The color of nutmeg was frequently used as well in contemporary plays. Thomas Middleton employed it in two of his plays; first, in *The Widow: A Comedy* he has Valeria's servant using nutmeg to describe a man's clothing, saying "he in the Nutmeg coloured band forsooth."[35] Next, in *Anything for a Quiet Life: A Comedy*, the character George describes his wife as having a "nutmeg hue."[36] In the same manner, Edward Howard's *A Man of Newmarket* features a Waiter assuring Trainstead of Madam Jacalin's affection, explaining that she has "heard [Madam Jacalin] commend just such a brown or Nutmeg-complexion as yours."[37] Clearly, contemporary English men and women were familiar enough with nutmeg to understand such comparisons to its color. Their familiarity with the spice is also evident in its presence in a total of thirty plays throughout the period (see Appendix).

The inclusion of nutmeg graters in seventeenth century plays further illustrates the active consumption of the spice. As Alan Davidson has explained, "the chemistry of nutmeg is such that aroma and flavour disappear quickly once a nutmeg is grated. Hence the profusion of nutmeg graters, intended to be used immediately before the need arises."[38] Because physical consumption of nutmeg is so closely tied to nutmeg graters, any mention of the grater is important as it shows that people knew how to include nutmeg in their diets. In *The Tragedy of the Dutchesse of Malfy*, John Webster illustrates that the public was acquainted with the tool, featuring Bosola explaining that "There was a Lady in France, that hauing had the small pockes, Flead the skinne off her face, to make it more leuell; And whereas before she look'd like a Nutmeg-grater, After she resembled a hedge-hog."[39] Henry Higden also uses a nutmeg grater to describe a person's face, having Leonora explain to her Aunt in *The Wary Widdow* that "his Face feels as rough as a Nutmeg grater."[40] While offering an excellent visual comparison, such usage also proves that nutmeg and nutmeg graters were both familiar items.

Just as playgoers clearly knew of the necessary steps required to consume nutmeg, they had comparable knowledge regarding sugar. Contemporary plays illustrate that sugar was widely known in English culture by the seventeenth century, as 116 plays discuss it in some manner. More telling, though, is that eight of these plays made mention of sugar in its conical, sugar loaf shape (see Appendix). This was the standard form contemporary consumers bought sugar in, which they would break apart with a hammer before using it.[41] Playwrights cited the shape of the assembled form of sugar loaf to create a visual for their audience. For example, Higden features the Master comparing "the peak of Tenariff," one of the Canary Islands, to "a sugar-loafe" in his *The Warry Widow*. It was also common for plays to make note of the molded and refined nature of loaf sugar. Mountfort's *The Successful Straingers*, for example, includes a character referring to another as having an expression that is "refin'd like loaf-Sugar," and William Congreve's *The Way of the World* features Mirabell exclaiming that she would "mold [her] boy's head like a sugar-loaf."[42] Clearly, if the English public knew the manner and shape that sugar was sold in, then they assumedly had some personal knowledge and even interaction with the product.

Similar to the public's knowledge of nutmeg and sugar, the manner of clove consumption, it often being "stuck" into other foods, appears to have been cemented in playgoers' minds. In *Aglaura*, for example, Sir John Suckling features Orsames describing love as "A mightie Prince, and full of curiositie—Harts newly sev'd up intire, and stucke with little Arrowes in stead of Cloves—."[43] While Thomas Dekker's *North-Ward Hoe* and Peter Anthony Motteux's *Love's a Jest* features cloves in "a gammon of bacon," cloves are most commonly presented with oranges, especially in the latter half of the seventeenth century.[44] William Cartwright uses Cloves in oranges to describe a woman's teeth, with Philostratus saying that the teeth looked "as if they were cloves stuck in an Orenge" in *The Siedge*.[45] Using cloves in an orange to flatter instead of insult, Sir P. Eitherside compliments Aurelia, stating "Dear

2. "Let the skie raine Potatoes"

Madam, your words have so pow'rfull an influence upon me, that I fear my breast wants room for the excessive joy; is stuck round with the darts of your Beauty, like an Orange that is stuck with Cloves" in D'Urfey's *The Royalist*.[46] In total, cloves appeared in twenty-four plays from the period (see Appendix). That they were often featured with other foods demonstrates not only that contemporary men and women knew what cloves were, but also they knew what foods they were typically paired with.

Tobacco appears to have infiltrated the national consciousness as well; it was included in 181 seventeenth century plays (see Appendix). Several of these plays made frequent reference to tobacco's smell and how it clung to those who smoked it, especially toward the end of the seventeenth century. Sir George Etherege's *The Man of Mode* has Mrs. Loveit complaining about the smell of four fellows, explaining, "their Perriwigs are scented with Tobacco so strong."[47] Mrs. Manley also addresses the problem of wigs retaining the smell of tobacco; in her *The Lost Lover* Wilmore exclaims that he stinks of "old Amorous Women" and concurring that "it be like our Perriwiggs, that retain the scent of Tobacco."[48]

Tobacco and brandy were also frequently mentioned together too. D'Urfey's *Trick for Trick* depicts Monsieur Thomas questioning a woman's morals upon hearing her referred to as a Gentlewoman. He scoffs, "this Gentlewoman—what Gentlewoman—? this Whore—Rogue, this Whore—Sirrah, let me have no corruption of Notions—But speak every thing in its Nature—by this Light, Gentlemen, a scurvy Suburb Whore, that smelt of nothing but Tobacco and Brandy."[49] Instead of insulting an alleged Gentlewoman, Congreve linked brandy and tobacco to attack soldiers. His *The Old Batchelour* features Belinda calling Bluffe a "monstrous filthy fellow" and then exclaiming "Good slovenly Captain Huffe, Bluffe, (What's your hideous Name?) be gone: You stink of Brandy and Tobacco, most Soldier-like."[50] Although smelling of tobacco has a negative connotation here, it is clear that the average playgoer would have been familiar with the lingering stench of it.

Allusions to tortoises and turkeys in contemporary drama prove to be the most interesting, though. Because plays commonly speak to the nature or behavior of these animals, it seems safe to assume that the English were well acquainted with them, possibly because they were eating them. Tortoises, for example, were featured in thirty contemporary plays; commonly discussed in relation to their speed, or lack thereof (see Appendix). Ben Johnson's play *Catline His Conspiracy* features Cethegus bemoaning the lateness of other characters and likening their tardiness to a "tortoyse speed."[51] Similarly, *The Hollander*, by Henry Glapthorne, includes a gentleman explaining that he likes his fires extinguished "with tortoyse speed," and *Don Sebastian*, by John Dryden, includes an Emperor accusing others of moving at "a Tortoise pace."[52] From such examples, it seems clear that contemporary English men and women fully understood the slowness of the tortoise.

They also had enough personal knowledge of the creature to know of its general appearance. There are many references to the shell of the tortoise and its ability to carry it on its back. More striking, though, are allusions to a tortoise's skin. While a person may have heard of a tortoise's slow speed or shell, the knowledge of the nature of its skin seems to indicate that the average playgoer had a more intimate understanding of the animal. And, just as the speed of a tortoise was used to insult other characters, so was its skin. Thomas Randolph's *The Jealous Lovers*, for example, has Phryne ranting that Asotus "has a skin as wrinckled as a Tortoyse."[53] Conversely, *The Comical History of Don Quixote*, by D'Urfey, comments on the dark color of a tortoise's skin, with a Hostess explaining to Sancho that a man has "a pair of Hands as black as the Skin of a Tortois."[54] Thus, between comparisons to the tortoises' speed, skin, and shell, it becomes apparent that seventeenth century playgoers were well acquainted with the animal.

Many comparisons were made about the qualities of turkeys as well. In fact, it was not uncommon for jealous or arrogant characters to be metaphorically referred to as turkey-cocks, the two apparently sharing the same behaviors. Shakespeare himself uses the comparison twice in his plays. In *Twelfth Night*, he features Fabian stating, "contemplation makes a rare Turkey Cocke" of Malvolio as he "jets under his advanced plumes." Then in his coauthored play *The Two Noble Kinsmen*, a country person mentions that his wife is "as jealous as a Turkey."[55] Similarly, in Dryden's *The Assignation*, Benito accuses Laura of "bristl[ing] up to me, and wheel[ing] about me, like a Turkey-cock that is making Love."[56] Such comparisons to the behavior of a turkey, along with mentions of turkeys being eaten at feasts, are found in thirty contemporary English plays (see Appendix). They demonstrate that turkeys were commonly kept and eaten in seventeenth century England, not at all surprising, since turkeys were first introduced to the country in the 1540s when a variety of poultry, both large and small, was typically eaten.[57]

The familiar way that these foreign foods were discussed suggests that playwrights assumed that the general audience had some previous knowledge of these products. Although the audience's familiarity with a foreign food does not prove it was being physically consumed, it seems that the only way they would have known about them is if they were being frequently encountered. Their integration into English culture demonstrates that the English were eager to reap the dietary benefits of their expanding transoceanic trade networks and burgeoning empire.

Foreign Foods, Gender and Class

Foreign foods, and especially foreign beverages like coffee, tea and chocolate, could also function as signifiers of a person's gender or class. In Peter Anthony Motteux's play *Love's A Jest*, Sir Thomas wonders "how thy drink at London now; for there are modes for drinking as for other things?" To this, Gaymood responds, "first, your Politicians drink Coffee; Wits, Beaux and Women, warm Tea, and some of 'em cold; We Rakes, drink Red, and then Small-beer; Bawds, Snapdragons; Whores what they can get, but Mead and Rhenish and Sugar to chuse; Stewards the best Champain, and their Masters the worst, Merchants smuggl'd Claret; Wenches Chocolate, and sometimes Dyetdrink."[58] Motteux's interpretation of what those in London were drinking seems to reflect actual trends that had emerged by the end of the seventeenth century.[59] Other playwrights support Motteux's notion of gender and social stratification based on beverage consumption as well, reflecting and reinforcing contemporary ideas about these foods.

Late seventeenth century plays do seem to label coffee houses as gathering spaces for the political, as historians like Brian Cowan have contended.[60] In *The City-Heiress*, for example, Aphra Behn includes a character that is said to be "tak[ing] up at Coffee-houses, talk[ing] gravely in the City, speak[ing] scandalously of the Government, and rail[ing] most abominably against the Pope and the French King."[61] Similarly, John Crown's aptly titled *City Politques* features a citizen of Podesta accusingly asking Craffy "who us'd to trouble themselves and others about State-affairs more then you Sir? Were you not such a tempestuous disputer in Coffe-houses, that as soon as ever you appear'd in one, both sides wou'd run away, our Friends out of envy, and our Enemies out of fear?"[62] This brings to light an interesting comparison; clearly here Craffy is being labeled as a politically minded man, yet earlier in the play he is called a pretender to poetry. The connection between the coffeehouse and poets, and perhaps poets and those who are political, is mentioned in several other plays of the period as well, including Thomas Porter's *A Witty Combat* and Congreve's *Love for Love*.[63]

Coffee itself was referred to in thirty contemporary plays, consumed most commonly amongst respectable men socializing with one another (see Appendix). *The Richmond Heiress* by D'Urfey, for example, features Stockjobb exasperated after his dealings with Hotspur, explaining he was leaving to "go and drink a Dish of Coffee with a good Neighbour, a Common Council-man, and Brother Stockjobber."[64] Also authored by D'Urfey, *The Famous History of the Rise and Fall of Massaniello, Part I* depicts Ursula irritated at the General and the Major, complaining that they were going to "parboil their Guts with Coffee" together.[65] Sir Charles Sedley's *The Mulberry-Garden* further illustrates men socializing over coffee, as Sir Samuel Forecast states to the Widow that he was "much bound to [her] for [her] Good opinion, and [came] to condole with [her]: [Her] Husband was an honest, prudent, and a Wealthy Gentleman, kept good hours, and even Reckonings, lov'd [him] well, and [they] have drank Many a Dish of Coffee together."[66] While these examples do not illustrate overtly political male coffee drinkers as Motteux suggested, they do demonstrate that coffee consumption was a primarily male activity. This, in a sense, fits with Motteux's assessment, since seventeenth century politicians were only males.

Other contemporary playwrights echo Motteux's notion that tea is popular amongst women of quality as well. *The Lost Lover* by Mrs. Manley, for example, explains in the Prologue that the audience may

2. "Let the skie raine Potatoes"

feel the "Lady" in the play should confine herself to "fringe and tea" instead of the actions of an "adventurer" as the play describes.[67] Similarly, in Colley Cibber's *Love Makes a Man*, Clodio brags that he has been wooing eleven different ladies, showering them with presents including tea.[68] Tea consumption amongst women was seen as a communal activity as well, as Congreve describes in his *The Double-Dealer* that the ladies went to "the Gallery; retired to their Tea, and Scandal."[69] In the same vain, the ladies in Thomas Southerne's *The Wives Excuse* are asked if they will "drink [their] Tea upon the Mount, and be the Envy of the Neighbourhood" and Oldwit orders the "womankind" in his presence to "pack away to [their] Cards, and [their] tea" in *Bury-Fair* by Thomas Shadwell.[70] Almost like wine in the twenty-first century, contemporary plays suggest that tea drinking denotes a level of sophistication, frequently consumed in a group setting of similarly respected females.

This is certainly not to say that men were not exhibited consuming the beverage; they were often illustrated taking tea with their wives or other females. In Sedley's *The Mulberry-Garden*, for example, Harry Modish tells Jack Wildish that to gain a good reputation a man must, amongst other things, have "a Dish of Tea after Dinner ... before the Ladies."[71] *The Lover's Luck*, penned by Thomas Dilke, also illustrates this, featuring Eager urging Collonel Bellair to go with him to "chat over a Dish of Tea with Vesuvia, [since] she's a merry Jade and will give [him] some account of the Intriegues of the Town."[72]

While depictions of men and women drinking tea together in such social situations was common, there were also a handful of references of woman using tea to slip their husbands opium. D'Urfey's *A Common-Wealth of Women*, for instance, opens with two paramours meeting and the woman stating that "after Dinner, 'tis always [her husband's] Custom to call for Tea, in which I cunningly infus'd a Dram or two of Opium, which made its Operation instantly; for after sneezing two or three times, and ... fetching a Rhumatick Cough from the bottom of his Lungs.... He fell fast asleep," affording her the opportunity to sneak away.[73] Dilke's *The Pretenders* features opium and tea in the same manner, with Widow Thoroshift recounting how "Lady Rampabout uses to infuse Opium into her Husbands Tea, and when the good old Knight is fast asleep in his chair of ease by the fire side, she very fairly receives her friendly visits without any danger of a discovery."[74] Assumedly, opium was not commonly slipped into an unknowing husband's tea, yet using tea as the vehicle for such a drugging speaks to the frequency that contemporary playgoers were consuming it. This is supported by the twenty-nine different plays that refer to the beverage during this period (see Appendix). Thus, by the end of the seventeenth century, tea drinking in teahouses and at home had obviously become an ingrained aspect of English culture.

Seventeenth century plays reveal that chocolate, too, was a somewhat gendered beverage when consumed publically, but its consumption and the chocolate houses that served it were not looked upon quite as favorably as tea or coffee houses. This is made clear in *The Way of the World*, where Congreve depicts the Coachman demanding "two Dishes of Chocolate and a Glass of Cinnamon-water" and Witwoud responds that the beverages "should be for two fasting Strumpets, and a Bawd troubl'd with Wind."[75] This resembles the advice offered in the play *The World in the Moon*. Here, Palmerin suggests that men who lie awake at night, should:

> First watch your Wives, and then your Money;
> And drive the Hornets from your Honey.
> For fear your Spouse your Crabs inoculate,
> Keep her from Beaus and House of Chocolate.[76]

Clearly, Palmerin believes that women frequenting chocolate houses will somehow be corrupted, an idea echoed by playwrights who comment on the clientele that went to these establishments. Mountfort, for example, describes in his comedy *Greenwich-Park* that "you can now ... pick up Whores at the Chocolate-House."[77] Contemporary plays suggest that there is a lack of morality amongst females who visit chocolate houses, especially when compared to their tea-drinking counterparts.

All gender divisions surrounding chocolate dissolve, however, when chocolate is consumed within the home. Many plays illustrate both men and women of quality drinking the beverage, especially in the morning. In fact, *The Adventure of Five Hours*, *Tarugo's Wiles*, *The English Frier*, *The Successfull Straingers*, *The Mock-Marriage*, and *The Reformed Wife* all feature a mixture of male and female characters ordering chocolate from their servants or being informed that their servants have brought them chocolate to drink.[78] Like tea, chocolate consumption was established by the end of the seventeenth century and was included by playwrights in thirty-two contemporary dramas (see Appendix).

Looking beyond the significance of whether a person consumed coffee, tea, or chocolate, it is extremely interesting that these three foreign substances were so integrated into seventeenth century English culture. Unlike foreign foods in medieval England, consumption of these products clearly evolved beyond a simple indication of wealth. While tea drinking carried an air of sophistication, a person's monetary resources, or lack thereof, did not factor into ideas about these consumers. Instead, popular opinion connected tea drinking to a person's virtuous character or moral fortitude. Because of this, it seems quite logical to conclude that coffee, tea, and chocolate were freely available to the public.

While many foreign foods were widely available to the average person during the seventeenth century, the spice cassia was still repeatedly illustrated as a product reserved only for the wealthy in the fourteen plays that mentioned it (see Appendix). This association between cassia and luxury may seem odd to modern readers, as cassia is similar to, but of lesser quality than, cinnamon. The luxurious status of cassia indicates that the seventeenth century English were importing it from Southern China where quality cassia was cultivated, although even this variety was still considered to be inferior to cinnamon.[79] Webster's *The Tragedy of the Dutchesse of Malfy* offers two examples of cassia's luxury status. In the first, Antonio states that "man (like to Cassia) is prou'd best"; if cassia remained "proud," it was likely too expensive for the average English consumer.[80] Secondly, the Duchesse is featured exclaiming that death does not terrify her, stating "what would it pleasure me, to haue my throate cut with diamonds? Or to be smothered with Cassia? Or to be shot to death with pearles? I know death hath ten thousand seuerall doors for men, to take their Exits."[81] Also linking cassia with luxury, *The Mvses Looking-Glasses*, by Thomas Randolph, depicts Banausus claiming that when he dies he will be "embalm'd with Mirrhe and Cassia, And richer unguents then th' Ægyptian Kings."[82] If contemporary playgoers viewed cassia in the same manner that they viewed diamonds, pearls, and the burial rights of Egyptian Kings, it was certainly not a product they would have had much personal experience with. That seventeenth century playwrights spoke of such products with such veneration, though, demonstrates that foods not discussed in such a manner were more commonplace. Cassia's luxury status acts as a marker, illustrating that many other foreign foods had trickled down the social ladder.

Foreign Foods and Medicinal Practices

Many foreign foods seem to have been quickly integrated into seventeenth century medical culture as well. As Cowan has noted, seventeenth century "orthodox medicine, which on the whole remained wedded to the Galenic paradigm, was not averse to accepting new and foreign drugs into its pharmacopoeia. The 'new worlds' brought to the attention of early modern Europeans were often portrayed as abundant in natural wealth ... it was only natural to expect these lands to be rich in useful medicines as well."[83] Because of this, some of the foreign foods referenced most frequently as excellent medicines were entirely new to the English and were being imported from the Americas. Others, such as spices, had been available to the English prior to the seventeenth century, but only via overland trade routes making them unaffordable to all but the very elite. Thus, contemporary plays highlight the trickling down of these curative products. In either case, though, the incorporation of entirely new foods and the newly cheap spices into medical thought demonstrates that the average person was acquainted with the curative powers these foreign foods were believed to have.

Spices are particularly prevalent in seventeenth century English drama, as it was believed they could help balance one's bodily humors. Because of this, the addition of spices to a beverage, most commonly some sort of wine, was popular and thought of as a restorer of health. In Margaret Cavendish, Duchess of Newcastle's play *Matrimonial Trouble, part I*, for example, one such concoction is ordered to cure a stomach made upset by a disagreeable meal. A Gentlewoman explains to a maid that: "in my Ladies stomach [the tough Posset-curd] proves as hard as stone; wherefore you must go and burn some Claret-wine

2. "Let the skie raine Potatoes"

for her, with Cloves, Mace, and Nutmegs, and make it very sweet with fine loaf-sugar."[84] A similar mixture of sherry, nutmeg, and sugar is included in three of D'Urfey's seventeenth century plays, all imbibed in the morning to ensure good health and "service" for the day.[85] That the usage of spiced wine to ensure health seems to have been common knowledge illustrates that the benefits of spices had become a part of English popular culture by this time.

Going beyond a discussion of the color of cinnamon, contemporary plays also note that the spice could act as a restorer of health. This is evident even in the early seventeenth century, as *West-ward Hoe*, written by Thomas Dekker, mentions the spice and its curative powers twice. In the first instance, Mistress Biralime endeavors to help the Earle, telling him to "drinke this draught of Cynamon water, and plucke vp your spirits."[86] Later in the play, Monopoly likewise tries to cure Clare after discovering her pulse racing. He orders "a draught of Cynamon water now for her, [which is] better than two Tankerdes out of the Thames."[87] Ben Jonson's *The Magnetick Lady* also refers to cinnamon water and, in fact, features a character claiming that it is better at curing "wenches falling in swoune" than anything a doctor could prescribe.[88] Thus, contemporary playgoers were familiar with the notion that cinnamon water could assist in restoring a persons overall health and wellness.

Like cinnamon water, gingerbread, made with several different spices and, in the seventeenth century, treacle, was used to cure a variety of different ailments and featured in forty contemporary plays (see Appendix).[89] For instance, the nurse Friswood asks Touch-wood in Brome's *The Sparagvs Garden* if he "will eate a peece of Ginger-bread for [his] Winde."[90] D'Urfey likewise included gingerbread in one of his plays, although he does not note that the food relieves flatulence. Instead, in *The Campaigner*, he features Bondevelt explaining that while visiting the Northern part of the globe, he will find very beneficial "commodities [that] warm the Stomach" such as "French Brandy, Irish Usquebaugh, and English Gigner-bread."[91] That gingerbread, a product that relied upon a variety of foreign foods, had been solidified as "English" demonstrates how entirely integrated into English culture it was. Not only did gingerbread represent an English culinary tradition, but contemporary plays illustrate that playgoers were so familiar with it that they were acquainted with its ability to cure flatulence and "warm" the stomach.

Entirely new foods from the Americas appear to have reached a similar status as well since, as Ben Johnson indicates, they were thought to be effective forms of treatment. In his play *Volpone*, Johnson includes a song, meant to advertise Volpone's miraculous oil, which states:

> Had old Hippocrates, or Galen,
> (That to their bookes put med'cines all in)
> But knowne this secret, they had neuer
> (Of which they will be guiltie euer)
> Beene murderers of so much paper,
> Or wasted many a hurtlesse taper:
> No Indian drug had ere beene famed,
> Tabacco, sassafras not named;
> Ne yet, of guacum one small stick, sir,
> Nor Raymvnd Lvllies great elixir.[92]

Here, Johnson juxtaposes three American products, tobacco, sassafras, and guaiacum, with the men whose work was the basis of English medical practices and theory. This illustrates that, like these great men, American products revolutionized English medicinal cultural. By using these men and ingredients as a marker to measure his own miraculous oil against, Volpone demonstrates to modern readers how highly regarded these products were.

Along with discussing the smell of tobacco, seventeenth century plays also commented upon the positive effects the plant was thought to have on the body. In *Technogamia*, Barten Holyday sums up the health benefits of tobacco through song, extolling:

> Tobacco's a Physician
> Good both for Sound and Sickly:
> T'is a Hot Perfume
> That expells Cold Rhewme,
> And makes it flow downe quickly.[93]

Tobacco's effectiveness in expelling rheum is similarly commented upon in the anonymously written *The Gossips Braule*, where a character seeks Spanish tobacco to cure his rheumatism.[94] While tobacco is also commonly discouraged and disparaged in plays, even King James I was famously opposed to the substance, some playwrights took on tobacco detractors.[95] Mountfort's *The Launching of the Mary*, for example, features

2. *"Let the skie raine Potatoes"*

a committee asking "Ist possible, to finde a man so blinde, so ignorant in any famous Comon wealth: that will, oppose the moderate vse of healthfull druggs, and Comfortable spices," one of these healthful drugs he mentions being tobacco.[96] Despite the negative attention tobacco consumption received, its place in the English pharmacopeia was solidified by the end of the seventeenth century.

Another foreign food that was especially popular for its curative qualities was plantains, featured in five plays from the period (see Appendix). Renowned for their abilities to cure wounds, plantains or plantain leaves were frequently used when there was some type of open sore.[97] Shakespeare and Fletcher's *The Two Noble Kinsmen* included an argument from their character Palamon that his "poor slight sores, need not a Plantain."[98] While neither of these plays identify whether it is the fruit or leaf of the plantain plant that is being used, *The Faithful Shepherd*, by Sir Richard Fanshawe, speaks of a poultice being made from a plantain leaf.[99] Even if only plantain leaves were being used in seventeenth century medicine, it is clear from contemporary drama that there was a firm belief in their ability to heal flesh wounds.

Although chocolate was not thought to cure ailments like other New World products, it was, like potatoes, thought to invoke desire in its consumers in the late seventeenth century. Amusingly, Edward Ravenscroft's *The London Cuckolds* features the Alderman Wiseacres explaining why he prefers young women to those of his own age, stating: "I am convinced that an old man can never love an old woman, that's for certain. Age is a sure decayer and renders men backward in their duty, therefore I marry a woman so young, that she may be a temptation to me when I am old. You may talk of Amber-cawdles, Chocolate, and Jelly-broths, but they are nothing comparable to youth and beauty, a young woman is the onely provocative for old age, I say."[100] Obviously, what a young woman could do for an old man was comparable to what chocolate could do for an old man with an old woman. Dilke echoes the notion that chocolate is a provocative product, with Eager telling Goosandelo in *The Lover's Luck* that a person would be very busy loving him, especially if they love "Provocatives, such as Shellfish, Cavere, Eringo-roots, Pistachoo-past, [or] Spanish Chocolate."[101]

While chocolate was clearly viewed as a lust-inducing product, D'Urfey provides some rather different insight about the food in his

Tastes of the Empire

The Famous History and Fall of Massainello, Part II. In it, Blowzabella's affinity towards chocolate and the effect it has on her shape is mentioned several times. Upon telling La Poop that she cannot dress in the morning until she has had her tenth dish of chocolate, La Poop exclaims: "Ah bless your Ladiship—you have de ver leetell Stomach—you soop, soop, soop—de pauvre quantity de Chocolate in de Morning, but you Eat nothing all de day long, besides dat is considerable. Ma foy you vill never put your shape in de fashipn, if you piddle, piddle—at dis rate." But while La Poop certainly attributes Blowzabella's shapely figure to her chocolate consumption, Blowzabella does not feel the same way, telling her "Plump—nay, if I am taken for one of the Lean ones, the Looker on sees double, and the Devil made the Spectacles; I'm sure I han't felt any Ribs I have this Ten years: And I weigh, *Sups her Chocolate*, let me see I weigh just three and fifty Stone, and two Pound."[102] While comical, it appears that by the end of the seventeenth century consumers understood what modern readers now know; chocolate is not healthy for the waistline.

Although plays do not prove that English men and women used spices, tobacco, plantains, or chocolate at all regularly to treat their bodies, the fact that these foods were widely known for their medicinal properties is nevertheless important. It demonstrates that despite the products availability to the average consumer, the public was actively intellectually consuming foreign foods by buying into the notion that these products could in some way restore or influence their health. Not only is the intellectual consumption of these foods reflected in seventeenth century plays, but it is also perpetuated through them as playwrights reinforced the idea that foreign foods could cure domestic bodies as well as nourish them.

Conclusion

Through the intellectual consumption of foreign foods in contemporary plays, then, it becomes apparent that the seventeenth-century English were increasingly engaging with extra-European products. This rise coincides with English transoceanic exploration and settlement, making it even more possible for foreign foods to be accessible in

2. "Let the skie raine Potatoes"

domestic markets. Foods from the New World were being introduced to Europeans for the first time and foods previously obtained from the Silk Road were being brought back to England at unprecedently low prices. Coupled together, the abundance of foods from east and west transformed England's culinary culture and the way consumers thought of these products. For the first time, the average English man and woman could consider, if not actually consume, such foods as if they were within their reach.

Not only do contemporary plays provide insight into how the English could think of and conceptualize foreign foods in their diet and pharmacopeia, they also bolster the idea that physical consumption was occurring as well. While it is clear that the audience of these plays were consuming foreign foods in mind if not in body, the casual way that playwrights reference these products would seem to indicate that they assumed the audience was already acquainted with them. Nowhere is an author seen explaining the curative properties of plantains, clarifying the plumpness of a pumpkin, or justifying why only a strumpet would consume chocolate; the audience is already expected to know such things. Although this common knowledge does not function as proof positive that physical consumption was occurring, it does demonstrate that intellectual consumption of imperial foods was widespread. Consequently, foreign foods and the impact they had on seventeenth century culture cannot be overlooked due to the lack of importation records proving physical consumption. As contemporary plays illustrate, the English were familiar with these products and consuming them quite regularly, in mind if not in body, decades before the dawn of the eighteenth century.

3

"The Queens Closet Opened"

Like many of the domestic texts of the seventeenth century, the anonymously published *The Court and kitchin of Elizabeth, Commonly Called Joan Cromwel the Wife of the Late Usurper* contains more than just recipes and cooking advice. In an interesting interlude between husband and wife, the text purports a domestic disturbance said to have taken place between Oliver Cromwell and Elizabeth over the availability of foreign fruits. The author prefaces this scene by explaining that, "...upon *Oliver's* Rupture with the *Spanyard* ... the Commodities of that Country grew very scarce, and the prizes of them raised by such as could procure them underhand: Among the rest of those goods, the fruits of the growth of that place were very rare and dear, especially *Oranges* and *Lemons*."[1]

Apparently, Cromwell had not factored in foreign produce when he sought war against the Spanish in 1656. Despite his best efforts, he was unable to take Hispaniola from the Spanish, an island John Morrill explains Cromwell was personally obsessed with.[2] The war also caused him acrimony at home, as the anonymous author describes Elizabeth was none to happy at how scarce oranges had become, writing:

> One day, as the Protector was private at dinner; He called for an *Orange* to a Loyne of Veal, to which he used no other Sauce, and urging the same command, was answered by his Wife, *that Oranges were Oranges now, that Crab Oranges would cost a Groat, and for her part, she never intended to give it*; and it was presently whispered, that sure her Highness was never the adviser of the *Spanish* War, and that his Highness should have done well to have consulted his Digestion, before his hasty and inordinate appetite of Dominion and Riches in the *West Indies*.[3]

3. "The Queens Closet Opened"

Evidently, the author intended to amusingly illustrate that foreign relations could have drastic effects on domestic diets. This humorous approach demonstrates how popular cookery books had become; as Robert Appelbaum contends, the text "takes the literature of cookery as a vehicle for satire, both attest[ing] to the growing literary presence of cookbooks in the public life of England and to the ability of mainstream literature to appropriate and hence contribute to its literary value."[4]

While the story recounted between Elizabeth and Oliver Cromwell regards obtaining access to foods from Spain at a time when relations between the two countries were strained, the tale shows that in seventeenth century English minds, foreign food consumption and foreign relations were intertwined. The connection between foreign land and foreign foods is especially visible as the English were beginning to conquer new areas. Due to advances in sailing capabilities, the English were able to form new trade routes that allowed them to gain what had previously been luxury products, such as spices, at unprecedently low prices. Coupled with entirely new food products from the New World, English food culture was forever changed.

This integration of foreign foods into English diets provided women with an especially intriguing prospect. Unlike their male counterparts, women were not afforded many opportunities to engage in activities that would help build the empire from the comfort of their own homes. By and large, it was men, for example, that funded expeditions that brought back foreign products to the domestic market. Where women did have power and influence, however, were areas within the domestic sphere, such as the kitchen. In fact, Sara Pennell claims that "it was the actors within the [kitchen], and their interactions with the objects therein—through good housewifery and supervised servitude—which constructed an ideal kitchen" rather than the equipment within it.[5] For this reason, the integration of foreign foods into cuisine fell directly under the control of women, for they determined what foods were to be bought and prepared for their family's consumption.[6]

While contemporary cookery books illustrate that many of these texts were published with a female audience in mind, they also demonstrate that foreign foods were being integrated into English cuisine at an unprecedented rate. Manuscript cookery books, more often than not kept by the female head-of-household, support both these notions.

Tastes of the Empire

As Jennifer Stine has noted, manuscript texts are important because they reflect the unique interests of their complier. Claiming they have much in common with contemporary commonplace books, she states that manuscript recipe collections "were compiled for personal use, or use by family or friends. While sections might be copied from other sources ... recipe collections were essentially unique documents, each shaped by its individual compiler.... They differ from other sorts of commonplace books in that they generally do not include other sorts of text besides the recipes themselves, though occasionally they are used to record births, deaths, or other sorts of lists."[7]

More than their uniqueness, though, manuscript cookery books prove that their printed counterparts were not just being published, bought, and collected as a form of entertainment; read and enjoyed by the "armchair chef," but the recipes included never used for cooking.[8] Instead, they demonstrate that recipes were passed down from mothers to daughters, shared amongst female friends, as well as copied from published cookery books, all of which indicates such recipes were actually being prepared. They contain "corrections, annotations, and greasy stains [that] show us that these texts were actively used in kitchens."[9] No matter the original source of the recipe, one must assume that if the time was taken to copy it into a person's private collection, it was intended that the recipe would be used at some point and the ingredients it called for consumed.

Taking manuscript and published cookery books together, then, it is evident that foreign foods were being integrated and consumed on a regular basis in seventeenth century England, in large part thanks to women. This integration of foreign foods into a family's diet allowed average housewives an opportunity to engage in an empire building activity. Thus, not only would foreign foods revolutionize English food culture, but they allowed women an area to participate in the growing of England's empire.

Gender, Class and Cooking

Gender historians have long contended that cookery and other kitchen related activities came under the female sphere of control. As

3. "The Queens Closet Opened"

Sara Mendelson and Patricia Crawford outline in their *Women in Early Modern England*, "housewifery involved women of middling and elite social status in a multitude of highly skilled tasks. Brewing and distilling, cooking and baking, and even the practice of medicine ('physick') were part of the labour preformed by the mistress of the household as well as her female servants."[10] Amanda Vickery echoes this point, contending that recipe books demonstrate that English women had a vested interest in the production and processing of foods that their household would consume.[11] Gilly Lehman furthers this argument in *The British Housewife*, establishing that seventeenth century women of all classes were involved in culinary activities, whether they themselves were doing the cooking or they were overseeing it. While at the English court there were professional male chefs, who more often than not were French, for the rest of the country, women were in charge of the kitchen and food preparation.[12]

Tracing trends made evident when examining early modern English cookery books, Lehman demonstrates that as the eighteenth century progressed, cookery books became more readily available to those farther down the social ladder, an idea that Ken Albala notes in his various works as well. Both scholars argue that, unlike cookery books published on the continent, there is reason to believe that even before the seventeenth century there was a genre of English cooking texts published with a female audience in mind.[13] Wendy Wall furthers this by contending "Only in England were women nominated in print to oversee a complex set of knowledges called 'housewifery,' blending herbal cultivation, textile making, anatomy, water purification, chemistry, medical care, manners, butchery, the preservation of foodstuffs, and the manufacture of goods. England, for a brief time, became the most active site for cookery publication in Europe and the only country marketing recipe books for women."[14]

Many of the titles of cookery books suggest women were the target audience for these texts, as well; in the seventeenth century alone there were over twenty different cookery book titles that directly referenced them. Nearly half of these titles purported to have advice coming from or meant for a lady, such as *The Ladies Cabinet Opened*, *The Ladies Cabinet Enlarged and Opened*, *The accomplished ladies rich closet of rarities*, *The Ladies companion* and *The accomplish'd ladies delight in preserving*.[15] Gentlewomen are featured similarly, although not as predominately, in titles like *The Gentlewomans Delight in Cookery, The gentlewomans cabinet unlocked*, and *A true gentlewomans delight*.[16] Another popular reference to women in these titles was their role as housewives, featured in texts like *The good huswifes iewell* and *The English hous-wife*.[17]

Such titles correspond with an interesting poem found midway through a contemporary manuscript cookery book. Written beneath a recipe for "Leek," the male author muses that:

> To help my Wife to be a cook
> I write receipts with this her book
> and hope to taste of some of these
> whenever her Ladyship doth please.[18]

While it illustrates that men did participate in the compiling of personal cookery books, it likewise demonstrates that the lady of the household chose and prepared the meals that her family would consume.

Although expensive ingredients or cooking equipment, like ovens, mentioned in cookery texts may make them appear as if they were meant for an elite female audience, the introductory material to some cookery books illustrate otherwise. In *The accomplished ladies rich closet of rarities*, for example, it states in the Preface to the Reader that the text includes:

> Approved Rules, Instructions and Direction for particular persons, whose ability and leasure may contribute in an extraordinary manner to the highest Acquirement, but such as are suitable to all degrees and capacities; such as must contribute to the Advancement of each Individual Female, to a Station that may render her acceptable in the eyes of the great ones, or at least create her a good repute, and pronounce her happy, though moving in a lower sphere.[19]

Similarly, *The Compleat Cook: or, the Whole Art of Cookery* notes in the introduction that the material covered is "full and plain, so that from the Maid to the Master Cook all may reap benefit."[20]

While there may have been other prohibitive factors that kept printed cookery texts away from English women farther down the social ladder, the cost of the text, for example, it is clear from such comments that authors envisioned the material in their text as important and accessible to women of all classes. Because of this, it seems

3. "The Queens Closet Opened"

unreasonable to presume these authors would have included ingredients, and especially foreign ones, in their recipes that they knew only middle to upper class women had access to.

As Lehman has argued, literacy rates and the affordability of cookery books were important factors that would have limited an author's audience despite their perception that they were writing for all of womankind. In his famous, and often contested, *Literacy and Social Order*, David Cressy contends that in London, where literacy rates tended to be higher than other regions of the country, almost eighty-five percent of the female population was illiterate in 1580, although by the 1720s only forty-five percent of the same group was unable to read.[21] While Cressy's study proves that female literacy was certainly on the rise, it still draws into question whether lower class women would have had the ability to read contemporary cookery books. Although Cressy does not compare female literacy at different levels of society, he does state that in the diocese of Durham at the beginning of the seventeenth century only seventeen percent of genteel society was illiterate.[22] Cressy's method of determining literacy based on one's ability to write their name is clearly problematic, and therefore Wall counters it, claiming that while women "recorded ways to prepare food and medicines, recipe books served as instruction manuals and draft pads for honing the mechanical skills of crafting letters and developing penmanship styles.... Recipe collections thus illustrate ways that women engaged in tactical handiwork in the home across different media, demonstrating a kitchen literacy that is too often invisible in the scholarly record."[23] Based on both Cressy and Wall's assessment, then, at the very least middle and upper class women would have had the means to comprehend the recipes in cookery books.

Published cookery books themselves likewise indicate that they were utilized predominately by middle to upper class women. If Tessa Watt's claim that approximately seventy five percent of a text's cost came from paper, then the lengthy size of many of these cookery books would indicate that their audience was one with a disposable income.[24] Because of the thoroughness and diverse recipes these texts endeavored to offer, the majority exceeded one hundred pages, but some were even as lengthy as two to three hundred pages. This was, in part, because many cookery books included medicinal and cooking recipes and even sections on religion, astrology, or miscellaneous information that related to other household tasks.

In addition to this, the vast majority of cookery texts feature recipes that call for the use of an oven and do not suggest any alternative to those farther down the social ladder who would not have had use of one. As Albala has noted, pies, the notorious pastry of the period that required an oven, "were not standard fare for most people; they immediately signaled wealth and affluence for a simple reason. Large pies had to be baked in an oven."[25] He does explain ways in which those without an oven could and likely did still produce foods like pies, but the fact that contemporary cookery books make no mention of any alternative seems to show that the authors wrote for oven owning women. Likewise, the plethora of pie recipes illustrates that they were almost a staple of the seventeenth century English cuisine, a fact that would likely have been true for middle to upper class households.

From all this, it is clear that published cookery books were being primarily bought and consulted by middling and upper class women. As part of their feminine duties, they were expected to be aware of the culinary preparations occurring in their kitchen, whether they were actually doing the cooking or not. This establishes a special relationship between the woman of a household and the ingredients in the recipes she was consulting. Since the preparation of meals fell into the female sphere of work, it was the mistress of the house who would have chosen to purchase foreign foods and integrate them into her family's diet. Once served, though, both male and female members of the family came together to enjoy the benefits of England's expanding empire.

Sugar

The foreign food that seventeenth century English men and women consumed the most was sugar, as contemporary cookery books demonstrate it was eaten in a variety of different dishes. Although sugar had been present in European cultures for centuries prior to this, it is still important to examine it as a "foreign food" since the production of New World sugar revolutionized the frequency that it was consumed. Sugar cane, the most popular source of sugar, is a plant native

3. "The Queens Closet Opened"

to South and East Asia. The cost to import sugar from there during the medieval period, however, caused sugar to be a luxury good, one that only the rich could afford.[26] Mintz claims that sugarcane "had reached England in small quantities by 1200 [CE]; during the next five centuries, the amounts of cane sugar available doubtless increased, slowly and irregularly." He goes on to further argue that sugar remained a luxury until 1650, when Europe saw the "development of the West."[27] While consumption was certainly on the rise throughout the sixteenth and seventeenth century, Mintz's dating of the transformation of sugar as a luxury to sugar as a necessity is slightly off. The plethora of recipes calling for sugar published before 1650 speak to the idea that it was no longer a product only for the rich. In total, recipes calling for sugar appear in no less than forty-four published cookery books during the seventeenth century.[28]

The number of recipes containing sugar during the period is countless, especially in recipes dealing with perservering or candying another food. What becomes obvious, though, is that sugar was being used often and not at all sparingly. This is true even at the beginning of the seventeenth century, as John Murrell's *A Daily Exercise for Ladies and Gentlewomen*, published in 1617, illustrates that those cooking with sugar had no qualms about using great quantities of it. His recipe "to make an excellent greene Paste without any colouring" calls for an equal weight of sugar and whole green apples. In another recipe, this time to make "Almond Paste," Murrell calls for one and half pounds of sugar.[29]

This trend continued throughout the period, with the anonymously published *The Queens Closet Opened*, first published in 1661 and later republished in 1696, calling for "one pound of fine sugar" in a recipe "to make Sugar Cakes."[30] In *The Gentlewomans Cabinet Unlocked* there is another recipe for a cake that, again, calls for one pound of sugar.[31] Since its being called for in pounds rather than a much smaller quantity, sugar cannot be viewed as a product that is being consumed sparingly.

Sugar was being used quite frequently in meat dishes as well. In Thomas Dawson's *A book of cookery*, it was necessary in recipes instructing how, amongst other things, "to boile a Neats tongue," "to smere a coney," "to boile a capon with sirrop," "to boyle Muggest," "to make boyled Meat after the French manner," "to stew calves feet," and "to shew [sic] a cock."[32] Similarly in the anonymously published *The compleat cook*, sugar was used in recipes for "mullets boiled," "calves feet stewed," "hare roasted," "pig roasted with the hair on it," and "sheeps tongues, deer tongues, or calves tongues fried." In a recipe for "venison stew'd a quick and frugal way," it explains "Slice the Venison of your Pot, Pye or Pasty; then put it into a Stewing-pan over a heap of coals with some Claret wine, a little rosemary, four or five Cloves, a little grated Bread, Sugar and Vinegar: having stew'd a while, grate on some nutmeg, and serve it up."[33] Since large amounts of sugar are not called for in these meat dishes, its use in them suggests that sugar could not have been terribly expensive, for if it could have easily been left out. This would also explain why a product previously seen as a luxury item would be featured in a recipe for venison designated as "frugal."

Similarly, sugar was used in a number of manuscript recipe books.[34] The Townshend Family's cookery book, for example, features recipes that call for sugar often and in large quantities, including a recipe "to make cakebread" that requires half pound of sugar, a recipe "to make a headghogg pudding," and instructions on preserving apricots, each calling for a quarter pound of sugar, respectively.[35] Another, this from an unknown family, includes sugar in recipes "to make gelly pippins," "to make syrup of marsh mallows," "to make macaroons," "to make muscadin comfits," for "superfine cakes" and for "Mrs Bennet's Wiggs," just to name a few.[36] This text also features a recipe explaining at some length how "to clarify sugar," with a note in the margin notating that it is "approved."[37] Also marked as "approved" are instructions on "how to boil up sugar" to fit different needs, explaining: "A full syrup is when it's of an Amber colour. Maonur Christis hight is when it draw between your fingers like a small thread. To boil it to a candy hight, you must stir it sometimes wth a stick, and as you stir it fling your stick from you, when yr sugar is high and it will fly from your stick in great flakes like snow."[38]

Seventeenth century cookery books seem to illustrate, then, that contemporary men and women were consuming sugar on a regular basis. Included in diverse recipes, sugar had become an English staple long before the turn of the eighteenth century, demonstrating that they

3. "The Queens Closet Opened"

were reaping the benefits of New World exploration and expansion earlier than scholars like Mintz have argued. While sugar production in the Americas would become a hot topic for English abolitionists later, since its production was dependent on slave labor, in the seventeenth century sugar production and slavery were not yet linked together in English minds.[39] Sugar was seen only as a once luxury good made affordable through the expansion of the empire.

Spices

Like sugar, the seventeenth century saw spices used in many recipes and in cookery books aimed at consumers that may not have had access to these flavorful products even one hundred years earlier. While countries east of Europe remained the primary suppliers of cinnamon, cloves, ginger, mace, nutmeg, and pepper, technological advances allowing for maritime transportation of these products back to Europe drastically reduced their prices. The only exception to this was Jamaican pepper, a new spice to Europeans who had only recently come in contact with it upon their arrival in the Americas. Because of the plethora of available spices, and the notion that they could help to restore heat to a person if their body's humors had become imbalanced, spices can be found in an array of contemporary recipes in both printed and manuscript form.

Although modern readers may think of English food as bland, it was not uncommon for a contemporary recipe to call for several spices to be used together. This was especially true in fish and meat dishes; Dawson's *A Book of Cookery*, for example, features recipes "to boyle a Leg of Mutton with Pudding" and "To boile a Neats tongue," both calling for "pepper and salt, cloves, mace, and cinnamon." Another recipe titled "to smere a Coney," requires "sinamon and nutmeg."[40] Similarly, *The Gentlewomans Delight in Cookery* includes a recipe for "A Haunch of Venison to Roast," where the venison is to be seasoned with "beaten cloves, mace, and a little nutmeg..." and served with a sauce that includes ginger and more cinnamon.[41] The text features another for "A Hare, to dress after the French Fashion," calling for pepper, sugar, cinnamon, and mace, and "To Roast a Salmon the best way," explaining that one should "take a Salmon, or any convenient part of him as the Jole or Rand, seasoned with Nutmeg, Sage, and Pepper; and stick at the same time the side with a few Cloves and some small stips of Rosemary: fasten it to the spit, and at first bath it with Claret alone; them with Claret and Butter and with what falls from it, together with an Anchovey and Juyce of a Lemon, make the Sawce and serve it up with Olives."[42]

The presence of multiple spices is also visible in recipes for cakes and pastries. *The Gentlewomans Cabinet Unlocked* contains a recipe entitled "To Make a Good Cake," which explains that "some nutmeg, cloves, and mace, cinnamon, ginger, and a pound of sugar" should be mingled together with "half a peck of flower" to start with.[43] In another, cloves, cinnamon, and sugar are combined in a recipe "To make a Pippin-Tart."[44] *The Compleat Cook* has spices used in a similar fashion, with recipes for "French Pudding" featuring cloves, mace, and nutmeg, and another for cheesecake using mace and nutmeg, along with an alarming eighteen egg yolks, and a recipe for "a waffle," requiring ginger, cinnamon, and sugar.[45] Comparable to the waffle, Cooper's *The Art of Cookery Refin'd and Augmented* includes instructions on "How to make Pancakes" and includes several spices. The recipe reads:

> Take twenty Eggs, with half the whites, and beat the half an hour or more with fine flour of Wheat, Cloves, Mace, and a little Salt, Creame, a little new Ale, or a spoonfull of Yest being warmed, and beat them well together; make it so thin as to run out of your spoon or ladle without any stop: this being done, cover it and set by the fire half an houre, or more, stiring it now and then; fry them with a quick fire (but not to hot) with a little Butter, and after you have fryed one or two, you may fry them without Butter as well as with it, and will be better, if you love them dry; scrape Sugar on them and serve them up.
>
> If you are loose in the Body you may make a Pancake of nothing but Eggs and Cynamon, and Salt beat well together; you may put in some Anniseeds (if you please) it will expel wind and take away the raw taste of the Egs or strew Carraway-comifts on it, being baked.[46]

While the one set of instructions actually functions as two separate recipes, it is interesting that both use spices in some shape or form.

Cinnamon, cloves, ginger, mace, and nutmeg appear in similar recipes in manuscript cookery books from the period as well. One very popular meat dish was "scotch collops," a recipe that appeared in at

3. "The Queens Closet Opened"

least eight different personal cookery books. Despite the fact that each recipe is a bit different, they all call for some combination of mace, nutmeg, pepper, and cloves.[47] Catherine Godfrey's recipe for "A Scotch Collop," for example, instructs:

> cut ye: lean of a leg of veale into very thin slices beat soundly on both sides lard one halfe of your collop with bacon season it a little with mace nutmeg pepper salt & a few sweet hers, fry & brown in sweet butter with 20 balls of force meat & clean out your pan & put in half pint of white wine with as much strong brother 2 anchovies 3 or 4 shallots 20 oysters, & let this stew a little & put y:e juice of a lemmon into your collops halfe a pound od sweet butter beat it thick with y:e yolks of 2 eggs serve it with sippets & garnish it with oysters forcemeat balls & lemmon sliced.[48]

Although Jane Parker's personal cookery book does not feature a recipe for scotch collops, her text has several meat recipes that use a combination of spices similarly to recipes in published texts. She includes instructions "to make a calves head pie," "to make neates tongues pies minced," "a made dish of rabbits livers," and "to coller beefe."[49] Hannah Biskar's book also features many recipes using several spices for a meat dish, including "to Season yo: meate for yo: mince pyes," "to make forced meat," "to make stake pye plaine," "to make a venson pastey," "to make a veale pye savery," "to make a turkey pye," "to coller elles," "to make a pye of Calves feete or Trotters," "to make a calves head pye," and "to make a chicken pye."[50] While it is clear that Mrs. Bisaker was quite fond of pies, her recipes, like the others, illustrate that it was common to use several spices at once when preparing dishes of flesh, fish, and foul.

Manuscript cookery books likewise reflect the common usage of a mixture of spices in cakes. Perhaps none better demonstrate this than Bridget Hyde's cookery book, a woman who seems to have been somewhat of a cake connoisseur. Her collection includes a recipe "to make a cake," "to make a plumb cake," "to make the Dutches Cake," "The Lady Frances Sandersons cake," and "Mrs Hurleys Receipt for a cake" All five cakes call for mace, cloves, and cinnamon, the last two adding nutmeg as well.[51] Although not featuring as many cake recipes, Amy Eyton's cookery book has similar recipes. Within her assortment of recipes are instructions "to make a cake Madam Manners way," calling for cloves, mace, nutmeg and cinnamon, "to make a good cake," using cinnamon,

83

cloves, and nutmeg, and "to make a larg cake," requiring mace, cloves, and nutmeg.[52]

Primarily featuring ginger, with cinnamon added in, recipes for gingerbread were also quite popular in contemporary personal cookery books; no fewer than seven different manuscript cookery books included at least one recipe for it.[53] One in particular featured a recipe for almond gingerbread just pages from another recipe for plain gingerbread, suggesting that gingerbread itself was popular enough that different versions of it were emerging.[54]

Pancakes seemed to have become a staple product by the seventeenth century as well, featured in several printed and manuscript cookery texts from the period. Oddly enough, though, the spices pancake recipes called for were quite different depending on their source. While pancakes in printed cookery books used a plethora of spices, recipes for pancakes in manuscript recipe collections consistently only call for nutmeg.[55] For example, one pancake recipe from an anonymous manuscript cookery book directs the reader to:

> Take one pound of sweet butter, put it in a quart of Creame, set it over the fire keep it stiring when it is melted, take it of then take 8 eggs scave out half the whites, beat them very well together, then put 3 spoonfulls of the best flower, into your eggs & beat them very well together, great in a whole nutmeg, so put your Cream to it stir it all together so let it stand a while before you bake it, put in a little salt.[56]

This could perhaps indicate that the spicier pancakes of printed cookery books were a newer invention. Conversely, it could suggest that many thought a basic mixture of cream, flour, eggs, and nutmeg was all a good pancake needed.

While cinnamon, cloves, ginger, mace, nutmeg, and pepper had long been present in England, Jamaica pepper, or what modern readers would identify as allspice, was an entirely new commodity. Earning its original name from Spanish explorers who encountered it in Jamaica at the beginning of the sixteenth century, it was labeled a pepper since its berries seemed to resemble those of that species. Jamaica pepper, however, is not a pepper at all; instead, it tastes like a combination of cloves, black pepper, nutmeg, and cinnamon, explaining why it later earned the name allspice. Although Jamaica pepper appears in only a handful of recipes prior to the eighteenth century, by the twentieth

3. "The Queens Closet Opened"

century the United Kingdom was ranked as the sixth largest importer of allspice.[57]

In 1682, Jamaica pepper appeared for the first time in two separate cookery books: John Collins' *Salt and Fishery* and G. Hartman's *The True Preserver and Restorer of Health*. The former contains two recipes that include the new Jamaican spice, both of which are attributed to one Mr. Richard Alcorne. The first of these describes how to pickle oysters and the second on how to preserve fish, such as eels, flounders, and soals, by marinating them in the "Italian manner."[58] The recipe for pickling oysters provides a bit more insight into Jamaican pepper, as the spice is included in a portion of the recipe that the author offers to the reader as a way to enhance the dish. This information comes at the end, after a method for pickling oysters has already been offered, and states, "but to render [the oysters] far more pleasant to the tast, and for longer keeping, instead of water and hot Hearbs, use White-Wine, Mace, or Jamaica Pepper, and if you please a little sliced Ginger, all to be simmered in the Pickle, which may continue longer on the Fire after the Oysters are taken out."[59] Thus, this New World spice is being used along with other ingredients to modify the taste of English culinary classics.

G. Hartman's cookery book also contains a recipe featuring Jamaica pepper that endeavors to elongate the life of the food it is added to, in this case Red Deer that "will keep a quarter of a year." What becomes interesting about this is that both regular pepper and Jamaica pepper are called for, seemingly illustrating that the seventeenth century English understood that, despite its name, it was different than the black pepper they had imported from the east for centuries. In fact, the recipe allows that Jamaica pepper may be substituted for nutmeg, further illustrating that they realized Jamaica pepper had become another resource in their spice cabinet rather than the same spice they had been using from a different part of the world.[60] This is important for it furthers the notion that the English were discovering there were many dietary resources that could be gained from an expanding empire and not just a means of obtaining cheaper food items they already had.

As in printed cookery books, recipes for Jamaica pepper in manuscript cookery books are few and far between. One calls for a handful of Jamaica pepper in a recipe to make mead.[61] In another, Jamaica pepper is used for "scotch collops," seemingly replacing other spices, as the only other one used is nutmeg.[62] Just as with printed cookery books, it appears that the seventeenth century English consumer was beginning to integrate the American spice into her repertoire.

The diverse types of recipes that spices were being used in suggests that transoceanic sailing made them attainable to the masses. This is supported by the fact that many of the recipes featuring them are found in books either written for or by women of average means, illustrating the affordability of these products. And because spices were no longer a luxury item, they were used in virtually every aspect of cooking. Not only does this show that the English were eager to consume foreign products, but also how quickly foreign foods could be integrated into a culinary culture.

Fowl and Fish

The most popular foreign fowl in seventeenth century England was undoubtedly the turkey. First introduced to Europe by the Spanish after they had conquered Central America in the early sixteenth century, turkeys appear to have been eagerly adopted into European diets. According to the *Oxford Companion to Food*, by 1541 turkeys in England "were cited amongst large birds such as cranes and swans in sumptuary laws [and] their prices had been fixed in the London markets by the mid 1550s."[63] The popularity of the turkey can be seen in contemporary published cookery books as well. The first text that a turkey appears in is *The Good Husvvifes Ievvell* by Thomas Dawson, first published in 1587. In a recipe entitled "To bake a Turkie and take out his bones," Dawson spends two thirds of a page describing in detail how one should disassemble the bird.[64] Only seven years later, *A Good Huswifes Handmaide for the Kitchin* was published without any indication of how to de-bone a turkey, only explaining, "Take and cleave your Turkie on the backe, and bruise all the bones: then season it with salt, and pepper grose beaten, and put into it good store of butter: he must have five houres baking."[65] It seems safe to assume that the lack

3. "The Queens Closet Opened"

of detail in the later recipe indicates that the English were quite familiar with turkeys, and therefore required no advice about cleaning and dressing them.

By the seventeenth century, then, recipes featuring turkeys had become numerous and rather diverse. In Gervase Markham's *The English hous-wife*, first published in 1631 but subsequently republished in 1637, 1649, 1656, and 1664, there are ten recipes relating to turkeys, including instructions on its basic baking, a sauce to make for a turkey, how to carbonado a turkey, what paste to use for a turkey, and during which courses the turkey should be served.[66] *The compleat cook* further broadens the scope of recipes pertaining to turkeys, including instructions on "how to bake a turkey in the French fashion," "to bake a turkey to be eaten cold," "to make a pottage of turkey farced," as well as when it was appropriate to eat turkeys.[67]

Manuscript cookery books likewise demonstrate that turkeys had become one of the main fowls in the contemporary English diet. In fact, no fewer than eight different recipe collections include a recipe for preparing a turkey.[68] One in particular provides insight into how turkeys were seen compared to other fowl. Written to the side of a recipe entitled "How to Pickle a Goose" is a note explaining, "Turkeys or ducks may be so done the more fleshy the better."[69] Another recipe in the same text further demonstrates that geese and turkeys can be prepared similarly, providing instructions on how to bake "A Dove Goose or Turkey."[70] A similar recipe can also be found in the Godfrey family recipes, which features a recipe "to season goose turkey & pidgeon pye."[71] Recipes such as these indicate that the English were able to quickly integrate turkeys into their diet because they were utilizing recipes already in existence. Unlike entirely new foods that would require new recipes, those already used for other birds, and presumably already in a family's cooking repertoire, could be used to prepare a turkey.

Because of the number of recipes in printed and manuscript cookery books for turkeys, the diverse ways they were eaten, and the variety of occasions they were considered appropriate, it is evident that by the seventeenth century turkeys had become a staple of English cuisine. Although turkeys were not a direct product of English exploration, their introduction to England from Spain illustrated the natural resources that the Americas had to offer. This demonstrated the material goods that could be gained from exploring the newly discovered continent.

Tortoises were also emerging as a popular "fish" during this period as well.[72] Tortoises, or what we would now call Sea Turtles, first became a staple for English seamen in the Caribbean who practically sustained themselves on them. As Archie Carr explains, "The vitamin hunger of sailors ... practically disappeared after the discovery of *Chelonia*, the green turtle. No other edible creature could be carried away and kept so long alive. Only the turtle could take the place of spoiled kegs of beef and send a ship on for a second year of wandering or marauding. All early activity in the new world tropics ... was in some way dependent on the turtle."[73] This popularity amongst seamen soon transferred back to England, as by the middle of the seventeenth century tortoises were showing up frequently in English cookery books.

The *Oxford Companion to Food* explains that according to a letter Horace Walpole wrote in 1789, the first consumption of sea turtles in England occurred in 1711. This is supported by the belief that Richard Bradley published the first recipe for dressing a sea turtle in 1732, a recipe that he claimed to have learned from a lady in Barbados.[74] However, this assessment does not fit with the six cookery books published between 1653 and 1694 that contain recipes pertaining to the consumption of the tortoise.[75] While tortoises certainly became more popular in the eighteenth century, it is still significant that, like many other foreign foods, they were already being consumed almost fifty years before the turn of the century.

One of the first cookery books that features a recipe for tortoises was François Pierre de La Varenne's *The French Cook* published in 1653. In it, de La Varenne includes three recipes for tortoises: the first being a pottage of tortoise, and the other two describing two different ways to dress a tortoise.[76] While all three recipes briefly describe the way that the tortoise should be properly dismembered, the third recipe on how to dress a tortoise explains what one should do if one finds the tortoise to have been a female and carrying eggs. De La Varenne states in that case, the reader should "save the Eggs whole, and stew them with the meat and liver in a dish with grated Nutmeg, a little sweet-herbs minced small, and some sweet butter; when stewed enough, serve it on fine white sippets, covering the meat with the upper shell of the Tortoise, and slices of Orange, or the juice thereof."[77] The English may have been interested in using as many edible parts of the tortoise as possible, but de La Varenne demonstrates that tortoise recipes had developed beyond the simple preparation that seamen would have carried out before eating them.

Although tortoises certainly did not have the same popularity that turkeys did prior to the eighteenth century, it is important to note that they were being consumed in England. Just as turkeys had grown in popularity during the sixteenth century, tortoises began to be featured more and more in recipes during the seventeenth century, especially since the many edible parts of the tortoise allowed it to be used for several meals. Both the turkey and the tortoise, then, worked to show that the New World offered more than just luxury food items. Just as early English navigators discovered the dietary value that the tortoise had to offer, English consumers began to realize throughout the seventeenth century that they could dine on new types of fish and fowl being discovered in other parts of the world. The turkey especially worked to illustrate the important products that the English stood to gain by supporting their expanding Empire. Not only did this new Empire bring wealth, luxury, and exotic new products, but it also brought resources that would make it easier and more convenient for the English to sustain themselves.

Pineapple, Potato and Pumpkin

Two new foreign fruits and a tuber made their mark on seventeenth century cooking as well. Although potatoes remained far more popular and accessible than either pineapples or pumpkins, the presence of all three in contemporary culinary culture indicates an eagerness to incorporate foreign foods into English cuisine. While all three would continue to grow in popularity into the eighteenth and nineteenth centuries, the potato would make the biggest mark on British history. The nineteenth century Great Famine of Ireland was due, in large part, to a potato blight that would not only cause starvation, but also a wave of immigrants fleeing the island. Although pineapples and pumpkins did not play as prominent a role in British history, their use in seventeenth century cuisine is still important.

The first European contact with a pineapple is believed to have occurred when Christopher Columbus "discovered" the fruit on the island of Guadeloupe in 1493. It is said that he took a load of pineapples with him back to Spain so that King Ferdinand could try them. Ferdinand allegedly responded well to the new fruit, although odd to imagine since reports indicate the pineapple had spoilt on the trans-Atlantic voyage. His successor Charles V, however, did not react similarly; it seems he did not find spoilt pineapple pleasant to taste or look at. The first English account of the fruit came from Sir Walter Raleigh, who dubbed it "the Princess of Fruit." Although Spaniards were the first Europeans to acquaint themselves with pineapples, the English were the first to grow them domestically. This feat was achieved by John Rose whom had an entire pineapple plant brought from the Caribbean to the Duchess of Cleveland's hothouse where it could ripen. Once ready, the pineapple was presented to Charles II, an exchange immortalized by the court painter in 1661.[78]

Coinciding with this royal event, pineapples appeared in twelve printed cookery books published in the second half of the seventeenth century.[79] Although pineapples were being eaten whole, at least by English royalty, the most common usage of pineapples was in recipes for pastries and deserts. In a recipe for "piramidia cream," the finished product is to be covered with "blown pineapple," although the recipe states that the cream may be eaten with or without the pineapple still on it.[80] William Rabisha publishes a recipe for pineapple tarts in his 1673 text, where two whole handfuls of pineapples are combined with peppins, cream, sugar, rosewater, and eggs. Later in the same book, pineapples are used in recipes for "cheesecake," "egg tarts," an "omelet made in the Oxford fashion," and an "omelet made in the Turkish fashion."[81]

Pineapples also found their way into meat recipes as well. In May's recipe describing different manners in which boiled meats may be dressed, pineapple seeds are suggested to add variety to a stew.[82] In another recipe for boiled meats, this one from 1673 and requiring chickens, pigeons, quails, larks, and bacon, pineapples are needed to boil with the meats and other herbs and spices.[83] Between meat dishes

3. "The Queens Closet Opened"

such as these, and the incorporation of pineapples into a variety of desserts, it seems that this New World "Princess of Fruit" was quickly becoming part of English culinary culture.

Exceeding the popularity of pineapples in desserts, however, was the potato.[84] Again first encountered by Spaniards who arrived in modern day Columbia in 1537, potatoes were not taken to Europe until 1550 and were not brought to Britain until even later. As the *Oxford Companion to Food* explains, "the arrival of the potato to Britain, despite the best efforts of scholars, remains something of a mystery, with tales involving Raleigh and Drake.... However, it is generally accepted that potatoes were introduced to the British Isles (including Ireland) during the 1590s."[85] This date, though, seems a bit late as Thomas Dawson's text published in 1587 included recipes for the tuber.

The most frequent usage of potatoes in printed cookery books was in meat dishes. John Murrell included such recipes in both of his seventeenth century cookery books, one being a recipe for a "marrow toast," where potato roots are boiled with the marrow toast along with other spices, and the other being a recipe for "boiling chicken in soup the common way."[86] Joseph Cooper, advertised as having been the chief cook to the late King, used potatoes similarly, including in a recipe "to boyl a Capon or Pullet with French Barley," which described that whole potatoes should be peeled and then boiled, among other things, in the barley.[87]

While potatoes appear most frequently with meat dishes, later seventeenth century cookery books begin to offer instructions on how to cook potato pies. One such recipe, from Mary Tillinghast's *Rare and Excellent Receipts*, states that three pounds of potatoes are to be peeled, placed in the center of the pie, and then covered with such preserves as cherries, gooseberries, barberries, grapes, and currants.[88] Although a recipe for potato pie is not included in the text, *The Compleat Cook* describes the occasions they are suited for, explaining that potato pies are excellent for non-fasting festival days in the spring and for the winter quarter.[89]

Like published cookery books, recipes featuring potatoes appear frequently in personal collections as well; using potatoes in a pudding seems to have been more popular in manuscript cookery books then their printed counter parts. One recipe for potato pudding, from the collection of Elizabeth Sleigh and Felicia Whitfield, features instruction for a potato pudding that is marked as "approved." It instructs the reader to "take half a pound of potattoes: boil & peel Them: then take suger & butter of each half a pound: mix these well together then brake in 8 eggs leave out 3 whites: bake it in a dish with a thin past round sides to make it rich put in sweetmeets."[90] Mary Bent's recipe for potato pudding reads similarly, except she adds rose water, nutmeg, and, if desired, bitter almonds.[91]

Recipes for potato pies were also frequent occurrences in manuscript cookery books. Both Mary Faussett Godfrey and Catherine Godfrey's recipe for "hartichoke or potato pye," for example, instructs "take ye bottoms of 12 boyld hartichokes and 12 yolks of eggs boyld hard 3 ounce of candid orange lemmon & citron sliced halfe a pound of reasons a blade or 2 of mace a little nutmeg sliced, a quarter of a pound of sugar put it into your pye with halfe a pound of butter."[92] While other recipes for potato pies offer different advice, the common difference is in the fruit added to the pie. The consistency in recipes for both potato pies and puddings suggests that these recipes had been in circulation long enough that the general public had adopted a universal way to cook them. This, with the popularity of potatoes in printed cookery books, demonstrates that by the turn of the eighteenth century, potatoes had been fully integrated into English culinary culture.

Although not as popular as potatoes or pineapples, the pumpkin did appear in a handful of cookery books in the latter half of the seventeenth century.[93] The first recipes, in Monsieur Marnettè's *The Perfect Cook*, include making a tart of the mellows of pumpkins, gourds, or melons and making an egg tart where pumpkins are substituted in for apples.[94] *The French Cook* features several recipes that include pumpkins as well, such as pottage of pumpkin with butter, pottage of pumpkin with milk, and a torte of pumpkin.[95] *The Compleat English and French Cook* also includes a recipe for a pottage of pumpkins and explains that this dish, as well as one for fried pumpkins, was acceptable to serve on Good Friday.[96] While the pumpkin did not appear as frequently as other foreign fruits and vegetables, it is apparent that they were being integrated into English cuisines, even incorporating pumpkin dishes into meals that could be prepared on days of religious fasting.

3. "The Queens Closet Opened"

This is supported by the fact that pumpkins were not featured in manuscript books of the period, suggesting that it was a new food that the English were still acquainting themselves with.

Chocolate

Although included in cookery books far less than other American products, it would be remiss to ignore chocolate, as drinking chocolate was popular during this period, especially amongst upper-class women. There were at least two recipes that featured chocolate during the seventeenth century, in texts from the 1690s. *The Accomplished Ladies Rich Closet of Rarities* explains that the beverage "Chocolate is made with Chocolate, Milk, Eggs, White-wine, Rose-water, and Mace or Cinnamon, which the Party fancies, they being all boiled together over a gentle fire; two ounces of Chocolate, eight eggs, a pint of White-wine, an ounce of Mace or Cinnamon, and half a pound of Sugar answering in this case a Gallon of Milk."[97] The other recipe featuring chocolate is found in *The True Way of Preserving and Candying* and describes how to make chocolate puffs.[98]

Likewise, there are only a few personal cookery books featuring recipes for chocolate.[99] Mrs. Carr's collection, for example, features a recipe "to make chocolate," but actually seems to be instructions for preparing cocoa nuts themselves. It explains that one should "take 20 pound of cacownutts ten pound of sugar one pound and 2 quarter of Cinamon 4 ounces of pepper 4 ounces of cloves 4 of nutmegs these must be beaten severally and afterwards be ground or beaten all together you must first take the cocownutss and parth them in a clean frying pan to take the husks off them."[100] More akin to the recipes found in printed cookery books, Mary Bent includes a recipe "to make a Chocolate pudding," explaining "take seven yolks of eggs and 4 whites beate them well then mix half a pound of Lofe sugar finely scaved a quarter of a pound of biskett half a pound of chocolate betwixt a pint and a gill of thick cream half a pound clarified butter mix these all together putt in a little sack and rose watter so bake it in a dish as you do others"[101]

While chocolate had not yet reached the popularity it would

obtain in later years, it is clear that the English had been introduced to and were consuming it on some level. The different dessert-type recipes that chocolate was used in during the seventeenth century, however, suggest that the English were beginning to experiment with it. Unlike other foreign beverages that had entered the domestic market, rum, coffee, and tea, for example, they were discovering that chocolate could be incorporated into edible recipes as well.

Conclusion

Judging from the inclusion of the plethora of foreign foods in contemporary cookery books, it is fair to say seventeenth-century English men and women were increasingly engaging with global products. This coincides with English transoceanic exploration and settlement, making it even more possible for foreign foods to be accessible in domestic markets. While there were other foreign objects being incorporated into seventeenth century English culture, for example furs and textiles, the consumption of foreign foods proves especially important. Unlike other objects of consumption, foreign foods impacted dietary culture, which played an important role in daily life. That women controlled such an important facet of consumption is also significant; it provided them an opportunity to act as agents of an expanding empire. Functioning within contemporary gender norms, women were able to incorporate foreign food products into their families' diet, exposing them to the benefits of England's burgeoning empire.

4

Foreign Additives in Domestic Remedies

Tracts and treatises regarding medicine and health had a long history of publication in England, but physician and astrologer Thomas Culpeper saw a gap in contemporary medical knowledge that needed to be filled. In his 1652 *The English Physitian*, he writes to the reader that previous medical authors:

> ... did much good in the study of this Art [of medicine], yet they and all others that wrought of the nature of Herbs gave not a bit of a reason why such an herb was appropriated to such a part of the body, nor why it cured such a Disease; truly my own body being sickly brought me easily into a capacity to know that Health was the greatest of all earthly blessings, and truly he was never sick that doth not believe it; then I considered that all Medicines were compounded of herbs, roots, flowers, &c. and this first set me on work in studying the nature of Simples, most of which I knew by sight before, and indeed all the Authors I could reade gave me but little satisfaction in this particular, or none at all.[1]

To remedy this lack of information, Culpeper set out to describe the health benefits that native English plants possessed. The approach proved extremely popular with the public, too. As Patrick Curry has noted, *The English Physitian* "sold widely at the time, and there have been over one hundred subsequent editions, including fifteen before 1700."[2]

But just as Culpeper was unsatisfied with the medical authors before him, Joseph Blagrave found *The English Physitian* lacking and incomplete. Because of this, he published a *Supplement or Englargement to Mr. Nich. Culpepper's English Physitian* in 1674, endeavoring to include products that Culpeper had ignored. Blagrave explains to his readers that he took "pains and care to add such English plants with their Virtues and use in Physick, which were wholly omitted in.... The

Tastes of the Empire

English Physitian. And likewise for further use and benefit of my Countreymen, I have inserted in the Supplemt, the virtues and use of such eminent and useful Tress, Herbs, Roots, Flowers, Fruits, Excrescencres of Plants, Drugs, &c. as are brought form any part of the world, and sold in our Druggists and Apothecaries Shops."[3] Blagrave used the same approach that Culpeper did in his text, describing various products and detailing the health and healing benefits that they offered. What sets the two authors apart was Blagrave's belief that a survey of strictly domestic products was not sufficient. That he saw the necessity of a text that included foreign additives illustrates that, at least by 1674, such products were being integrated into contemporary medicinal culture and, according to him, were available in the domestic marketplace. Not only do contemporary medicinal recipes support both ideas, but the fact that Blagrave's text was subsequently republished three years later demonstrates that foreign foods were being integrated into seventeenth century medicinal culture at a growing rate.[4]

The use of these new, foreign plants, spices, and other additives in medicine was especially important to contemporary woman, no matter their class, as they were the center of their family's medical knowledge and care. Looking at England's early modern medical culture, Andrew Wear explains "social historians of medicine … have confirmed that medical expertise was widespread across society. Lay medical practice was centered on the family. Patients often treated themselves, and the women members of the family especially were the sources of medical knowledge and treatment."[5] He notes that remedies for ailments were located "in the female culture of medicine, which was a major component of the provision of medical care and treatment available in early modern England. The manufacture of remedies was one of the household skills expected of women."[6] Because of this, a female would have chosen ingredients used in any remedy.

Wear contends that the female dominated sphere of medicine was not affected by the increase in published medical tracts and treatise by male "physicians," who tended to write for other male physicians. Instead, he suggests that "distinctions between lay [predominately female] and medical [predominately male] readerships were blurred and both groups might read works which were ostensibly for the other."[7] This was especially true as more medical books were being published

4. Foreign Additives in Domestic Remedies

in English than in Latin. He argues that, "the more extreme learned physicians aimed for a cadre of physicians fluent in Latin ... books in English, they believed, diluted such practices."[8] English books, however, were being increasingly demanded by a public that saw Latin medical texts in a similar vein as Latin Bibles, both of which they viewed as attempts to keep the general public ignorant of ideas they felt they had a right to.[9]

Speaking to this duality of England's seventeenth century medical culture, Jennifer Stine has presented the idea that "household medicine was being discovered from both within and without in the early modern period: from within in the sense that women who had no doubt long practiced medicine locally began to extend their role and to create a written literature documenting their practices; and from without in the sense that their practices were of great interest to others in seventeenth-century society. This included members of the scientific community."[10] Furthering this, Alun Withey claims "recipe collections were a point of conjunction between oral and literate medical cultures ... [they were] repositories of family and community knowledge and lore, as well as congeries of inherited and imported knowledge derived from literate sources."[11] Michelle DiMeo and Rebecca Laroche likewise note that it was not uncommon for such medical knowledge to pass from one generation of females to another.[12] While acknowledging the growing number of paid, male, medical professionals who were researching, writing, and practicing during the seventeenth century, Stine contends that medical knowledge and practice were still dependent on female centered communities of knowledge and the doctoring they enabled women to preform.

To add to this, Stine argues that the household itself remained the center of medicine. She states that, "a central feature of medical care in early modern England is that it was both given and received within a house. Advice on a medical condition might come directly from a member of the household, or it might come from neighbors, friends, physicians, or others.... Medications could be made within the home, purchased without, or both, but they were usually administered at home."[13] She contends that it is this "domestic context of early modern medicine that sets the stage for the extensive involvement of women ... [as] houses were a center for women's activities."[14] While there may have been a growing number of technically trained physicians, their work was still dependent on female doctoring or care within the household.

That women played such a central role in contemporary medical culture is vital to understanding their connection to and relationship with the foreign ingredients entering the domestic pharmacopeia. As the head of their family's medical knowledge, women would have selected cures used to restore health to an ailing body. This choice allowed women a unique interaction with England's expanding empire, as it was female demand for medicinal, extra-European products that would influence their importation. Although historians, including Stine, have often contended that foreign products did not have any great effect on seventeenth century medical culture, Blagrave's text and the growing rate at which foreign products were used in contemporary medical cures prove otherwise. While many medicinal recipes certainly relied on tried and true ingredients that grew naturally in England, foreign additives were being incorporated into medicine at an increasing rate throughout the seventeenth century as a result of their inclusion in cures that contemporary women concocted.

Humoral Theory

Plants, flowers, herbs, and other food products were frequently used in early modern English medicine as the discipline still relied heavily on the Hippocratic treatises, composed by several authors between 420–350 BCE, and the writings of Galen, a second century Greek physician. To demonstrate why such texts were still important to sixteenth and seventeenth century Europeans, Wear explains that during the Renaissance, humanists, wishing to better contemporary medicine, believed a return to "the *prisca medicina*, the pure ancient medicine of the Greeks" would provide long lost cures and medical insight. While the Hippocratic treatises and Galen's writings had informed medieval medical practitioners, humanists felt that, through myth and mistranslations, the original ideas of the texts had been lost. For them, "going back to the pure founts of medical wisdom, medicine, it was believed, would be improved. Just as the reformation of religion

4. Foreign Additives in Domestic Remedies

involved a return to the original word of God, the Bible, so the reformation of medicine would take place through better knowledge of the words of medicine's founders."[15] Thus, because of the revival of these ancient texts, the seventeenth century English had become reacquainted with their teachings and advice.

This was especially true of Galen's teachings, whose ideas regarding humor theory played an important role in contemporary medical practices and even how daily diets were constructed. Wear explains that for Galen, "four humors or fluids—blood, phlegm, yellow bile or choler, and black bile or melancholy—made up the body and ... they were the products of the combination of the four qualities of hot, cold, dry, and wet that Aristotle, the Greek philosopher, had stated were the primary constituents of the world."[16] Blood was believed to be hot and wet, phlegm cold and wet, yellow bile and choler hot and dry, and black bile and melancholy cold and dry. Galenic medicine held that every person possessed a unique mixture of these humors, influencing their health, personality, and appearance. Depending on the dominant humors, a person was choleric (hot and dry), melancholic (cold and dry), phlegmatic (cold and wet), or sanguine (hot and wet).

There were other factors that could contribute to a person's bodily humors, too. The season of the year, for example, could influence humors, the winter promoting cold and dryness, the spring hot and wetness, the summer hot and dryness, and the fall cold and wetness. According to believers in Galenic medicine, a person's age could also influence their humors. Children were more likely to be hot and wet, the youth hot and dry, adults cold and dry, and the elderly cold and wet. Gender likewise played a role in a person's humors. As Sara Mendelson and Patricia Crawford have noted, Galenic medicine saw man as hot and dry and woman as cold and moist and, because of this, "man was active, woman passive; man was energetic, brave, and strong, while woman was gentle, tender, kind, and timorous. Anatomically, women were less healthful because their passivity subjected them to diseases."[17]

Because there were so many factors that could influence a person's bodily humors at any given time, scholars and authors studied and classified foods and medicines by their humoral nature. Such classifications were frequently included in published texts, too, so that the general public had access to this knowledge.[18] The idea was that to remain healthy, individuals needed to regularly consume foods opposite to their countenance as a form of preventative medicine. For example, individuals who were naturally melancholic should strive for a diet of mostly hot and wet foods, avoiding those that were cold and dry. This was important, as "poor digestion produced by too much food or by food unsuitable to an individual's constitution was understood to be the origin of many diseases and humoral disorders."[19] Thus, it was vital that each person understood their body and its unique humoral balance. Because every diet would have to be developed with a person's individual constitution in mind, contemporary thought held that most people could determine their own diet just as well as a trained physician could.[20]

Seventeenth century men and women used spices and perfumes in particular as a form of preventative medicine. As Paul Freedman has explains in his *Out of the East: Spices and the Medieval Imagination*, medieval thought, which carried over to the early modern period, held that fragrance and health were related; they believed inhaling the scent of sickness could prove infectious.[21] He notes that especially where the plague was concerned, contemporary English men and women were obsessed with the notion that "foul odors ... caused the onset of epidemics, [and thus] aromatic products were the obvious means of prevention."[22] Because of this, strong smelling spices and fragrant perfumes, including resin, frankincense, ambergris, castoreum, musk, and civet, were used to keep the plague at bay.[23]

While food products were used to maintain a person's health, medicinal cures were sought when injury or illness were at hand. As Wear explains, contemporary medical remedies relied heavily on plants, animals, and minerals to fix ailments. He states such ingredients were essential in early modern English medicine, noting that "they formed a large part of the published medical literature, and they constituted practically the only type of medical information that lay men and women set down on paper."[24] Culpeper not only proves Wear's assertion, but further explains the importance of herbs, plants, and other natural ingredients in his 1653 *Culpeper's Complete Herbal*. He notes that natural ingredients, those produced by the earth, worked because they "manifestly operate, either by heat, coldness, dryness, or

4. Foreign Additives in Domestic Remedies

moisture," a combination that was required to cure the human body.[25]

Because a person's health depended on the food they consumed and the natural ingredients they had to cure their ailments, Wear argues that there was a general European desire to expand and gain more of both. He states that as "exotic foreign remedies ... came into Europe from other continents," an idea emerged that new foods and medicinal resources existed in other parts of the globe. This formed "part of the commercial justification for exploration and settlement, being seen as precious commodities alongside gold and silver."[26] This demonstrates, perhaps more than anything, how seriously contemporary English men and women took humor theory and how important consumable resources, both domestic and foreign, were to them.

Spices

Spices were fairly common ingredients in pre-early modern medical culture. Freedman notes that Europeans valued spices in particular for two reasons; firstly, spices were seen as possessing hot and dry humors and therefore ideal for tempering cold and wet diseases or foods, which most meats and fish were.[27] Secondly, they considered spices to be digestive aids. He states that in the Middle Ages, "there was a purgative idea of how the body should digest food and the main worry was stagnation: the failure of the system to absorb what was nourishing and to expel expeditiously what was not. To the degree that spices stimulated the bowels, was all for the best."[28] Because of the continuation of such ideas established in medieval medical culture, the use of spices in the seventeenth century only increased as transoceanic trading made them cheaper and more accessible in the domestic market.

Since a decrease in prices allowed for an increase in the use of spices, seventeenth century medical culture also saw an increase in the number of remedies calling for multiple spices at once. The usage of several spices in one recipe is likely due to the fact that they were all, to a degree, seen as humorally hot and dry and therefore could cure similar ailments. Two cures used a variety of spices particularly popular in seventeenth century medicine: aqua mirabilis and Dr. Steven's water. Recipes for aqua mirabilis can be found in a handful of published texts, including Thomas Brugis's 1640 *The Marrow of Physicke*, the anonymously published *The Ladies Cabinet Enlarged and Opened* of 1667 and *The Queens Closet Opened* of 1696.[29] Recipes for it can be found in at least ten manuscript cookery books from the later seventeenth century as well.[30] While there are slight variations between recipes, they all require the combination of a plethora of spices, including galangal, cloves, ginger, mace, nutmegs, cubebs, cardamoms, and cinnamon, and some sort of wine.

Brugis provides insight into the benefits of aqua mirabilis, explaining:

> this water helpeth much the lungs, and healeth them if they be much wounded, or perished, it suffereth not the Blood to putrifie, so that there shall be no need of phlebotomy, it is good against Phlegme, and Melancholy, and expelleth Rheume mightily, and purgeth the Stomack: it conforteth youth in his owne estate, and gendreth a good colour, and conserveth their visage, and memory; it destroyeth the Palsey of the Liver, and Tongue; and if the said water be given to a man, or woman laboring towards death, one spoonful relieveth: of all the Waters artificiall, this is counted the best, and in the Summer use once a week fasting, the quantity of a spoonful, and in Winter as much more.[31]

Not only does Brugis's explanation demonstrate his high opinion of the elixir, but it also illustrates that aqua mirabilis could be used both to cure a body in distress and to strengthen the countenance of an already healthy person.

Dr. Steven's water was likewise popular in seventeenth century medicine. Recipes for it were not only published in the same books that featured aqua mirabilis, but also Thomas Dawson's 1650 *A Book of Cookery*, J.S.'s 1687 *The Accomplished Ladies Rich Closet of Rarities*, and G. Hartman's 1695 *The True Preserver and Restorer of Health*.[32] Dr. Steven's water is found in no less than five manuscript texts throughout the period as well, although there is no consensus to the exact spelling of the illustrious doctor's name.[33] Like aqua mirabilis, Dr. Steven's water calls for a variety of different spices, including ginger, galangal, cinnamon, cloves, mace, and nutmeg which are to be put in a gallon of Gascon wine and left to stand for sixteen hours. *The Ladies Cabinet Enlarged and Opened* provides interesting insight into the mixture, first outlining its benefits and then providing details about

4. Foreign Additives in Domestic Remedies

Dr. Stevens himself. It explains "the principle use of this water, is against all cold diseases, it preserveth youth, comforteth the stomach, cureth the stone of what nature soever, using but two spoonfuls in seven days. It preserved Doctor Stevens, ten years bed-ridden, that he lived to ninety eight years."[34] How a bed-ridden doctor created the water is not explained, but the notion that it could heal cold diseases is made clear.

While Blagrave did not mention either aqua mirabilis or Dr. Steven's water in his text, he did outline the benefits of various spices and how they often functioned very similarly to one another. He, for example, notes that he saw very little difference between nutmeg and mace, noting that both are hot and dry, are "somewhat astringent, and are good to stay the Lask: they are effectual in all cold griefs of the head of Brain, for Palsies, shrinking of Sinews, and diseases of the Mother, they cause a sweet breath, and discuss wind in the stomach or bowels … provoke urine, increase sperm, and are comfortable to the stomach; they help to procure rest and sleep being laid to the temples, by allaying the distemper of the Spirits."[35] He further notes that, "the thick oyl that is drawn from both Nutmegs and Mace is good in pectoral griefs, to warm a cold stomach, and help the cough, and to dry up distillations of Rheum falling upon the lungs."[36]

Contemporary medical recipes support Blagrave's analysis of nutmeg and mace and their curative properties. Beginning in 1640, Brugis's text features nutmeg in several medicinal recipes, including remedies for "Hollands Powder for the Cholicke," "A powder for the falling sickness," "a very good balm," "Catholicum simplex," as well as in aqua mirabilis and Dr. Steven's water.[37] A.M.'s 1656 *Queen Elizabeth's Closet of Physical Secrets* added to this, including nutmeg in recipes for a "julep for the cough" and "for the trembling of the heart."[38] The number of published texts featuring nutmeg multiplied beginning in the 1660s, with *The Ladies Cabinet Enlarged and Opened* (1667), *Choice and Experimental Receipts in Physick and Chirurgery* (1668), *The Closet of the Eminently Learned Kenelm Digby* (1669), *Kitchin-physick* (1676), *Vade Mecum* (1680), *The Accomplished Ladies Rich Closet of* Rarities (1687), *The True Preserver and Restorer of Health* (1695) and *The Queens Closet Opened* (1696) all calling for the spice in at least one of their medicinal recipes. Most of these remedies focused on curing the body of a cold disease, as "A Remedy against an Ague" from Hartman's

Tastes of the Empire

The True Preserver and Restorer of Health did. The remedy instructs the reader to "take a large nutmeg, grate half of it, and mix it with the yolk of an Egg beaten, then put to it five or six spoonfuls of Plague water; shake it well together, and let the Patient drink it an hour or two before the Fit, or as soon as he perceives that his Nails begin to change blew; repeat this until it be cured."[39]

Blagrave's assessment that the oil of nutmegs could cure various ailments was seemingly a new idea, as only one other published text from the seventeenth century, Brugis's 1651 *Vade Mecum*, mentions its benefits. It explains that "this oyl being drunk with wine driveth down womens months, and also the quick and dead fruit; the same it doth if it be given in a spoone with a little sugar; being taken with wine it takes away all paines of the head comming of cold."[40] Although it does not explain the benefits of nutmeg oil, a contemporary manuscript recipe book details in a rather lengthy recipe that to make this, one should take broken nutmegs, boil them in Malmsey, mix in fresh butter, and set the mixture in the sun for four to five days. After this, the concoction is to be boiled again, poured through linen, and left in the sun again. Once another straining has been completed, the result is nutmeg oil.[41] Because of the lack of other recipes detailing how to make nutmeg oil or even listing its benefits, it seems likely that the oil was just being introduced and experimented with in contemporary medicines.

As Blagrave's explanation of nutmeg and mace highlighted, the similarity between the two spices meant they were often used very similarly. Just as with nutmeg, Brugis's 1640 *The Marrow of Physicke* included mace in recipes for "A plaister very excellent for sciatica," "to make a pretious water," "to make an electuary called Hiera Simplex," along with recipes for Dr. Steven's water and aqua mirabilis.[42] Unlike Blagrave's recipes calling for nutmeg, though, he never features mace singularly, only in tandem with other spices. While inconsequential in the five recipes that Brugis uses mace in, other contemporary texts, including *Queen Elizabeths Closet of Physical Secrets* (1656), *The Ladies Cabinet Enlarged and Opened* (1667), *The Last Legacy* (1668), *Kitchin-Physic* (1676), *The Accomplished Ladies Rich Closet of Rarities* (1687), and *The True Preserver and Restorer of Health* (1695) all fail to include mace in a recipe where several other spices are not also being used. Because this usage is so drastically different than that of nutmeg, a

4. Foreign Additives in Domestic Remedies

spice that Blagrave explains is essentially its equivalent, it would appear that either nutmeg was favored over mace in medicinal culture or the curative properties of mace were still being realized.

The only exception to this was the use of "mace-ale," a substance never described but presumably a mixture of some amount of mace with ale. Thomas Cock features it in *Miscelanea Medica*, one of his two texts published in 1675, and includes it in an exchange between two physicians, one seeking advice from the other. When the first recounts seeing a man afflicted with "the Bloody flux" and admitting "what to do with him, I know not," the second suggests giving him "a good draught" of one of several beverages, including "egg-caudle, mace-ale, mull'd Sack, or burnt Claret."[43] The only other reference to mace-ale during the period came from the 1696 anonymously published *The Queens Closet Opened* in a brief recipe "For Womens Swounding fits after Deliver of Child." It instructs to "take the powder of white Amber as much as will lye on a three pence and give it in Mace-Ale warm."[44] Although mace-ale is mentioned only twice in seventeenth century medical literature, and for completely different ailments, the mixture would go on to grow in popularity.

Cloves were another spice often included in contemporary remedies and cures. Again noting that, like other spices, cloves are hot and dry, Blagrave explains that they "comfort the head and heart, strengthen the liver, and stomach, and all inward parts that want heat, they help digestion, break wind, and provoke urine, the Portugal women use to distill the Cloves while they are fresh, which make a sweet and delicate water, profitable for all passions of the Heart, and weakness of the stomack."[45] While this assessment would suggest that the seventeenth century English were consuming some sort of clove water, similar to what the Portuguese women were making, there is no indication that such a liquid was being used.

As many of the same texts that featured nutmeg and mace illustrate, the English were consistently using cloves in medicinal recipes, especially in the latter half of the century. Brugis's *The Marrow of Physick*, for example, featured several recipes calling for cloves, including "oleum Benedictum," "to make oyle of swallows," and "a drdge powder that purgeth choler."[46] Perhaps the author that provides the most insight into the medicinal usage of cloves, though, was the philosopher, courtier, and Chancellor to Queen Henrietta Maria, Sir Kenelm Digby.[47] In his 1668 *Choice and Experimental Receipts in Physick and Chirurgery*, he includes cloves in recipes for "all sorts of fluxes," "for a lossnes," and a "excellent water for gangrene," remedies similar to what other contemporary authors included them in.[48] His 1669 text, *The Closet of the Eminently Learned Kenelme Digbie*, however, uses cloves in several recipes of the same type. They are featured in "an excellent white meathe," "Mr. Webbes Meath," "Metheglin composed by my selfe out of sundry receipts," "hydromel as I made it weak for the Queen Mother," "to make white metheglin of the Countess of Dorset," and "to make white Meath."[49] Of these six recipes, two are for meathe, a water-based elixir, and three for metheglin, a mead-based liquid, both meant to preserve the body's health. That Digby consistently included cloves in such remedies demonstrates that he thought cloves were effective in achieving health.

More popular than cloves, nutmeg, or mace, however, was cinnamon. Blagrave describes the hot and dry spice as being:

> very aromatical; it is very cordial, it comforteth the Heart, and stengthneth a weak Stomach, it easeth the pains of the Cholick, especially the distilled water of it, the stopping of urine, and it stays the superabounding flux of Womens Courses; it causeth a good colour in the Face, makes a sweet breath, and good against the poison of venomous beasts, it is much used to stay looseness and binde the body: the distilled water there of is most effectual; but the Chymical oyle thereof is much more hot and piercing.[50]

Contemporary texts illustrate it was not only used with other spices in aqua mirabilis, Dr. Steven's water, and various other remedies, but, as Blagrave indicates, cinnamon water and cinnamon oil were seen as valuable medicinal products themselves. In total, more than half of the published seventeenth century medicinal texts included cinnamon or its derivatives in remedies.

While cinnamon water was frequently mentioned in seventeenth century medical literature, recipes for it were not quite as common in published texts. The anonymously published *The Ladies Companion* of 1653, however, does provide instructions on how to make the liquid. It explains that one should "take a quart of white wine, a quart of rose-water, a pinte of muskadine, half a poun of cinomon bruised, as you do for spocras, lay the cinomon to steep in the wine twelve hours,

4. Foreign Additives in Domestic Remedies

stirring them now and then; after that put them in a Lembike, and still them with a measurable fire, and theof you may draw three pints, if you will not have it strong, instead of Muskadine in so much of Rose water or white wine."[51] Recipes to make the water were far more common in manuscript texts of the period, as six different texts include at least one entry describing how to make the substance.[52] This discrepancy between the number of recipes for cinnamon water in published and manuscript texts could be due to the fact that authors expected readers to already have knowledge of how to prepare the water, knowledge they would have kept in their private recipe book.

Published texts do indicate, however, that cinnamon water was believed to be especially beneficial to expectant mothers. Two texts from the 1650s by A.M., *A Rich Closet of Physical Secrets* and *Queen Elizabeths Closset of Physical Secrets*, advocate giving pregnant women cinnamon water when they are unwell, especially in the later stages of pregnancy.[53] Published at approximately the same time, Thomas Chamberlayne's *The Compleat Midvvife's Practice* of 1653 includes cinnamon water in a paragraph explaining "how to expell the cholick from women in child-bed." He writes that, "there are some women, who the same instant they are in Travel [labor], are taken with cholick." In this situation, he states "the woman ought to take these Remedies; two ounces of oil of sweet almonds, with an ounce of cinnamon-water."[54] Although none of the texts explain why cinnamon water, or even cinnamon, played such an integral role in the health of pregnant women, it is clear that by the mid seventeenth century it had become a tenet of medical practice.

Cinnamon oil was not nearly as popular as cinnamon water, although Blagrave was not the only author to understand its virtues. John Hester's 1631 *The Secrets of Physick and Philosophy* included nearly four pages about the substance, not only describing how to make it but also its virtues. To create "oyl of sinamon," he instructs the reader to "take sinamon as much as you will, and stampe it grossely; then put it into a glasse with pure Aqua vita, and so let it stand five or six dayes, then distill it with a small fire, and there will come forth both oyle and water, the which you shall separate one from another, for the oyle will sinke to the bottome."[55] Extolling the oil in much the same manner that Blagrave did, Hester adds that it is "special for the heart and head, in so much that if a man lay speechlesse, and could scant draw his winde, it would presently recover him again."[56] He also contends that "this oyle is of such operation and vertue, that if a man drinke never so little, he shall feele the working in his fingers and toes with great marvell: and therefore to be short, it pierceth throw the whole body, and helps all diseases."[57] Two manuscript recipe books from the mid seventeenth century also mention oil of cinnamon, one providing instructions on how to make it and the other in a recipe to restore a person from any faintness.[58]

Taken together, the use of nutmeg, mace, cloves, and cinnamon in contemporary medicine demonstrates that the English valued foreign products, seeing them as more than just new, exotic ingredients to dabble with. Spices had been present in England long before the seventeenth century, yet new trade networks caused a drastic decrease in their price. The frequency and manner that they were medicinally consumed illustrates that, unlike previous centuries, spices were a staple of the English pharmacopeia and economically accessible to the majority of the population.

Plantains

Although there were foreign fruits being integrated into English diets, the only one that may have been used in medicinal recipes was the plantain.[59] While it is impossible to discern the exact regions the English were importing plantains from, that they were being referred to in medicinal recipes at all is important. Although Blagrave fails to mention them in his text, other contemporary authors illustrate that plantains were a staple of seventeenth century medical culture, including them in remedies in nearly half the texts from the period.

John Partridges's 1631 *The Widows Treasure*, features plantains in several remedies, including a cure for the ague, a disease of the gums or throat, and for "the heat in the back."[60] While Patridges's text includes plantains in seemingly unrelated remedies, other texts featured them in a similar, sporadic fashion. *A Book of Fruits and Flowers* from 1656, for example, includes plantains in cures "for the canker in the mouth" and "to kill the ring-worm" and *The Ladies Cabinet*

4. Foreign Additives in Domestic Remedies

Enlarged and Opened, published in 1654 by the Earl of Forth and Brentford, includes them in "a water for outward or inward wounds," "a remedie for the spitting of blood," "a cullesse to stop the bloudy flux," "an exceeding good remedie against the yellow jaundice," "an approved good medicine for running of the reins," and "to kill the wild fire."[61] Although such recipes seem to suggest that plantains were used rather randomly, other collections commonly feature plantains in remedies for skin related afflictions and for ailments specific to women.

Beginning in the mid seventeenth century, plantains were especially popular in recipes meant to treat dermatological issues. Burgis's *The Marrow of Physick*, for example, features plantains in remedies for "an ointment for the face after the Poxe ... and which mightily cleares the skin," "unguentum de calcantho, good for ulcers ... and evil flesh," "to make greene salve," "a salve for all manner of wounds, and sores that be curable," "a water for rednesse, and pimples in the face" and "a cataplasme for the Kings Evill, or the Tumour called Scrophula."[62] Similarly, Gervase Markham's 1656 *The English House-Wife* includes plantains in a water to wash a sore, an ointment for a burn, a bath for broken joints, and an oil of swallows for bone pain, amongst other things.[63] Likewise, the 1696 *The Accomplished Ladies Rich Closet of Rarities* calls for plantains in cures for filthy ulcers, to take away freckles, and to cool the liver and heart.[64] Published the same year, *The Queen's Closet Opened* features plantains in "a receipt for the Kings Evil, Fistula, for Breasts, Legs, or Other Sores."[65] This last remedy, as well as Burgis's for the same affliction, proves particularly interesting since scrofula, referred to as the King's Evil, was a notorious skin disease in medieval and early modern England. Prior to this, it was believed the only way to cure scrofula was to obtain a coin from the monarch that he had touched, hence the reference to the King in the recipe title. The practice, however, was completely abandoned by the early half of the eighteenth century presumably, at least in part, because more successful remedies had been found. That plantains were used in one such recipe speaks volumes to the important status this foreign food had gained in English medicinal culture.

Contemporary manuscripts also featured plantains in remedies for wounds. One such recipe collection, circa 1625, provides instructions for a "balsam for wounds," where one handful of plantains are called for.[66] Another, from approximately the same time, compiled by Anne Brumwich, likewise includes plantains in a recipe for a balsam that promises to cure "any grooms wound profondly."[67] While an anonymously kept manuscript text does feature plantains in a recipe for a "wound drink," more interesting is its use in a recipe "to fasten teeth." It instructs the reader to boil plantains with a variety of other ingredients and put it "every night a quarter of an hour especially on that side the tooth decay."[68] Clearly, seventeenth century medical thought held that plantains were good for curing wounds. While not a wound in the traditional sense, it is possible the belief that they could heal a cut or sore influenced the thought that they would help restore rotting teeth.

Plantains were also being used in recipes relating to women's health. In Culpeper's 1651 *A directory for midvvives*, he states that feverish woman who were lying in should add either plantain leaves or roots to their diet.[69] Using plantains in the aftercare of a woman who has just given birth, *The English Midwife Enlarged* states in a section titled "of remedies for the brests and lower parts of the Belly of women newly deliverer" to "after 10 or 12 days fortifie the parts with a decoction of province roses, plantain leaves and roots, and Smith's water."[70] Another recipe, this time from Mrs. Elizabeth Hirst's private collection compiled toward the end of the seventeenth century, features plantains in a recipe "against ye Mother," yet does not explain how or when it is to help her. It simply instructs the reader to:

> take plantane, succor, burrage, agrimony, violet leaves of each one hadfull, boyle them in 6 pints of water, till they be consumed then straine them and to the liquor put halfe an ounce of bruis'd cloves & half a pound of white sugar candy, sit it on the feir til the sugar be dissol'd then clarrifye it with the white of an egg and straine it againe when it is cold put a quarter of pint of white vinegar to it drink of it 3 spoonfulls at a time the first and last thing you do.[71]

While all three recipes are rather different from one another, they similarly illustrate that a foreign product was being incorporated into a variety of remedies. Perhaps the most curious remedy featuring plantains from the period is in one for horses, featured in G.L.'s 1691 *The Gentleman's New Jockey*. In a cure for "the canker in the nose," the text instructs the reader to boil together plantain juice with white wine vinegar, rue, honey, and "roach allom," and apply it as "hot as the horse will endure."[72] " Obviously, by the turn of the eighteenth century,

4. Foreign Additives in Domestic Remedies

plantains had been fully integrated into English medicinal culture if they were being used in veterinary medicine as well.

Guaiacum, Muscadine, Sarsaparilla and Sassafras

Several New World plants also appear in seventeenth century medicinal recipes. Since domestic herbs and plants held a firm place in the English pharmacopeia, it seems logical that the English would look to similar products abroad when seeking to expand the number of ingredients they had at their disposal. While American plants like guaiacum, muscadine, sarsaparilla, and sassafras did not appear in as many remedies as various spices or even plantains did, their inclusion proves that the English were integrating foreign products more and more as the century progressed and their access to such goods increased.

One such American plant was guaiacum, a flowering shrub native to the Caribbean islands. Blagrave informs his readers that its wood, bark, and gum are "hot and dry, and are used for all cold flegmatick and windy humors, and are effectual against the Epilepse, Falling Sickness, Catharrhs, Rheums, and cold distillations on the Lungs, or other parts, Coughs and Consumptions, the Gout and all Joint-aches, and many other like diseases, and to make teeth white and firm." Despite this, though, Blagrave is most taken with the plant's ability to cure syphilis. He explains that, "most particularly it is appropriated to the cure of the French-pox by drinking the decoction of the wood and bark." Because of this, he concludes his discussion on guaiacum with instructions on how to make an extract of it, which he states is "not unpleasant to take and most effectual for the French-pox."[73]

Even though Blagrave insisted that guaiacum was an excellent cure for syphilis, the contemporary remedies that feature the plant, two written before and two after the publication of Blagrave's text, do not mention the disease. Guaiacum first appeared in Partridges's *The VViddovves Treasure* in a recipe "for the Strangary," a syphilitic symptom. The recipe calls for a pound of guaiacum, beaten into a powder, and indicates that it may be attained from an apothecary, explaining that one should follow his directions regarding the use of it.[74] In the Earl of Forth and Brentford's text, one pound of guaiacum is needed for "a diet for the patient that has ulcers of wounds that will hardly be cured with Ointments, Salves, or Plaisters."[75] Adding to this, Johanna Saint John mentioned guaiacum in a remedy in her personal recipe collection, listing it as the first of a series of ingredients for a "fume to be taken in a pipe."[76] In another recipe collection, this time compiled by an anonymous owner, guaiacum is featured alongside two other New World plants, sarsaparilla and sassafras, in "a drink for the weakness of the eyes."[77] Though these are only four recipes from the period that include guaiacum, the notion that English apothecaries would be able to offer advice regarding its use and that it could cure the dreaded "French pox" bolsters the idea that this plant was beginning to be incorporated into contemporary medical culture.

The use of sarsaparilla, native to Central America and the Caribbean, was also seen throughout the period. Blagrave devoted nearly three pages of his text to it, explaining that sarsaparilla does not promote heat so much as it does dryness. He states, "it is much used in many kinds of diseases; as in all cold fluxes from the head and braine, rhuems, and catarrhes, as also in all cold griefs of the stomack and mother. It helpeth not only the French disease, but all manner of aches in the sinews or joynts; all running sores in the legs, all flegmatick swellings, tetters or ringworms, and all of spots, and foulness of the skin."[78] He also provides the reader with a brief history of how sarsaparilla has been consumed. Blagrave explains:

> the manner of using it is, and hath been divers: in former times it was used beaten to powder, and so drank; others used to boyle it so long until it became tender, which being beaten or broken, was afterwards strained into the decoction, making a kinde of drink like cream. Some others, and that most useually, boyled it in water, to the half, or the consumption of the third part as they would have it stronger or weaker; and that either, by it self or with other things proper for the disease it was intended for, and others also put it amongst other things into drink; either Beer or Ale new tunned up, to drink after it hath stood three or four dayes for Physick-drink.[79]

This description not only demonstrates the various ways that sarsaparilla was prepared and ingested, but that there was already a tradition of it being used for medicinal purposes in England by the later seventeenth century.

Despite this, the majority of the texts that feature sarsaparilla come from the latter half of the period. Supporting Blagrave's idea that the

4. Foreign Additives in Domestic Remedies

plant was useful against syphilis, *Queen Elizabeths Closset of Physical Secrets* of 1656 includes a remedy for the "French Pox," in which sarsaparilla is mixed with a variety of other ingredients, boiled in spring water, and given to the patient three times a day.[80] Published approximately ten years later, William Drage's *A Physical Nosonomy* outlines that when "sweaters" are needed to expel moisture from the body, "a decoction of sarsaparilla is best."[81] Perhaps it is because of the invocation of sweat that G. Hartman's *The True Preserver and Restorer of Health*, features sarsaparilla in several "diet" drinks, such as "a famous cure of a desperate Dropsie by a Diet of Garlick, preformed by D. Farrar, upon an Eminent Lord," which calls for twelve ounces of the plant. Hartman's text also includes the plant in a recipe for "an electuary to comfort the spleen and stomach"[82]

Two manuscript texts, both from the later seventeenth century, echo the notion that sarsaparilla was seen as a plant that would draw moisture from the body. Bridget Hyde's recipe collection features the plant in two remedies, one entitled "an excellent receipt for ye dropsy and all sorts of watrish humours" and the other "a good medicine to purge and dry up superflious humours and nourishing after ill humors be evacuated."[83] Similarly, Elizabeth Jacob's collection includes "an excellent dyet drink prescribed by Dr Buttler to be used three dayes together taken between eight and nine in the morning and three or four in the afternoon go wither you will so you keep warm this may be taken thrice in the yeare or as often as you can gett green scurvey grass." The recipe instructs the reader to take three ounces of sarsaparilla, along with an array of other herbs, and put them into "a linen bagg, and tie them up in four gallons of new beere, put a stone into the bagg, to cause it to sink, and the first two days squeeze the bag that the juyce may go into the drink, the fourth day drink of it a good draught." The remedy concludes by stating that, "it is a most soveraigne remedy against most disesases, especially any infection or cold in the stomach."[84] Taken together, the recipes featuring sarsaparilla demonstrate that English medicinal culture believed in the plant's ability to dry out and draw moisture from the body.

Sassafras, found in North America, was being used similarly to sarsaparilla, and sometimes even in conjunction with it. Blagrave explains that sassafras, sometimes referred to as "ague-tree," is a hot and dry plant good in "cold rheums and defluxions of the head, on the teeth, eyes, or lungs; warming and drying up the moisture and strengthening the parts." He notes that "it is thought to be good in plague-time, to wear some thereof continually about them, that the smell thereof may expel the corrupt and evil vapours of the Pestilence: It is generally used in all the diseases that come of cold, raw, thin and corrupt humours; the French disease, and other of the like foul nature; the Indians use the leaves being bruised to heal their wounds and soures."[85] While Blagrave does not explicitly point out the similarities between sassafras and sarsaparilla, the parallels in the curative properties of the two plants illustrate why they would have been used together.

Like sarsaparilla, sassafras is found in recipes meant to draw moisture from the body. For example, *Queen Elizabeth's Closset of Physical Secrets* of 1656 features a recipe for "infants troubled with wind and phlegm," explaining that sugar candy should be "bruised" in it and given to the child.[86] Sir Kenelm Digby features the plant in such recipes in both of his 1660s texts, first including it in "a great and approved cure of the dropsie" and "a great electuary" in *Choice and Experiment Receipts in Physick and Chirurgery* and then calling for sassafras in "a receipt to make a tun of metheglin" and "to make white Metheglin of the Countess of Dorset."[87] Similar recipes are found in personal recipe collections, with remedies featuring sassafras including "Dr Tabors Ague Medicine," "for a consumption cough," and "An approved Medecine called the Purging to be taken every Spring & Fall from the first of April to the end there of and from the Middle of September to the Middle of October."[88] Like sarsaparilla, sassafras had clearly become a standard ingredient in remedies against cold and wet ailments.

Muscadine, a grapevine species that is indigenous to modern southeastern Florida, is another plant seen in a handful of later seventeenth century English cookery books. Blagrave, however, fails to mention it in his text. Although medicinal recipes featuring it had already appeared in texts prior to the publication of his, it is possible that the usage of muscadine was still somewhat new, causing him to overlook it.

Used in a wide variety of remedies, muscadine is first found in *Queen Elizabeth's Closset of Physical Secrets* in a liniment for a mothers stomach and a "water for a consumption," which calls for three pounds

4. Foreign Additives in Domestic Remedies

of the plant.[89] A few years later, William Rabisha's 1661 *The Whole Body of Cookery Dissected* proposes that muscadine, combined with other herbs, eggs, and wines, can cure a weak stomach.[90] In 1667, *The Ladies Cabinet Enlarged and Opened* calls for muscadine in "A Bath to comfort the brain" which explains that the reader should, "take a quart of muscadine, sweet marjoram a handul, rosemary tops one handul, and a few cloves, boil them upon a soft fie to the one half, and bathe the head therewith often in the spring and fall of the lead, drying it in with hot napkins."[91] Two recipes featuring the plant also appear in the 1696 *The Queens Closet Opened*. Interestingly enough, all these recipes call for large quantities of muscadine, with it even functioning as the primary ingredient in remedies like "a bath to comfort the brain."

Medical cures including muscadine can also be found in three manuscript texts from the latter seventeenth century. The most curious of them is Johanna Saint John's recipe for "snayle water for a consumption," a rather long recipe that begins by instructing the reader to take "house snayls 3 pound taken out of the shels & washed in muscadine."[92] Although not requiring snails, Edward and Katherine Kidder include muscadine in a remedy "for ye collick or wind in ye body," an anonymous collection of family recipes feature it in a remedy entitled "plague water," and an inhabitant of Harrow-upon-the-Hill featured it in an unnamed remedy for joint pain.[93] The smattering of remedies that featured muscadine towards the end of the century indicate that the English were only beginning to experiment with its medicinal benefits.

Taken together, guaiacum, sarsaparilla, sassafras, and muscadine illustrate that the English were using foreign plants in their remedies similarly to how they used domestic herbs and vegetation. While some were being utilized more than others, their inclusion in medicine demonstrates an awareness that the conquering of new lands could provide new cures. Their usage also proves that the importation of foreign products was revolutionizing the English pharmacopeia.

Tobacco

The most popular foreign plant, however, was tobacco; it was referenced in more than ten contemporary texts featuring medicinal recipes. Blagrave tells his readers that it is "of a stupefying quality: it is held to be available to expectorate tough phlegm out of the stomach chest and lungs; the juice thereof made into a syrup, distilled water of the herb drank with Sugar, the same also helps to expel worms in the stomach and belly ... the seed hereof is much effectual to ease the pains of the teeth, and the ashes of the burnt herb to cleanse the gums and teeth, and make them white." He also notes that "the liquor that distilleth therefrom is singular good to use for cramps, aches, the gout and sciatica, and to heal itches, scabs, and running ulcers, and foul soures whatsoever. The juice is good for all said greifs, and likewise to kill lice in childrens heads."[94]

Interestingly enough, John Chamberlayne writes rather differently of tobacco in his 1682 text *The Natural History of Coffee, Thee, Chocolate, Tobacco*. He states that he is "confident that [tobacco] is of the poysonous sort, for it Intoxicates, Inflanes, Vomits, and Purges; which operations are common to poisonous plants." He supports this by arguing oil of tobacco is poisonous, explaining that "every one knows that the Oyl of Tobacco is one of the greatest Poysons in nature, a few drops of it falling upon the tongue of a Cat, will immediately throw her into Convulsions, under which she will die.... I can speak it upon my own certain knowledge, having kill' several animals with a few drops of this Oyl."[95] Noting that even King James I, "both writ and disputed very smartly against [tobacco] at Oxford," he claims that "some anatomists tell us most terrible stories of sooty brains, and black Lungs, which have been seen in the dissections of Dead Bodies, which when living had been accustomed to Tobacco."[96] Despite all this, Chamberlayne does concede that it has been known to cure ulcers, sores, toothaches, and "violent pains of the head," though.[97] While accepting it can be used to cure some ailments, Chamberlayne was obviously not as supportive of tobacco usage as Blagrave was.

Contemporary recipes do support Blagrave's explanation of the plant, while also illustrating the different medicinal benefits tobacco could offer and the variety of ways it could be consumed. In a recipe describing the virtues and uses of tobacco, the Earl of Forth and Brentford states in his 1654 text that one should "take of the green herb and roote three pound and an half, stampe it in a mortar with a little salt, then put it in a glasse with six ounces of spirit of wine, and set it a

4. Foreign Additives in Domestic Remedies

whole month in horse dung to putrifie; then distil it in Balneo til all the substance be come out; and put as much Oleum Sulphuris into it as will make it tarte and then keep it close from air." By drinking this concoction, the Earl claims a person can be cured from a fever, ulcer, or scabs.[98]

Many other remedies used tobacco in an attempt to cure some skin affliction, like a scab, yet they favored topical application as opposed to the drinking of an elixir. *The Marrow of Physicke*, for example, explains that using the juice of "English tobacco" makes an excellent salve for fresh cuts.[99] Published nearly thirty years later, *The Ladies Cabinet Enlarged and Opened* includes a recipe to make oil of tobacco, which the text states is a precious skin balm.[100] Such remedies could be due to the idea that, as *Queen Elizabeths Closset of Physical Secrets* points out in a remedy for erysipelas, the English learned how to treat skin afflictions with tobacco from Spaniards and Native Americans who used the juice from it to expel poison.[101]

Several manuscript texts include recipes featuring tobacco in oils or ointments as well. In an anonymously kept English medical notebook from the first half of the century, the writer provides instructions on how to make "an ointment of English tobacco" and also includes a remedy "for the itch" that includes tobacco as an ingredient.[102] Similar cures for "the itch" featuring tobacco are found in two other anonymously kept texts as well.[103] While it does not include tobacco in a remedy for a skin affliction, Elizabeth Jacob's text features a recipe "for the tooth ach" in which tobacco and sugar are used.[104] Interestingly enough, a similar remedy can be found in *The Gentleman's New Jockey*, which advises farriers to "annoint gums with the oyntment of tobacco" for any horse that has "pains in the teeth or jaws."[105] Such a transition from human to horse remedies seems to indicate that that tobacco must have alleviated human tooth pain and therefore why it would have been used on the animal.

As Blagrave pointed out, tobacco was thought to cure a variety of different ailments and could be consumed a variety of different ways. While there are recipes for the usage of tobacco and its juice, none of these remedies speak of smoking tobacco, yet smoking of tobacco in pipes was commonplace in seventeenth century England. Because of this, it is safe to assume tobacco was used more frequently than the evidence suggests. Thus, not only had tobacco become a part of English leisure activities, but it had become an established ingredient in English medical culture as well.

Chocolate and Coffee

While there are many references to coffee and chocolate in seventeenth century literature, Blagrave and his contemporary Chamberlayne arguably devote the most time discussing their medicinal usages and providing recipes for them. Going beyond recipes for leisurely consumption, they note that both are known to influence the body's constitution. Although both spend much more time on chocolate than on coffee, their analysis proves that by the end of the seventeenth century, the English were beginning to view both as more than just exotic treats.

Blagrave begins his section on chocolate by stating that the public already knew of the virtues of the substance, and therefore he did not need to repeat them. Chamberlayne's text, published some ten years after Blagrave's, proves a bit more useful in discerning the medical benefits of it, though. Referencing many of the travel writers who had been to the New World and encountered chocolate there, Chamberlayne writes that they all agree "that the cacao nut has a wonderful faculty of quenching thirst, allaying Hectick heats, of nourishing and fatning the body." Although some feel cacao is too oily, he explains that "the bitterness of the nut makes amends, carrying the [oil] off by strengthening the bowels." He concludes by deciding chocolate is "proper for Lean, Weak, and Consumptive Complexions: it may be proper for some breeding Women, and those persons that are Hypocondiacal and Melancholly."[106]

Although Blagrave does not list the medical benefits of chocolate as Chamberlayne did, he does provide different recipes for different constitutions. He states that the reader should take it "for a rule that one receipt cannot be proper for all Persons; therefore such a drink [as is a] common drink in publick houses, may receive more hurt than good by it; therefore every one may make choice of ingredients, that they may be usefull for the complexion of the body." He writes that a

4. Foreign Additives in Domestic Remedies

standard recipe for chocolate requires "to every 100 of cacao's, two cods of long red pepper, one handful of anniseeds; one cod of Campeche or logwood, two drams of cinnamon; almonds and hasel-nuts of each a dozen, white sugar half a pound." However, those who "are of cold or moist constitutions, and are troubled with a very cold stomach and liver" should add some black pepper and "tanasco," an Indian root that he likens to Madder. If a person is prone to "chronick diseases, macilent bodies, or are inclinable to be infirm ... it is very proper and convenient that sugar be put into it."[107] From the various recipes for chocolate that Blagrave offers, it's evident he felt cocoa was good for the body and, when combined with other ingredients, could be made appropriate for all consumers.

Blagrave is somewhat less enthusiastic about the benefits that coffee can offer, though. While noting that many argue coffee can increase a person's "watchfulness" and can bring about sobriety in a drunken person, his tone suggests that he remains skeptical of both claims. He argues that "certainly if there had been any worth in it, some of the ancient Arabian Physicians or others neer those parts, would have recorded it: But there is no mention made of any medicinal use thereof, by any Author either Ancient or Modern." Despite this, he does include instructions on how to make coffee, telling the reader to "take a gallon of water and sit it in a pot of Tyn, or any other vessel close cover'd, set it upon the fire and let it boyl; when it thoroughly boyles, put into it a quarter of a pound of the powder of the coffee-berry, stirring it well together, so let it boyl a quarter of an hour, and your coffee is ready to drink, then pour some of it into a smaller pot covered, and keep it always ready before the fire."[108]

Countering this, Chamberlayne finds many positive benefits of the beverage, even suggesting that it may have been the famed "black Broth of the Spartans." He writes that, "in several Headachs, Dizziness, Lethargies, and Catarrhs, where there is a gross habit of the body, and a cold heavy constitution, there coffee may be proper."[109] He notes coffee "is said to be very good for those, that have taken too much drink, meat, or fruit ... as also against shortness of breath, and rheum, and it is very famous in old obstructions, so that all the Ægyptian, and Arabian Women, are overv'd to promote their monthly courses with Coffee, and to triple constantly of it all the time they are flowing."[110]

119

Chamberlayne also explains that coffee has a reputation, at least in Persia, of making "men Paralytick, and does so slacken their strings, as they become unfit for sports, and excercises of the Bed, and their Wives recreations." He states that "the Persians are of an opinion that Coffee allays their natural heat; for which reason they drink it, that they may avoid the charge, and inconveniences of many children."[111] As Chamberlayne describes it, Persian men used coffee almost as a form of birth control, although he notes that he fears English men may avoid the beverage because of these rumored effects.

While seventeenth century medicinal texts are not wrought with remedies and cures utilizing chocolate and coffee, the information that Blagrave and Chamberlayne provide in their respective texts illustrate that both beverages were believed to have medical usages. Along with tea, coffee and chocolate were popularly consumed in the growing number of coffeehouses springing up across the country, proving that contemporary English men and women were consuming these beverages on a regular basis. Whether they were doing so because of a fad fueled by an interest in exotic products or to reap the medicinal benefits of the beverages is hard to tell.

Conclusion

Judging from the numerous foreign foods in contemporary medical recipes, seventeenth-century English men and women were increasingly engaging with foreign products. Unlike other objects of consumption, foreign foods impacted household medicinal culture, which played an important role in daily life and health. While male medical professionals did treat patients and author treatises, contemporary medicine was centered in home and relied on the female head of household. More often then not, it was she who would diagnosis and work to cure an ailing family member. Even when a male physician was brought in, she was responsible for the upkeep of the patient once his diagnosis had been made. Because of this contemporary female doctoring, foreign ingredients were used in remedies at a woman's discretion. That women controlled such an important facet of consumption is significant; it provided them an opportunity to act as agents of

4. Foreign Additives in Domestic Remedies

an expanding empire. Functioning within contemporary gender norms, women were able to incorporate foreign ingredients into their families' cures and remedies, exposing them to the benefits of England's burgeoning empire. It allowed them to act as agents of change at home, curing the ailing bodies of their family members, as well as abroad, encouraging the growth and expansion of the English realm.

5

Vices and Virtues
Tobacco, Chocolate, Coffee and Tea in Print

In 1685, J.C.B.'s *Rebellions Antidote: or A Dialogue Between Coffee and Tea* endeavored to persuade the public to abandon alcohol and consume coffee or tea instead. The one-page discussion between coffee and tea describes how wine, ale, and beer have morally corrupted society, positioning themselves as the respectable alternative to these alcoholic beverages. Railing against the debauchery of wine, ale, and beer, coffee is featured saying:

> 'Tis Wine and Ale and eke the Grape
> Has spawn'd this spurious bestial rape;
> What is't but there produce, what horrid fact
> But Wine and Ale and Beer will act;
> Death Hell and Judgment hand in hand
> With them and theirs do always stand'
> Rapes, Murders, Thefts, and thousand Crimes
> Are gender'd by foul Ale and Wines;
> These are but Trifles to the woe
> That Wine and Ale, and Beer can do.[1]

Coffee and tea agree to fight against the evils of their alcoholic counterparts, saving contemporary English society in the process. The tract closes using coffee as a creative acronym, stating:

> C ome frantick Fools leave off your Drunken fits,
> O bsequiens be and I'll recall your Wits,
> F rom perfect madness to a modest strain,
> F or farthings four I'll fetch you back again.
> E nable all your mene with tricks of State,
> E nter and sip then attend your Fate.

5. Vices and Virtues

> Come Drunk or Sober for a gentle Fee,
> Come ne'r so Mad I'll your physican be.[2]

Not only are coffee and tea being suggested as healthy alternatives to wine, ale, and beer, but the author is clearly contending that coffee will assist the body in recovering from drunkenness. Obviously written to bolster the consumption, and sales, of coffee and tea, the tract endorses both beverages and the medicinal effects they offer.

Like J.C.B., many contemporary authors took to print to discuss the vices or virtues associated with foreign products, especially tobacco, chocolate, coffee, and tea. These four became extremely popular with the English public, arguably more than any other foreign food introduced during the sixteenth or seventeenth centuries. The first of these to reach the English market, tobacco, had an established tradition of English consumption by the turn of the seventeenth century. While there is no clear evidence of when tobacco was first introduced to England, Iain Gately contends that it was certainly "in use in England by 1571."[3] He claims that an English tobacco craze caught on quickly, perhaps due to Sir Walter Raleigh's fondness of it, as Raleigh's "mannerisms were widely imitated," especially by those in the "higher strata."[4]

Tobacco's popularity did not mean it was cheap, though. Gately states that in 1598, "tobacco cost £4 10s. per pound. By way of comparison, a mug of ale cost a penny and a young whore with good teeth was less than a shilling a throw."[5] It was because of this that by 1590 efforts were made to grow tobacco domestically and by 1630, "great parts of Gloucestershire, Wiltshire, and Worcestershire were given over to tobacco plantations."[6] Domestically grown tobacco could never replace American tobacco, though. In 1618, London imported 20,000 pounds of Virginian tobacco; in 1627, 500,000 pounds; and three years later, triple that amount.[7] Because of this steady increase, Carole Shammas has argued that by 1670, there was enough tobacco in England for twenty five percent of adults to have at least one pipeful of it a day.[8] To accommodate this, there were no fewer than sixty-six tobacco pipe makers in England by 1699.[9]

Chocolate appeared in the domestic market some seventy years after tobacco in 1640, the English learning of it from the Spanish who were regarded as the best authorities on the drink.[10] Marcy Norton has claimed that chocolate's "historical significance ... transcends chocolate itself. That dark, stimulating beverage served as a 'gateway' drink for those other ones—coffee and tea—that would overtake their predecessor in popularity across all European countries, except Spain, by the end of the seventeenth century."[11] She contends that early coffee vendors also sold chocolate, "perhaps persuading their readers that this was a variant but related beverage."[12]

Kate Loveman's analysis of chocolate consumption seems to support this, as she claims that by 1650, London had a number of chocolate sellers, many of which also sold coffee. She further notes the price of contemporary chocolate, explaining that in 1662 one Henry Stubbe sold his "chocolate-royal for 6s 6d per pound and his 'ordinary Chocolatat' at 3s 8d; in the same year, the coffee-house of 'Morat the Great' in Exchange Alley sold 'ordinary' chocolate at 2s 6d per pound."[13] She claims, though, that ready-made chocolate served by the dish at a coffee or chocolate house was cheaper, as most charged a penny a dish.[14]

Although Loveman notes that there is an overall absence of quantitative data on chocolate sales in the seventeenth century, she claims it can be inferred that "drinking chocolate as a habit rather than as an occasional medicine appears to have taken hold first among wealthy hispanophiles, courtiers, and metropolitans with strong mercantile or diplomatic ties. Alongside the public consumption of the drink in coffee-houses, there was also a less visible growing market for chocolate pastilles or tablets to be prepared at home."[15] It was not, she claims, a beverage that "trickled down" from the aristocracy, but instead one that was bought by the gentry as well. Despite this, chocolate consumption was ultimately dwarfed by the English appetite for coffee in the later seventeenth century and tea in the eighteenth century.[16]

The first coffee vendor in England was a Jewish man named Jacobs who opened a coffee house, called the Angel, in Oxford in 1650.[17] Pasqua Rosée founded London's first coffee establishment some two years later in 1652, and, as Brian Cowan contends, "the national English virtuoso community began to eagerly investigate the properties of this strange new beverage."[18] Cowan notes that coffee first came to England in small quantities from Levant or Mediterranean merchants, but "five years after the foundation of the first coffeehouse in London ... [the East India Company] ordered their Surat factor to send ten tons of

5. Vices and Virtues

coffee back to England for domestic sales."[19] This continued throughout the seventeenth and into the eighteenth century, as in 1708 the East India Company's director commented that coffee was still in great demand in England.[20]

Coffeehouses, too, gained in popularity throughout the 1600s. Cowan argues that such establishments began as centers for news culture, where news and coffee were packaged together as a way to attract costumers.[21] Customer acquisition was still a concern of coffee vendors in the 1660s, as they were still endeavoring to "carve out a niche in the London retail market." Because of this, the Turk's Head offered free coffee on New Year's Day 1663 to all "gentlemen willing to give the new drink a try, and promised to continue doing so."[22] Although precise numbers of London coffeehouses do not exist, Cowan contends that there were at least sixty-five coffeehouses in the city by 1702 and 551 by 1734.[23]

Coffee was not just consumed in coffeehouses, though. William Ukers argues that in the mid seventeenth century, it was "the custom" for English people to buy coffee beans, "dry them in an oven, or to roast them in an old pudding dish or frying pan before pounding them to a powder with mortar and pestle, to force the powder through a lawn sieve, and then to boil it with spring water for a quarter of an hour."[24] In the later seventeenth century, European coffee connoisseurs also used the "Turkish combination coffee grinder with folding handle and cup receptacle for the beans, used for grinding, boiling, and drinking ... first made in Damascus in 1665."[25]

Coffee consumption was surpassed by tea in the eighteenth century, though. Cowan notes that "around 1700, it has been estimated that coffee consumption per capita was about ten times as great as that of tea.... By the 1720s, the value of the tea imported into Britain was substantially higher than the value of imported coffee."[26] Tea was first imported to London from the Dutch in 1657. Jane Pettigrew and Bruce Richardson explain that, "when the East India Company wished to present a casket of tea to Charles II and his queen, Catherine of Braganza, in 1664, they had to buy it from Dutch merchants."[27] While the English were soon importing their own tea, the trade was slow to start. Pettigrew and Richardson note that "in 1678, 5,000 pounds [of tea] was enough to cause a glut on the London market. Although imports continued, by the end of the 1680s a regular trade with China still had not been established."[28] According to them, one reason for this was the high price of tea, citing the Countess of Argyll's 1690 household accounts that show tea cost more than £26 per pound.[29] Also noting its expensiveness, Kate Colquhoun explains that there was only two varieties of tea leaves available to seventeenth century English consumers: Bohea, which "could be topped up with water several times" and Green, which "was lost if it was used more than once."[30]

Although originally sold in London coffee houses, a traditionally male space, tea drinking within the home became popular amongst women.[31] Pettigrew and Richardson claim that tea was made fashionable with females because of Queen Catherine's fondness of it. They explain that when she arrived in England in 1662 to marry Charles II, she brought with her a casket of tea and consumed it as an "everyday beverage."[32] Because of this, they argue that there was a gradual increase in tea drinking in the home through the last part of the seventeenth century.[33] English tea consumption continued to rise in the eighteenth century, with 18 million pounds of tea consumed a year by 1779.[34]

With English popularity of tobacco, chocolate, coffee, and tea in mind, it is no wonder contemporary authors took to print to discuss these products and the consumption of them. While some simply offered praise for them as J.C.B. did, others informed readers about where they could purchase these items in and about London. Functioning as early modern advertisements, such tracts and treatise demonstrate that tobacco, chocolate, coffee, and tea were available in the London marketplace and that their physical consumption was actually occurring there during the seventeenth century.

Although not all tracts featured directions to vendors, the virtues discussed in print encouraged consumers to consider and engage with the product being discussed. Even though J.C.B.'s dialogue does not tell readers where they can purchase coffee, his tract would have caused them to think about the beverage and encouraged them to seek it out when they needed to recover from being overly intoxicated. Thus, authors like J.C.B. demonstrate the manner in which a product was being thought of by society and whether contemporary ideas held that the consumption of tobacco, chocolate, coffee, or tea was a vice or a virtue.

5. Vices and Virtues

And, as seventeenth century tracts and treatise illustrate, not all foreign products were thought of positively. Detractors of coffee and tobacco wrote just as vigorously as those who endorsed their consumption, providing true insight into seventeenth century ideas about both products. The debates that circled around the usage of coffee and tobacco, however, still speak to the extent of their consumption. Surely, scholars, physicians, businessmen, and, in the case of tobacco, King James I, would not have taken to print to vilify these products if a significant portion of society was not frequently consuming them.

Thus, contemporary discourses concerning tobacco, chocolate, coffee, and tea provide insight into contemporary English ideas about the products and how frequently they were being consumed. It did not matter if the text in question sought to educate its reader or advertise a certain vendor's wares, as both offer implicit proof that consumption of these foreign goods was occurring. Tracts and treatise demonstrate that tobacco, chocolate, coffee, and tea were popularly consumed and discussed in seventeenth century English culture, despite whether their consumption was being supported or contested.

Tobacco

Unlike chocolate, tea, and coffee, which rose to popularity in the mid to latter half of the 1600s, tobacco was already entrenched in English culture at the dawn of the seventeenth century. Tobacco received far more negative press than chocolate, coffee, or tea ever did, though; even King James I took to print to warn his subjects against the dangers of its usage. Numerous tracts and treatise both advocating for and against tobacco were published in the seventeenth century, together demonstrating how popular the plant had become.

Contemporary authors indicate that the debate over the healthfulness of tobacco consumption was established well before 1600. Doctor Bellamy, for example, opened his 1602 *A New and Short Defense of Tabacco* by endeavoring to explain to his readers where he fit within this larger debate over the herb. He contends that, "perceauing how vehemently (yet without iust cause) the vse of Tabacco hath of late beene by common speech detracted, & by diuerse, publikely written

Tastes of the Empire

against, [the author] desireth herein briefly, by his owne example and experience ... to satisfie and direct his friends and countrimen, in the practice, and taking of that hearb."[35] Obviously, Dr. Bellamy felt that he needed to explain why he would write a tract detailing the benefits of tobacco when so many before him had spoken against it, indicating that tobacco had been fully integrated into English culture well before 1600.

Acknowledging that he is using his own knowledge of tobacco to speak of the medicinal benefits that it offers, Bellamy writes that tobacco opens and dries the body, functioning as an excellent purging and expelling agent. Wishing to provide readers with a personal example, he writes "in processe of weekes, well I wot, it hath forced out of my braines, through the great middle suture of my scull, at an emunctorie, not much aboue the toppe of my eares, by times, more yellow, bitter, corrupt, choloricke moisture, I am sure, then three gill cuppes could containes, before it left that course of purging. This humour was the primarie and principall occasion (as I take it) of all my former inueterate fluxes and destillations."[36] Bellamy estimates that what tobacco purged from his body had been the source of ailments that had plagued him for the last fifteen years. This, then, explains why Bellamy felt the need to support tobacco consumption and further explain its medicinal benefits, as he understood it to have curative properties that other contemporary drugs could not offer. It also provides insight into how those who supported tobacco consumption understood its ability to restore one's health.

King James I also took to print to weigh in on contemporary tobacco consumption. Unlike Bellamy, though, he was entirely against the product, calling into question any health benefits associated with its intake. Noting in his 1604 *A Counterblast to Tobacco* that it was from Native Americans that we learned of tobacco, he asks his countrymen to:

> ... consider what honour or policie can move us to imitate the barbarous and beastly maners of the wilde, godlesse, and slavish Indians, especially in so vile and stinking a custome.... Shall wee, I say, without blushing, abase ourselves so farre as to imitate these beastly Indians, slaves to the Spaniards, refuse to the world, and as yet aliens from the holy Covenant of God? Why do we not as well imitate them in walking naked as they doe? in preferring glasses, feathers, and such toyes, to golde and precious stones, as they do? yea why do we not denie God and adore the Devill, as they doe?[37]

5. Vices and Virtues

Lambasting tobacco for its foreignness, James found it appalling that his fellow countrymen would be attracted to such a foreign and unchristian product.

As Gately interestingly notes, "tobacco was a natural adversary for James" as the royal had made it his personal mission to fight witchcraft, so much so that "an average of 400 witches per annum were burned in the latter years of James's Scottish reign." Gately claims, "In addition to [tobaccos] visible hell-fire associations when smoked, the tobacco plant had a family tie to witchcraft. Witches' favourite potions for flying were compounded from tobacco's cousins in the *Solanaceae* order—belladonna and henbane.... Indeed tobacco was known for a brief period of time as henbane of Peru."[38] In this sense, not only was tobacco a foreign plant from the unchristian people of the Americas, but it also had connections to satanic forces the King had been battling for years.

James further attacked the healthfulness of tobacco consumption as well. He contends that one cannot reason tobacco is good against cold and wet humors, like rheumatism, simply because of the nature of the plant. And while he notes many have claimed tobacco is hot and dry, James himself argues differently. He states that, "tobacco is not simply of a dry & hot quality, but rather hath a certaine venomous facultie joined with the heate thereof, which makes it have an antipathie against nature, as by the hatefull smell thereof doeth well appeare. For the nose being the proper organ and conovoy of the sense of smelling to the braines ... doeth ever serve us for an infallible witnesse, whether that odour which we smell, be healthful or hurtful to the braine."[39] Citing the noxious smell tobacco produces, James claims that something beneficial to the body could not smell so displeasing.

King James finishes his tract by chastising the reader, claiming that by abusing tobacco they are shaming the country. He argues that ones "abuse thereof [is] sinning against God, harming your selves both in persons and goods, and raking also thereby the markes and notes of vanities upon you: by the custome thereof making your selves to be wondered at by all forraine civil Nations, and by all strangers that come among you, to be scorned and contemned."[40] While James' hatred for tobacco is unmistakable, his verbiage indicates that tobacco consumption was rampant in England by the time he was writing. Surely it would take a large number of tobacco consumers for James to fear that other foreign countries would look down on the English for their usage of it.

Edmund Gardiner's *The Triall of Tabacco*, published in 1610, illustrates that James was not the only one to criticize tobacco. After explaining how the plant grows in the Americas, Gardiner writes "it was first brought into Europe out of the prouinces of America ... but being now planted in the gardens of Europe, it prosperth very well, and cometh from seedin one yere to beare both floures & seed. The which I take to be better for the constitution of our bodies, then that which is brought from India, and that which is growing in the Indies, better for the people of the same country."[41] Not only does Gardiner demonstrate that by 1610 tobacco was being grown in Europe, but he puts forward the idea that domestically grown tobacco was better for English people as it was more suited for their bodies.

His assertion that domestically cultivated tobacco is good for the English body fits with his overall assessment of the plant, as he states "tabacco is a noble medicine, and fit to be used."[42] He does note, however, that its consumption can be dangerous for some. Claiming tobacco is excellent for those with too much moisture in their body, he cautions those with drier constitutions to avoid it altogether. He states that any that "are in all respects resembling the physiognomie and shape of Enuie ... must in any wise banish tobacco farre from them, as a thing most pernicious."[43] This contemporary notion that tobacco could be helpful to people with excessively wet bodies, yet hazardous to their arid counterparts, provides insight into the debate surrounding the health benefits of the plant. As Gardiner demonstrates, not only was the foreignness of the plant causing people to question its legitimacy, but also its dual effects on the human body.

The distrust of foreign tobacco is an idea especially touched on in C.T.'s 1615 *An Advice How to Plant Tobacco in England*. Chief amongst the author's arguments is that the Spanish have been essentially poisoning the English with the tobacco they grow in the Americas and then sell to them. He claims that, "since the Spaniards have observed, that the English respect but two things chiefly in Tobacco, to wit, the colour, and the biting in the nose, they have added poyson to the painting, and annoynted the leaves of their Tobacco with the

5. Vices and Virtues

common sublimate; by which, though it doe not worke at the instant; yet may the one halfe of all Gentlemen of England, and many thousands of others be easily poisoned in one yeare."⁴⁴ If that had not disgusted his readers enough, C.T. offers further details regarding the vile Spanish tobacco. He writes:

> Besides these harmefull mixtures, if our English which delight in Indian Tobacco, had seene how the Spanish slaves make it up, how they dresse their sores, and pockie ulcers, with the same unwasht hands with which they slubber and annoynt the Tobacco, and call it sauce per los perros Luteranos, for Lutheran dogges; they would not so often draw it into their heads and through their noses as they doe: yea many a filthy flavour should they find therein, did not the smell of the hunny master it.⁴⁵

C.T.'s assessment is clearly influenced by the animosity between the English and Spanish, explaining that the ill will between the two is actually contaminating the tobacco those in England are consuming. Using such criticisms of Spanish tobacco as a catalyst for English cultivation of the plant, C.T. demonstrates that tobacco may have gained a poor reputation in contemporary culture because of its connection with the Spanish.

Despite this, he illustrates that tobacco was being frequently consumed, and most especially by contemporary English gentlemen. He reports that he has "heard it reported, by men of good judgment, that there is paid out of England and Ireland, neere the value of two hundred thousand pounds every yeare for Tobacco."⁴⁶ Because of alarming prices and the dangers of Spanish tobacco, C.T. advises his readers to grow the herb domestically, explaining that if done right, English tobacco will be of similar quality to that grown in the New World.

He explains that one of the keys to growing tobacco domestically is the soil. He notes that "the ground must be naturally fertile ... and that which hath not borne any other but grasse; for if you sow your seed in ground enriched with dung, except you stay two yeare at least, til the dung and the vapour be consumed, your Tobacco will retain the savour of it."⁴⁷ He also states that tobacco seeds must be planted between September and April and, once grown to a stalk, should be watered once a day. The greatest care must be taken when harvesting the tobacco, too. C.T. cautions against cutting the leaves too soon, otherwise the tobacco produced may be harmful.⁴⁸

Tastes of the Empire

Weighing in on the healthfulness of tobacco usage, C.T. cites the plethora of people who consume tobacco worldwide as evidence that it cannot be bad for the body. He argues "it is taken in all America, even from Canada to the Straights of Magellan, in all Affrica upon the coast, from Barbary to the Cape of Good Hope, and so till you come to the mouth of the Red Sea; it is also used in most of all the kingdoms of the East Indies."[49] Thus, in C.T.'s estimation, the smoking of tobacco was not strictly an English fad. His overall analysis of the herb and his encouragement of domestic tobacco production demonstrates that he saw tobacco consumption as a fixture of contemporary culture.

Doctor Tobias Venner also notes the popularity of tobacco, taking issue with its usage in *A Briefe and Accurate Treatise, Concerning, the Taking of the Fume Tobacco*, published in 1621. He writes that many contemporary Englishmen are commonly taking tobacco, "through a pipe, for that purpose, into the mouth, and thrust foorth againe at the nostrils, and is of some also sucked into the stomacke and breast" to ward off cold and moist diseases.[50] He notes that the English learned this from Native Americans, yet had taken to consuming tobacco in a much different manner. Venner claims that those in America only used tobacco when their bodies were especially weak or tired to help them sleep; their English counterparts, however, smoked tobacco in excess with little thought to their health.

Acknowledging that tobacco can, on occasion, help with rheumatism, Venner bemuses that "mee thinks I heare many that are not by nature rheumaticke, nor of a colde temperature of body, lovers of this fume, or that I may more rightly speake, abusers, and luxuriating in this kind of evil, for clocking of their vicious custome."[51] Clearly, he finds that tobacco is being used much more than medically necessary, and takes issue with any kind of recreational usage of it. That he is so alarmed by this, though, speaks to how frequently and regularly the English must have been consuming the plant, whether they believed it was aiding in their health or not.

John Lacy's 1669 *Tobacco, A Poem* also highlights the notion that English tobacco consumption had become ubiquitous. Lacy devotes half of his first stanza to Walter Raleigh, the man he credits with teaching the English about tobacco, and the other half to rhymes about the wonders of the herb. He writes:

5. Vices and Virtues

> Hail Thought inspiring Plant! Though Balm of Life!
> Well might thy Worth engage a Nation's Strife;
> Thou sweet Amusement of the Old and Young,
> Say why remain thy healing Powers unsung?
> Exhaustless Fountain of Britannia's Wealth,
> Thou Friend to Wisdom, and thou source of Health;
> At Morn and Night, thy kindly Influ'nce shed,
> And o'er the Mind delightful Quiet Spread.
> Thou mak'st the Passions due Obedience know,
> And regular the swift Ideas flow;
> The mighty Raleigh, first thy Virtue taught,
> And prov'd Himself thy generous Aid to Thought.
> Calm'd by thy Pow'r;–His mind through ages run,
> And shew'd how Men and Manners first begun;
> Defy'd Affliction's most tormenting Weight,
> And viewed serene, the impending Stroke of Fate;
> With Thee shall live for ever Raleigh's name,
> Nor Thou the least of his immortal Fame.[52]

While illustrating how profitable tobacco had become for the Empire, Lacy also makes clear that tobacco was good for the mind and body. Its association with Walter Raleigh only seems to heighten Lacy's opinion of the plant.

In his second stanza, Lacy points out that both men and women were consuming tobacco. He writes, "To either Sex thy generous Power extends, Damon and Celia are alike thy Friends."[53] Arguing that contemporary men and women partook in its usage, Lacy illustrates how universal tobacco consumption had become. Noting that tobacco had a "generous power" to extend, Lacy also references the many benefits that the smoking of tobacco can bring to the consumer.

While some contemporary authors were skeptical of tobacco and its usage, and a few even went as far as to vilify it, tracts and treatise discussing the plant, whether positive or negative, show how entrenched it had become in seventeenth century English life. Whether it was the unhealthiness of the plant or its foreignness that garnered it so much negative attention varied from author to author, yet together they seem to be speaking to a wide audience of tobacco consumers. Although it is impossible to say whether these consumers partook in tobacco for the health benefits it offered or simply because they enjoyed it, it is clear that this New World plant had become a staple of English culture.

Chocolate

The drinking of chocolate was first popularized in Europe after Hernán Cortés successfully introduced cacao beans to Spain in 1528. From there, knowledge of it spread throughout Europe, where demand increased during the seventeenth century.[54] Because of this, the first English publications describing chocolate and its benefits come from Spanish texts that were translated into English. While such texts do not speak directly to English consumption habits, they demonstrate how those in England understood the benefits of the product and why they should wish to consume it.

The first English treatise on chocolate was published in 1640, entitled *A Curious Treatise of the Nature and Quality of Chocolate*. The text was actually a translation of the Spaniard Antonio Colmenero de Ledesma's text by Don Diego de Vadesforte. Colmenero de Ledesma explains to the reader that such a treatise is necessary, as "the number is so great of those, who, in these times, drinke chocolate, that not only in the Indies, where this kinde of drinke hath its orginall; but it is also much used in Spaine, Italy, and Flanders particularly at court. And many doe speake diversly of it, according to the benefit, or hurt, they receive of it."[55] Because of chocolate's popularity and the discrepancy in knowledge surrounding it, Colmenero de Ledesma seeks to inform his readers about the true nature and qualities of the beverage.

He begins by stating that cocoa is humorally cold and dry and explaining the effects it could have on the body because of this. Noting that everything can be over consumed, he advises that a person "must onely take five or six ounces in the morning."[56] He also offers his opinion on a contemporary debate over whether what is left in the cup after drinking chocolate should be consumed. He tells the reader to observe "that there are earthy parts in the cacao, which fall to the bottom of the cup, when you make the drinke, divers are of the opinion, that, that which remains, is the best and more substantiall; and they hurt themselves not a little, by drinking of it. For besides, that it is an earthy substance, thick and stopping, it is of a melancholy nature; and therefore you must avoid the drinking of it."[57]

Colmenero de Ledesma concludes his treatise by noting that

5. Vices and Virtues

"chocolate makes most of [the people] that drinke it, fat."[58] He reasons this is because "the many unctuous parts, which are in cacao, are those, which pinguife, and make fat; and the hotter ingredients of [chocolate], serve for a guide, or vehicall, to passe to the Liver, and the other parts, until they come to the fleshy parts; and therefore finding a like substance, which is hot and moyst, as is the unctuous part, converting itself into the same substance, it doth augment and pinguife."[59] He does follow this opinion with a disclaimer, making clear he is not a physician and perhaps such subjects should be left for them to answer. Despite this, his perception that those who drink chocolate, for whatever reason, gain weight is interesting. Taken together, his treatise highlights that even in the early half of the seventeenth century, the English were learning to consume chocolate from their Spanish counterparts who, as Colmenero de Ledesma states, frequently consumed the beverage.

Colmenero de Ledesma's *A Curious Treatise of the Nature and Quality of Chocolate* was followed twelve years later by another of his texts, *Chocolate: or, An Indian Drinke* translated by Captain James Wadsworth. While most of the text is identical to his previous treatise, the title page of *Chocolate: or, An Indian Drinke* explains that it was "printed by J.G. for Iohn Dawkins, dwelling near the Vine Tavern in Holborne, where this Tract, together with the Chocolate it selfe, may be had at reasonable rates."[60] Clearly, the publisher understands that in extolling the benefits of chocolate through print, customers who bought the text may return to his London establishment to purchase it after reading of its greatness.

The translator of the 1640 *A Curious Treatise of the Nature and Quality of Chocolate*, Don Diego de Vadesforte, contributed to *Chocolate: or, An Indian Drinke*, as well. In a preface "to the Gentry of the English," Vadesforte writes that "the ensuing tract, I many yeares since translated out of the Originall Spanish ... since which time, [chocolate] hath been universally sought for, and thirsted after by people of all degrees (especially those of the Female sex) either for the Pleasure therein Naturally residing, [or] to cure, and divert diseases."[61] Vadesforte's note to his readers proves important for two reasons. In writing specifically to "the English gentry," it would appear he sees them as the class most actively engaging in chocolate consumption. Also, his assertion that females especially desired chocolate demonstrates women were the primary English consumers of this foreign food even as early as the mid seventeenth century.

Vadesforte goes on to include a poem about chocolate, writing it is for "every individual, man, and woman, learn'd, or unlearn'd, honest, or dishonest: in the due praise of divine chocolate."[62] Like Vadesforte's introduction, the verses seek to demonstrate the universal appeal that chocolate has. It reads:

Doctors lay by your Irksome Books, And all ye Petty-Fogging Rookes
Leave Quacking; and Enucleate, The vertues of our chocolate

Let th' Universall Medicine, (Made up of Dead-mens Bones and Skin,)
Be henceforth Illegitimate, And yield to Soveraigne Chocolate

Let Bawdy-Baths be us'd no more, Nor Smoaky-Stoves but by the whore;
Of Babilon: since Happy-Fate, Hath Blessed us with Chocolate

Let old Punctaeus Greaze his shooes, With his Mock-Balsome: and Abuse
No more the World: But Meditate, The Excellence of Chocolate

Let Doctor Trigg (who so excells), No longer Trudge to Westwood-Wells:
For though that water Expurgate, 'Tis but the Dreggs of Chocolate.

Let all the Paracelsian Crew, Who can extract Christian from Jew;
Or out of Monarchy, A State, Break all their Stills for Chocolate.

Tell us no more of Weapon-Salve, But rather Doome us to a Grave:
For Sure our wounds will Ulcerate, Unlesse they're wash'd with Chocolate.

The Thriving Saint, who will not come, Within a Sack-Shop's Bowzing-Roome
(His spirit to Exhilerate), Drinkes Bowles (at home) of Chocolate

His spouse when she (Brimfull of sense), Doth want her due Benevolence,
And Babes of Grace would Propagate, Is always Sipping Chocolate.

The Roaring-Crew of Gallant-Ones, Whose Marrow Rotts within their Bones:
Their Bodyes quickly Regulate, If once but sous'd in Chocolate.

Young Heires that have more Land then, When once they doe but Tast of it, (Wit,
Will rather spend their whole Estate, Then weaned be from Chocolate.

The Nut-Browne-Lasses of the Land, Whom Nature vayl'd in Face and Hand,
Are quickly beauties of High-Rate, By one small Draught of Chocolate.

Besides, it saves the Money lost, Each day in Patches, which did cost
Them deare, untill of Late, They found this Heavenly Chocolate.

Nor need the Women longer grieve, Who spend their Oyle, yet not conceive,
For 'tis a Helpe-Immediate, If such but Lick of Chocolate.

Consumptions too (be well asur'd), Are no lesse soone then foundly cur'd:
(Excepting such as doe Relate, unto the purse) by Chocolate.

Nay more: It's virtue is so much, That if a Lady get a touch,
Her griefe it will extenuate, If she but smell of Chocolate.

5. Vices and Virtues

The Feeble-Man, whom Nature Tyes, To doe his Mistresse's Drudgeries;
O how it will his minde Elate, If shee allow him Chocolate!

Twill make Old women Young and Fresh; Create New Motions of the Flesh,
And cause them long for you know what, If they but taste of Chocolate.

There's ne're a Common Counsell-Man, Whose Life would Reach unto a Span,
Should he not Well-Affect the State, And first and last drinke Chocolate.

Nor e're a Citizen's chast wife, That ever shall prolong her Life,
(Whilst open stands her Posterne-Gate) Unless she drinke of Chocolate.

Nor doth the Levite and Harme, It keppeth his Devotion warme,
And eke the Hayre upon his Pate, so long as he drinkes Chocolate.

Both High and Low, both Rich and Poore, My Lord, my Lady, and his ____
With all the Folkes at Billngsgate, Bow, Bow yours Hammes to Chocolate.[63]

While Vadesforte certainly makes clear that chocolate consumption transcends social class, his poem also highlights the medical benefits associated with drinking chocolate. Not only is its usage by doctors referenced several times, but Vadesforte also contends chocolate is good for washing wounds, stimulating ones spirit and elevating the mood, regulating the body, causing conception, and increasing ones natural beauty.

His rhyme also shows that by the 1650s, the English were already consuming chocolate within their homes. Framing domestic chocolate drinking as an activity for a saint who wishes to stay away from the debauchery of public establishments, the fact that consumption was occurring in the home is important. It highlights that the beverage was being consumed whether or not there were local coffee or chocolate houses that served it, illuminating the idea that it was more than just a public phenomena.

Including verses from Vadesforte's poem, the anonymously published *The Vertues of Chocolate East-India Drink* of 1660 similarly lauds the beverage. The one page document lists that "by this pleasing drinking, health is preserved, sickness diverted, it cures consumption and cough of the lungs; it expells poyson, cleaneth teeth, and sweetneth the breath; provoketh urine; cureth the stone and stranguary, maketh fat and corpulent, faire and aimeable, it cureth the running of the Reins, with sundry other desperate diseases."[64] Despite all this, the author concludes, "it is impossible to innumerate all new and admirable effects then producing every day in such as drink it, therefore I'le leave the judgement of it, to those who daily make a continuall proofe of it."[65] To assist those who wish to consume chocolate on a regular basis, the bottom of the sheet explains to the reader that the drink is "sold by James Hough at M. Sury's neare East gate."[66] Thus, the virtues of chocolate were extolled so that London readers would want to purchase it for themselves, perhaps from James Hough.

While not explicitly advertising chocolate, Philippe Sylvestre Dufour's *The Manner of Making Coffee, Tea, and Chocolate* of 1685 endeavored to explain the benefits of chocolate and promote other American products that should be used with it. Translated by John Chamberlayne, Dufour notes in the Preface that much of the information included in the text about chocolate comes from Colmenero de Ledesma, yet his own opinions about it "will be well accepted by all good men."[67] After explaining that cocoa, by nature, is humorally cold and dry, Dufour discusses the "other ingredients [used in] making your confection of chocolate." He notes that some put black pepper in their chocolate, but, being hot and dry, this combination "does not agree but with those whose Liver is very cold." To support his assertion, he writes an

> ... eminent Doctor of Physick of the University of Mexico is of the same opinion ... that black pepper was not very proper in Chocolate, to prove his opinion, and to make manifest that the pepper of Mexico, called Chile, is far the better, tried this experiment in the Liver of a Sheep, in half of which having put black pepper, and in the other half pepper of Mexico, in four and twenty hours he found that part, wherein the black pepper was, quite dryed up, but the other, that had the Mexico pepper, moist and juicy as if nothing had been put therein.[68]

In encouraging the combination of chocolate and chili pepper, Dufour not only advocates for the consumption of chocolate, but also the inclusion of another New World food product in the recipe as well.

Dufour does the same with vanilla, discussing its consumption with chocolate. He states that in chocolate confections, "every body ... puts therein certain little straws, or as the Spaniards call them Vanillas de Campeche ... [they] seem to have deduced their name from a certain Town call'd Campeche, which is in the Province of Yucatan in New Spain, as likewise a kind of Brasil wood, which they call the Wood of Campeche, which the Dyers employ very much in their trade, and of

5. Vices and Virtues

which there is great abundance brought in to Europe." While noting that this wood "has nothing of affinity with our vanilla which are used in making the chocolate," it is nevertheless interesting that, according to Dufour, this Brazilian wood played an important part in contemporary European dying.[69] His insights also illustrate that vanilla, an American product, was seen as a necessary ingredient when preparing chocolate.

Printed five years after Dufour's text, the anonymously authored sheet *The Virtures of Coffee, Chocolette, and Thee or Tea* devotes half a page to the benefits of chocolate. It states that "it's a great cordial both for Aged people, middle-aged and young, it nourisheth the child in the womb, it's a great corroborator, and it doth not only warm and comfort the coats of the stomach, but it doth nourish and restore nature where it is debilitated and depraved."[70] It also contends that, "for any man that doth travel upon the Road, (as such there are that cannot eat in the morning,) let them but drink a dish or two of this, and they may travel by the strength of it many Miles. All which things are sufficiently known, and can be proved by many who now live in the City of London, to their own experience, for above these thirty years."[71] Although praising the strength that chocolate gives a person, the author reveals that, while it has been popular in London for more than thirty years, those outside of the city may not have been as familiar with it.

The author leaves the reader with information on how to obtain chocolate as well. The page concludes with a note, warning that "the reader may take notice, that there are many who pretend Skill, and do prepare both Coffee and Chocolette, but either for want of Judgment in compounding, buying of bad commodities, or not being at the charge for doing it well, do vend that which is false made up. But if any man hath both occasion for that which is good indeed, and really and truly prepared and compounded, let them repair to Samuel Price in Christ Church Hospital."[72] Guised as information about the virtues and benefits of chocolate, the tract, like others, endeavors to promote the product as it is prepared and sold by one particular vendor.

The handful of treatise praising chocolate and its virtues published from 1640 onward illustrate that English consumption was occurring at a growing rate. This is further supported by the details regarding individual sellers that some of these tracts feature, demonstrating that chocolate was widely available in the domestic marketplace. Thus, not only were the English considering the benefits of chocolate consumption, but physical consumption was occurring at a frequent enough rate for retailers to advertise it.

Coffee

More popular than chocolate, though, was coffee. In the seventeenth century, coffee and coffeehouses were the height of fashion. It is perhaps because of this popularity that coffee was taken to task by a handful of authors, with attacks against it stemming from a distrust of its foreign and unchristian origins.

Because of the rise in coffee houses and coffee consumption in general, several advertisements for the product were published. Two of the earliest advertisements, published in 1652 and 1660, respectively, were virtually identical to each other. Both titled *The Vertue of the Coffee Drink*, and penned by an anonymous author, describe in a single sheet how the Turks drank it, and the health benefits associated with its consumption. They contend that coffee assists with digestion, "quickens the spirit and make the heart light," eases the pain of sore eyes and headaches, and prevents drowsiness and miscarriages in pregnant women."[73]

Despite this, the two tracts differ in two places. Firstly, the vendor they instruct readers to visit is not the same. The 1652 tract states that, "this drink is to be sold at the Raine-Bow in Fleet Street, between the two Temple Gate" whereas the 1660 sheet reads "it is to be sold by James Bough at Mr. Surge a taylor by Queens Cott Corner."[74] Because the latter appears to be an addition to the original text and included at the bottom of the page, it seems likely the anonymous author of the 1660 advertisement simply plagiarized the 1652 tract. The second difference between the two texts is that the 1660 version closes by telling the reader that, "there are many thousands in London who have received much benefit by this drink."[75] Judging by this author's estimation, by the mid seventeenth century thousands of Londoners had consumed coffee, illustrating that it was quickly being incorporated into England's urban culture.

5. Vices and Virtues

With a very similar title to the two advertisements, N.D.'s *The Vertues of Coffee* of 1663 seeks to educate readers about the beverage instead of endeavoring to sell it to them. Addressing the reader as "Gentlemen," N.D. writes that after consuming coffee himself, he wished to know more about it, but could not gain knowledge of its virtues "by discourse with those who sold of it, nor others which drank thereof dayly."[76] He explains that this lack of knowledge is what drove him to write his text. If his assertions are correct, though, and contemporary consumers and vendors of coffee did not know of its virtues, then one is lead to believe they were not drinking the beverage for its health benefit. While the two anonymous advertisements published prior to N.D.'s text suggest that coffee was good for the body, N.D.'s analysis suggests consumers were not aware of or concerned with coffee's medicinal properties. Instead, they consumed the beverage for other reasons, perhaps indulging in its newness, its taste, or the socialization consuming it in a public setting offered.

This latter notion, that drinking coffee with a group of peers was attractive to contemporary society, is one that N.D. actually touches on twice in his tract. He also opines that the communal act of drinking coffee is a blessing, since it replaces the similar consumption of beer, ale, and wine. He explains that in Arabia, Egypt, and "other places of the Turks dominion," coffee is sometimes served instead of wine, claiming it is "generally sold in all their tap houses."[77] He later claims that besides all the health benefits coffee has to offer, "it is found already that this Coffa Drink hath caused a great sobriety amongst the Nations; for whereas formerly Apprentices and Clerks with others used to take their mornings draught in Ale, Beer, or Wine…. They use now to play the goodfellows in this Wakeful and civill Drink. Therefore the worthy gentleman Sr. James Muddiford who introduced the practice hereof first to London deserves much respect of the whole nation."[78] More than any other virtue it possesses, N.D. believed that increasing English sobriety is coffee's greatest quality. Important though is that he still anticipates that consumers will partake in coffee consumption with each other. This lends to the idea that, as far as N.D. was concerned, the English participated in coffee drinking to socialize with each other rather than to achieve any medicinal benefit.

Published seven years later, the anonymous *The Nature, Quality, and Most Excellent Vertues of Coffee* likewise endeavored to teach the public about the benefits of coffee. Although it does not explicitly advertise a certain coffee shop or vendor, the single page document clearly encourages and endorses the consumption of the foreign beverage. Before extolling the many health benefits of coffee, the author first notes that coffee is of a hot and dry temperament. He argues previous reports that it was cold and dry were confusing the coffee berry, which he claims is cold and dry, with the beverage once it had been prepared. He likens this to two local English crops, noting "our barely, which is the coldest of all our grains, yet when it maulted it becometh hot: and chalk, when burned and made into Lime, being exceedingly hot."[79] By comparing the medicinal qualities of this foreign product with popular domestic goods, it is clear the author wants his readers to fully understand the virtues coffee has to offer.

Turning to the various ailments coffee can cure and benefits it can bring to the human body, the track offers a lengthy list of its virtues. It claims that the beverage can expel wind, strengthen the liver and cure it of any disease, heal itches and scabs, refresh the heart, increase appetite, stimulate the brain, take away pains in the spleen, promote urine flow, and wards off rheumatic pain. It also contends that "the steem [from coffee] is good for rheumes in the eyes, and for pains and noise in the ears, and for dullness of hearing; it is good for the falling down of the pallat, and for the squinzie, if from a cold rheume; it is good for difficulty of breathing, the consumption, Ptisick, and all rheumes falling upon the lungs."[80] Attempting to offer advice about when one should consume coffee to achieve one of its many medicinal effects, the author explains that "this drink may best agree with our constitutions onely in the spring, summer, autumn, and winter; and as to the time of day, at any time till within two or three hours of your going to bed, for its operation will not last above two or three hours. You may not fear any hurt by the due and moderate use of it."[81] The diverse ailments the author promises coffee will cure, coupled with his claim that it is appropriate for all seasons and awake hours of the day, proves that the tract is endeavoring to endorse the beverage.

Because of the unending praise the author offers about coffee, he concludes his tract with a verse by Robert Morton explaining how the wonders of coffee cannot be put into words. It reads:

5. *Vices and Virtues*

> To raise our Coffee in a Verse or two,
> Is more then all the peopled World could do;
> Whose rare transcendent Vertues so extend,
> It cannot be within a Poem, penn'd.
> Let this suffice (though many it displeases)
> Our wholesome liquor helpeth most Diseases.[82]

Although not adding any further insight into the beverage, it is interesting that coffee is referred to as "our wholesome liquor." For an English author to refer to coffee as an English drink as early as 1670 demonstrates how quickly and completely it was adopted into contemporary society. While some still published tracts to better educate consumers about the coffee they drank, it is clear that consumption was occurring frequently enough for it to be dubbed English, whether they knew of the virtues of the beverage or not.

The idea that the English public was frequently consuming coffee is further supported by two tracts, both published in the early 1670s, which advise people to stay away from the beverage altogether. The first of these was the anonymously published *A Broad-side Against Coffee; or, the Marriage of the Turk* of 1672. The sheet begins by stating "coffee, a kind of Turkish Renegade, has late a match with Christian water made," with the following verses explaining how the two came together, but that their union would result in a divorce.[83] Continuing to play on this idea that the two beverages had entered into a relationship, the author writes:

> For this indeed the cause is of their stay,
> Newcastle's bowles warmer are than they:
> The melting nymph distills her self to do't,
> Whilst the slave coffee must be beaten to't:
> Incorporate him close as close may be,
> Pause but a while, and he is none of he;
> Which for a truth, and not a story tells,
> No faith is to be kept with Infidels.
> Sure he suspects, and shuns her as a Whore,
> And loves, and kills, like the Venetian Moore;
> Bold Asian Brat! with speed our confines flee;
> Water, though common, is too good for thee.[84]

While humorous, the author's analysis illustrates almost an obsession with the foreignness of coffee. Phrases like "slave," "Infidel, "Venetian Moore," and "Asian Brat" reveal that, unlike the reference to "our coffee" in *The Nature, Quality, and Most Excellent Vertues of Coffee*, coffee was still seen as a foreign beverage with an un–Christian background. Because of this, even water, the most common English drink, was too good for it. While the tract discusses the union between coffee and water, the author conveys the notion that any English person, no matter their class, is too good for this foreign beverage.

From the relationship of water and coffee, the tract turns to mocking physicians and the idea that coffee is good for one's health. The author writes:

> A Coachmen was the first (here) Coffee made,
> And ever since the rest drive on the trade;
> Me no good Engalash! and sure enough,
> He plaid the Quack to Salve his Stygian stuff;
> Ver boon for dr stomach, de cough, de Physick,
> And I believe him, for it looks like Physick.[85]

Again focusing on the foreignness of the beverage and those who introduced it to England, the author ties the sale of coffee and the advertisement of its health benefits together. Although it is the original vendor who is to have "plaid the Quack" in order to enrich his sales, the tract suggests he was only the first of many to do so. Thus, not only should coffee be avoided because of its foreignness, but also the inauthentic health benefits ascribed to it.

Another anonymous tract against coffee was published two years later, this one titled *A Satyr Against Coffee*. Instead of focusing on the foreignness of coffee, the nine-verses of the text attack the beverage for a variety of other reasons. Opening with a warning to "avoid, Satanick Tipple! hence, Thoa murther of Farthings, and of Pence; And midwife to all false intelligence!" coffee is decried for its cost and fallaciousness.[86] The author goes on to label it "a swill that needs must be accurst, And of all sorts of Drink the very worst, By which the Devils Children (Lies) are nurst."[87] Although many of the verses, including this one, lambast coffee for no particular reason, one line in the text offers up an explanation. Describing it as a "sifter of the common sewer," the author writes that coffee "robs the Vintner and undoes the Brewer."[88] This gives credence to the idea that coffee was seen as an alternative to alcoholic beverages, a notion authors of previous tracts and treatise had encouraged in their respective texts. While the author of this satire remains nameless, it seems plausible he profited from the sale and consumption of alcohol and saw coffee as competition.

Interestingly enough, *A Brief Description of the Excellent Vertues of that Sober and Wholesome Drink, Called Coffee*, also published in 1674, takes on the criticisms raised by both *A Broad-side Against Coffee* and *A Satyr Against Coffee*. Instead of attacking the foreignness of coffee, it praises it, explaining, "arts, and all good Fashions first [began]" in Arabia, as the country is "where Earth with choicest rarities is blessed."[89] It also contends that coffee is good for healing the stomach, curing sadness, easing dropsies and gout, aiding digestion, and "maintaining a friendly entercourse" between the heart, liver, and brain.[90] Because of this, the author advises the reader to "do but this rare Arabian cordial use, And though may'st all the Doctors Slops Refuse."[91]

The tract also furthers the idea that coffee is a better beverage choice than its alcoholic counterparts. After claiming that coffee is stronger than wine and "conquers old sherry, and brisk Claret Charm," the author concludes his assessment of coffee with:

> In Breife, all you who Healths Rich Treasures Prize,
> And court not Ruby-Noses or blear'd Eyes,
> But own sobriety to be your Drift,
> And love at once good company and Thirst;
> To Wine no more make wit and coyn a trophy,
> But come each night and frollique here in coffee.[92]

While clearly proposing that coffee is good for one's health and a life of sobriety is preferable, the closing lines illustrate that the author is advertising coffee consumption in an establishment, presumably a coffeehouse. Perhaps those who argued for the abandonment of alcohol for coffee were in fact advocating that consumers who normally visited inns, taverns, or alehouses begin to frequent coffeehouses instead. Seen in this light, tracts that considered coffee and alcohol as alternatives to one another could in fact be functioning as advertisements for the establishments that sold such beverages.

Nearly ten years later, Dufour's *The Manner of Making of Coffee, Tea, and Chocolate* endeavored to further educate the public about coffee rather than engage in a discussion of whether one should drink coffee or alcohol. After describing at some length the coffee bean itself,

Dufour offers interesting insight into how coffee is being consumed in Amsterdam. He states that there, "this drink is sold with great commendation of the publick, for it preserves the radical moistness, strengthens the stomach, cures sore eyes, pains in the head, catharrs, palsie, gout, the dropsie, 'tis good against the scurvy, breaks the stone, and eases women with child."[93] Though Dufour does discuss Arabian consumption habits of coffee as well, he indicates that coffee drinking was not an English specific fad, but instead a trend that swept Europe. From his estimation, it is clear that coffee had become entrenched in European culture by the end of the seventeenth century.

This is echoed in Samuel Price's 1690 *The Virtues of Coffee, Chocolette, and Thee or Tea*, which begins the section on coffee by stating, "the nature, places, and manner of [coffee's] growth, and what it is, I shall not insist upon to acquaint you, as being too tedious, and for that it hath been already by several set forth."[94] While Price goes on to discuss the health benefits of coffee, in his estimation the public was already aware of the plant and its origins. This awareness indicates that, whether the average person was consuming the product or not, coffee had become a familiar product in English society.

Wishing to advertise the benefits of his wares, Price spends nearly half a page discussing how coffee could better one's health. Like other authors before him, he notes it is good against the stone, scurvy, gout, dropsies, and blood corruptions, it expels wind, and it strengthens the heart, liver, and stomach. He mentions in particular that "by the constant drinking thereof it cured a learned Bishop of this Kingdom, who had been left off as incurable by some of the most ablest Physicians of England (by drinking thereof, as he was advised, with sugar-candy)."[95] It is perhaps because coffee had become so common and widely known that Price felt the need to include this story. Without such a testament, his advertisement would have read like all those before him, promising coffee could cure virtually all ailments.

The tracts and treatises attesting to the health benefits of coffee along with those texts published against its consumption illustrate that coffee had become a staple of seventeenth century English culture. Despite its foreignness, coffee was being sold and consumed quite frequently, whether due to an English fondness for its taste or a desire to reap the medicinal benefits many claimed it possessed. No matter the

5. Vices and Virtues

reason, it is clear that coffee had become an important part of contemporary culture.

Tea

Tea was growing in popularity throughout the seventeenth century, although tracts and treatise concerning it did not appear quite as early as they did for chocolate and coffee. In fact, tea was virtually unheard of in Europe before the seventeenth century.[96] Despite its later appearance, though, contemporary tracks and treatise prove the English were eager to learn about tea and incorporate it into their culture.

Thomas Garway's *An Exact Description of the Growth, Quality, and Vertues of the Leaf Tea* of 1660 provides insight into its cultivation, the history of its consumption in England, where to purchase it, and the benefits of drinking it, all on a single page. Noting that most tea comes to the English from China, Garway explains those who live there "gather [tea leafs] every day, and drying them in the shade, or in iron pans or over a gentle fire, till the humidity be exhausted, then put up close in Leaden pots, preserve them for their drink tea ... at meals, and upon all visits and entertainment of private families, and in the palaces of Grandees."[97] Wishing to educate the English public about how tea is gathered, Garway also demonstrates that in Asia tea consumption transcends class boundaries.

Because of this, Garway endeavors to convince his audience that tea no longer needs to be seen as a luxury product in England. He explains that formerly, "in England, [tea] hath been sold in the Leaf for six pounds, and sometimes for ten pounds the weight, and in respect to its former scarceness and dearness, it hath been only used as a Regalia in high treatments and Entertainments, and presents made thereof to Princes and Grandess till the year 1657." According to Garway, it was then that he bought a quantity of tea and began to publicly sell it. He advertises that "to the end of that all persons of eminence and quality, gentlemen and others, who have occasion for tea in leaf may be supplied; these are to give notice, that the said Thomas Garway hath tea to sell from sixteen to fifty shilling the pound."[98] Although advertising his own business, Garway's tract proves that by the mid seventeenth century, tea was readily available to the English, even shedding light on its contemporary price.

The advertisement would not be complete, though, without insight into why the public should want to consume it. Set apart from the rest of the text on the page, Garway writes in italicized font that tea "is moderately hot, proper for Winter or Summer. The drink is declared to be most wholesome, preserving in perfect health untill extreme Old Age." Following this, he lists the virtues of tea, stating it helps with headaches, cures obstructions, strengthens the memory, drives sleepiness away, and improves the health of diverse organs, including the spleen, kidneys, lungs, stomach, and brain. He notes this is especially true when drank with milk and water, as the combination is known to "strengthen the inward parts."[99] While tea's ability to cure such ailments is doubtful, it is interesting that tea was already being consumed with milk, something the English would become known for in future centuries.

Some fifteen years later, J.C.B. authored *Rebellions Antidote: or a Dialogue Between Coffee and Tea*. Though the tract takes an interesting approach to promoting tea, also intriguing is the gendering of both beverages that occurs in the text. Coffee refers to tea as a "dear sister" and "dearer than a wife," choosing in both instances to place tea in feminine roles. Similarly, tea refers to coffee as a "noble sir."[100] Assumedly, tea was referred to as a female because it was thought of as a drink primarily consumed by women.

In the same year, Dufour echoed some of J.C.B.'s sentiments in his *The Manner of Making of Coffee, Tea, and Chocolate*, expressing that tea was better than liquors "which being drunk with excess, either weaken or quite deprive [people] of their understanding, whereas Tea fortifies them." Quite the opposite of alcohol, Dufour states that one of tea's "excellent properties" is that it makes "one that is drunk become sober."[101] Taken together, both *Rebellions Antidotes* and Dufour's text seem to indicate that the notion of replacing alcoholic beverages with tea was one that was popular in contemporary culture.

Besides his discussion of tea and alcohol, Dufour's text focused on how tea was cultivated and consumed in China and Japan. He explains that tea:

5. *Vices and Virtues*

> ... is not to be purchased in any country of the world, but only two Provinces of China, where it grows, one whereof is called Nanquin, whence comes the best Tea, which they call Cha, the other is the Province of Chinchean, in these two Provinces, there is as much care taken in the crop of this lead as there is in our Vintages. It grows here in so great abundance that they have enough thereof to furnish the rest of China, Japan, Tarquin, Cochinchina, and several other Kingdoms, where they so ordinarily make use of Tea, that those who drink it but three times a day, are the most moderate, others take of it ten or twelve times a day, or to say better, every hour.[102]

Not only does Dufour wish to educate his readers about Chinese tea cultivation, but he also endeavors to enlighten them about Asian tea consumption. While not explicitly advertising the product, the implicit suggestion is that Europeans could frequently consume the beverage like their Chinese and Japanese counterparts.

Dufour also briefly mentions how tea was entering the European, domestic marketplace and the prices being paid for it. He states that tea is beginning "to be known in some countrys of Europe, by the means of the Hollanders, who bring it from China, and sell it at Paris for thirty Franks the pound which they buy in this country for eight pence or ten pence, and yet I perceive that it is commonly very old and naughty." Not satisfied with the quality of the product that the Dutch were supplying, Dufour laments that "tis thus that the French and English suffer strangers to enrich themselves in the East-India trade, whence they might draw all the best commodities of the world, if they had but the courage to undertake it as well as their neighbors, who have less means to prosper therein then our Country-men."[103] Shedding light on Europe's initial reliance on the Dutch for tea, Dufour's analysis also highlights the contemporary idea that European countries needed to expand their trade networks and control so that their consumers could enjoy foreign goods.

Five years later in 1690, Price published his tract extolling the virtues of coffee, chocolate, and tea. Like other contemporary authors, Price explained that tea, or thee as he notes the French spelled it, was a "wholesome herb [that would] preserveth in health till very old age, it maketh the body active and lusty, it helpeth headache and heaviness thereof, Lippitude, Distillatious, and difficulty of Breathing, weakness of the Ventricle, pains of the Bowels, Lassitude, it is also good for the stone, and for any sharp Rheums whatsoever."[104] Providing directions to his shop, Price encourages the reader to visit him if they wish to purchase good quality tea. While it is clear Price's only intention was to publicize the virtues of tea to gain costumers, it illustrates contemporary ideas about tea and that it was available to consumers, at least in London.

J. Ovington's 1699 *An Essay Upon the Nature and Qualities of Tea* also indicates that by the end of the seventeenth century, tea had become quite accessible to the average English consumer. In explaining why he felt the need to write an essay on tea, Ovington states that:

> this Western World has been induc'd of late to encourage the Importation of [tea], and make some experiments of its admirable Effects, either out of curiosity, because of its novelty; or out of pleasure of gratifying the palate; or because of some medicinal vertues, with which it is pregnant. And since the drinking of it has of late obtain'd here so universally, as to ... become both a private Regale at Court, and to be made use of in place of publick Entertainment, which has greatly rais'd the character, and gain'd it a singular repute.[105]

His assessment of tea consumption proves interesting in its practicality. While stating that European consumption of the product is increasing its importation, he acknowledges that there are consumers who may be indulging in it simply because of its newness. Instead of attributing tea's popularity to its curative powers, he also reasons that others may simply like the taste of it. He does demonstrate, though, that whatever a person's reason are to drink the beverage, the practice of doing so had become common, done universally both at home and in public.

After spending a good deal of his text describing the different varieties of tea available to those in China, Ovington shifts to focus on the health benefits of tea drinking. He includes a verse, entitled "of Tea, commended by Her Majesty," that reads:

> Venus her Myrtle, Phoebus has his Bays;
> Tea both excels, which she vouchsafes to praise
> The best of Queens, and best of Herbs we owe,
> To that bold Nation, which the way did show
> To the fair Region, where the Sun does rise;
> Whose rich Productions we so justly prize.
> The Muses friend, Tea, does our Fancy aid;
> Repress those vapors which the Head invade;
> And keeps the Palace of the soul serene
> Fit on her birth-day to salute the Queen.[106]

5. Vices and Virtues

The Queen mentioned is never named, but Ovington notes that she herself had praised tea. This, coupled with its ability to maintain the body, is a strong endorsement for the foreign beverage. Although Ovington does not explicitly write his essay to cajole readers into buying a product he sold, his opinions about tea and the benefits of drinking it encourage its consumption.

Because of the health benefits associated with tea drinking, authors of tracts and treatise encouraged contemporary English men and women to partake in its consumption. Whether they were seeking to educate the public about this new beverage or promote their own sales, authors were clearly speaking to a public they understood to be friendly to tea drinking. Although it is impossible to tell if the English were drinking tea to cure their ailments or simply because they liked the taste, the notion that they were frequently consuming the beverage is clear.

Conclusion

Seventeenth century tracts and treatise concerned with chocolate, tea, coffee, and tobacco demonstrate that the English were consuming these products on a regular basis, both in body and in mind. Authors who wished to inform the public about the benefits of these foreign goods highlight contemporary ideas about them and why countless men and women chose to indulge in them. Vendors who advertised their wares by writing about the virtues of these products did this as well, but also prove that chocolate, tea, coffee, and tobacco were readily available for purchase within the London marketplace. Together with texts that spoke against coffee or tobacco, the plethora of information available to the average consumer about these products not only indicates that they were being thought of and considered often, but being consumed physically as well.

Conclusion

"Tell me what you eat: I will tell you what you are."[1]

If people are what they eat, then seventeenth century English men and women were certainly members of an expanding empire. Consuming foods like sugar, cocoa, and potatoes and drinking chocolate, coffee, and tea solidified a reciprocal culinary relationship between England and the lands it was colonizing and trade routes it was establishing. Not only did they include foods from other parts of the world into their daily diets, but contemporary popular culture illustrates they were captivated by these products as well. Thus, they were not only eating the empire, but consistently and repeatedly imagining it as well.

This connection is made especially apparent when examining the diaries of Samuel Pepys. Beginning in January 1660 and ending in May 1669, Pepys meticulously recorded the events of each day, including the foreign products he encountered. His entries over the decade not only illustrate that he was physically consuming foreign foods on a somewhat regular basis, but that he was also afforded the opportunity to imagine and mentally consume them as well. While this definitively illustrates that Pepys was a man reaping the benefits of England's culinary empire, it also points to the notion that others must have been doing the same thing as well. As Robert Latham has noted, Pepys' diaries are particularly useful as they show "both an individual's experience and the multiple experiences of his society.... At [their] best, [they] amount to something approaching a total transcript of experience."[2] If Pepys' testament to culinary life in the 1660s can be applied to other Londoners or even other English men and women, then clearly they were consuming their way to becoming the largest global empire the world would ever see.

Conclusion

Foreign foods are present in Pepys' diary from the very first entry. On January 1, 1660, he notes that he and his wife dinned at home and that she "dressed the remains of a turkey, and in the doing of it she burned her hand."[3] Within that first week of January, Pepys enjoyed turkey three more times in the form of a "turkey-pie" as he dined at the homes of his acquaintances.[4] In the next few weeks, between January 8th and February 6th, he reports consuming turkeys another three times; one of these originally a live gift that his wife killed herself.[5] Interestingly enough, though, Pepys only references eating a turkey one other time that year, on December 23rd, and only five other times over the course of his diaries: on December 26, 1661; December 20 and 31, 1663; December 23, 1664; and January 1 and December 23, 1665.[6] It's entirely possible that turkey had become associated with the winter months, and perhaps even the Christmas season, explaining why so many of these references come in December and why Pepys does not seem to be eating turkey year round.

However, it still seems odd that all reference to the bird stopped after 1665. While it's possible that Pepys stopped eating turkeys after this point, the more logical conclusion is that his consumption of them had become so commonplace that he no longer felt the need to comment on it. As Latham notes, "Pepys' concern with the large events of the world outside himself made it impossible for him to indulge for too long in personal trivia.... His version of the daily round of living obviously excluded much of what was routine."[7] That turkeys had become "routine" to Pepys rings especially true when considering the details he provides in the entries where they are referenced. While he notes that he ate a turkey or a turkey-pie, he does so as an aside to demonstrate what his hosts served him or to denote some action undertaken or injury endured by his wife. From this, it's not hard to conclude that Pepys frequently ate the foreign fowl even more than his diary acknowledges.

The same can be said about Pepys' consumption of sugar. While he surely ingested the sweet substance frequently, as it had become quite common in English society by then, he writes of it less than twenty times in his diaries. Perhaps some of this can be attributed to the fact that Pepys himself did not prepare food for his household, so his interaction with the product as it was incorporated into dishes

Conclusion

would have been limited, although he does mention buying sugar and sugar-loafs a handful of times. Instead, the majority of his references to sugar relate to adding it to some kind of wine or ale. A particularly interesting example of this involves Pepys taking his own supply of sugar with him to a tavern on June 10, 1663. He writes that he and three friends went "to the Half-Moone taverne, I buying some sugar and carrying it with me, which we drank with wine."[8] Although the type of wine paired with the sugar is not mentioned here, on other occasions Pepys notes that he added it to white wine, Rhenish wine, and, in March of 1669, a wine made from orange peels.[9]

Similarly, there are several entries that detail Pepys' consumption of beer or ale with sugar.[10] Perhaps the most interesting of these references is an ale, sugar, and butter concoction that was meant to ease his physical discomfort. On October 12, 1663, Pepys writes:

> ... and yet when I came home and try to shit, the very little straining, which I thought was no straining at all at the present, did by and by bring me some good pain for a good while. Anon, about 8 a-clock, my wife did give me a Clyster which Mr. Holland directed, *viz.*, A pinte of strong ale, four ounces of Sugar, and two ounces of butter. It lay while I lay upon the bed above an hour, if not two. And then, thinking it quite lost, I gave me three or four more excellent stools and carried away wind—put me into excellent ease.[11]

Whether this is how, or even why, Pepys normally consumed sugar with beer or ale is unclear, but it is quite obvious that he believed the mixture relieved him of his discomfort on that day. Although he notes the ingredients in this "clyster," Pepys also includes that his wife was the one who prepared it for him, highlighting the more distant relationship men like Pepys had with these foreign products. Perhaps a diary written by Elizabeth Pepys, preparer of culinary and medicinal recipes in her household, would have better provided an idea of how ubiquitous these foreign goods were in seventeenth century culture.

Like sugar, the foreign spices that had made their way into English kitchens were disproportionately acknowledged in Pepys' diary entries. Pepper, cloves, nutmeg, and mace are mentioned in a handful of places, but mostly as commodities related to the business transactions of the East India Company.[12] One of the few entries that diverge from this pattern once again illustrates that Pepys ingested a foreign product in a medicinal recipe at the instruction of a woman. On March 12, 1660,

Conclusion

he writes "I ... took a thing for my cold by Mrs. Bowyers direction, *viz.* a spoonful of honey and a nutmeg scraped into it and so take it into my mouth, which I found did do me much good."[13] As before, Pepys reports being satisfied with the effectiveness of the remedy, perhaps explaining his need to include it in his entry. He again demonstrates to modern readers, though, that foreign foods had certainly become part of the seventeenth century pharmacopeia and that they fell under the female sphere of knowledge.

Another foreign and medicinal product that Pepys references is tobacco, an herb that had become so popular that he also notes the establishment of tobacco-shops and Tobacconists in the city.[14] Pepys first describes in 1661 how tobacco made a Mr. Chetwind "fat and lusty" where he was once "consumptive," yet it is his illusion that the plant could stave off the plague that proves especially intriguing. He writes that seeing houses marked with "a red cross upon the door," a sign of the plague, "put me into an ill conception of myself and my smell, so that I was forced to buy some roll-tobacco to smell and to chaw—which took away the apprehension."[15] And as Pepys details, tobacco was considered restorative to other animals, too; he explains how tobacco saved a horse that looked like it was going to "drop down dead" when the coachmen "blew some tobacco in his nose; upon which the horse sneezed, and by and by grows well."[16] Certainly the medicinal properties of the plant had to have been widely known by that point, perhaps because of its association with warding off the plague, for few would have thought to use tobacco smoke to cure a horse if it was not common knowledge that it had restorative powers over humans. While Pepys only references the herb a handful of times, and only indicates that he "chawed" it once, his diaries still demonstrate that tobacco had become part of London's 1660s society and medicinal culture.

Pepys demonstrates that chocolate was also thought to have restorative properties, although no claims are made to its ability to bring horses back to life. He does note in 1661, though, that it helped him cope with the effects of a hangover. He writes on April 24th that he "waked in the morning with my head in a sad taking through the last night's drink, which I am very sorry for. So rise and went out with Mr. Creed to drink our morning draught, which he did give me in Chocolate to settle my stomach."[17] All of the chocolate that Pepys writes

Conclusion

of drinking was for his morning draught, although this is the only reference to its use to cure a hangover, and oddly enough the majority of these draughts were consumed in the company of the same Mr. Creed.[18] Mr. Creed, as Kate Loveman contends, was "an advocate of chocolate: more than once he served it to friends in his chamber."[19] This may explain why so many of Pepys' interactions with chocolate feature him; it could also be the case, though, that Mr. Creed had more of a disposable income, as Loveman also notes that "chocolate bought in box or tablet form for preparation at home was a great outlay" in the 1660s.[20]

Despite these morning draughts, though, Pepys only mentions consuming chocolate in the early 1660s, assumedly because, like turkeys, it too became a routine part of daily life. This is further supported by Pepys' references to the coffee-houses he frequented, establishments that sold both coffee and chocolate. In fact, Pepys' last reference to chocolate describes that he went "to a Coffee-House to drink Jocolatte, very good."[21] While home made chocolate was quite costly, it was much cheaper when prepared in an establishment. With this in mind, it seems logical that Pepys continued to indulge in the beverage in a manner that became routine and cost effective.

Although Pepys no longer referenced chocolate after 1664, his diaries demonstrate that he was a frequent patron of coffee-houses, where he could have consumed either chocolate or coffee, throughout the decade. He notes that he visited a coffee-house no fewer than ninety one times over the course of his entries, fifty eight of those visits occurring between 1663–1664.[22] Interestingly, though, Pepys rarely wrote of his own consumption of the beverage. One of these rare occurrences took place on March 30, 1664, where he wrote that he drank some of Lady Carteret's "Coffee; which was purely made with a little sugar in it."[23] From this, it seems logical to conclude that Pepys was at least a casual consumer of the hot beverage, for how else would he have the knowledge to speak to the pureness of the coffee Lady Carteret served? Despite the lack of direct references to his coffee consumption, Pepys' frequent visits to coffee-houses certainly gave him access to the substance. Cheaper than chocolate, coffee could be bought for "a penny a dish" in a coffee-house, increasing the likelyhood that Pepys was at least a moderate coffee consumer.[24]

Conclusion

Even if Pepys took it upon himself to regularly frequent coffee-houses and not consume either chocolate or coffee, his diaries still demonstrate how common such establishments had become and show that he was consuming these products in mind if not in body. While there are certainly some Londoners who would not have had the opportunity to frequent such businesses, perhaps because of socio-economic barriers, Pepys' entries work to illustrate that coffee-houses had become so ubiquitous that they were part of popular culture. Patrons could physically consume coffee or chocolate by visiting coffee-houses, but bystanders could also consume these products mentally through their imagination.

Similarly, the plays that Pepys recounts seeing illustrate that he was intellectually consuming foreign foods on a regular basis. Contemporary plays were steeped in references to foreign goods and Pepys, being a regular playgoer, would have been exposed to such products. Pepys attended so many plays, in fact, that on December 31, 1661, he writes "I have newly taken an oath about abstaining from plays and wine, which I am resolved to keep according to the letter of the oath, which I keepe by me."[25] While Pepys did keep to his oath initially, his avoidance of theatrical performances did not last. From 1660–1669, he attended a total of fifty-two different plays that featured a reference to at least one foreign food (see Appendix); many of these plays he viewed more than once. Even though Pepys never mentioned eating foods like potatoes, tortoises, or plantains, his attendance at plays that discussed these products illustrates that he was consuming them in mind if not in body. His accounts speak to what the culinary climate of 1660s London was like, illustrating that English men and women were in some form consuming food from the empire on a daily basis.

This incorporation of extra-European products into contemporary life was occurring at an unprecedented rate. English controlled lands in the Americas brought entirely new foods to the domestic marketplace. To add to this, familiar foods, such as spices, from the Far East became affordable for the first time due to transoceanic trade routes. As Pepys attests to, a rise in consumption of both new and established foreign foods is evident in various aspects of English culture. Together, cookery books and texts extolling the virtues of these products indicate that they were actually being ingested. On top of this

Conclusion

physical consumption, travel narratives and plays demonstrate foreign foods were also being thought of and imagined.

Despite this, scholars have by and large ignored foreign foods in seventeenth century England. Extensive work has been done by food historians on the emergence of spices in medieval European diets and culture, yet such studies do not stretch into the seventeenth century when spices where losing their luxury status and becoming attainable by more than just the elite. Although they provide a complete picture of the introduction of spices to Europe and how they were consumed by medieval men and women, they alone do not provide a full understanding of the history of English spice consumption, let alone how they were consumed alongside other foreign products.

Similarly, studies that have focused on a particular foreign food, coffee, chocolate, or pineapple, for example, do not speak to how consumption of that product fits with the growing popularity of foreign foods in general. While providing a detailed history of one foreign food and how it was integrated into English culture, the broader English desire for extra European products is left undeveloped. Therefore, they are not able to illustrate the culinary revolution that the plethora of foreign foods in the English imagination and marketplace caused.

Although a few scholars, such as Troy Bickham and Carole Shammas, have noticed the transformative effects that foreign foods had on English culinary culture, they contend that foreign foods were not consumed with any frequency before the eighteenth century. It is certainly true that for many foreign foods, English consumption grew exponentially throughout the eighteenth and nineteenth centuries. Yet such growth does not negate the fact that consumption was already occurring in the seventeenth century. Ignoring the decades before foreign foods became commonplace in English diets only provides a partial picture of English consumption, disregarding the initial introduction of the product or any intellectual consumption that occurred prior to when it was first ingested.

This intellectual consumption, the thinking, contemplating, and imagining of foreign foods, illustrates that seventeenth century men and women understood and were associated with a variety of foreign foods. Such consumption provides insight into what the English learned about a particular product from the people they were importing

Conclusion

it from, how the food was first introduced to them, and what the ideas, beliefs, or opinions that they commonly held about it were. Intellectual consumption demonstrates that the English consumed foreign foods mentally just as often, if not more than, they were actually ingesting them.

Through the commentaries of travel narratives and plays, two genres of popular culture where foreign foods were popularly discussed, one can discern how the English first learned of these products and how and why they should be ingested. For foreign foods like sugar and tobacco that had become common place in contemporary culture, they also offer information about physical consumption habits. But even those foods that were still proving difficult to access domestically, such as the pineapple and other New World fruit, were being talked about and discussed in travel narratives and plays, showing that there was an intellectual consumption occurring even when physical consumption was not possible.

Intellectual consumption also works to support the idea that people were eating foreign foods when they became affordably available in the domestic marketplace. Although seventeenth century cookery books were ripe with foreign foods, declaring physical consumption actually occurred based on recipes alone is, as many scholars have noted, problematic. Such a verdict does not take into account that recipes could have been collected and included in cookery books as much to entertain the reader as to instruct them on how to prepare a meal or remedy. That such foods were also being talked about and discussed, though, supports what contemporary cookery texts indicate; foreign foods were being quickly integrated into English culture, whether physical consumption was occurring or not.

Both published and manuscript cookery books, together with medical texts of the period, indicate that as the seventeenth century progressed, foreign foods were being physically consumed as well. This is not only evident in their integration into the English diet, but also their pharmacopeia. Whether it was sugar or spices being used more often because they had become affordable or entirely new American foods like potatoes, turkeys, or chocolate becomes unimportant, as in both cases the English were engaging with foreign products at a previously unparalleled frequency. The regular inclusion of these foods in domestic culture demonstrates that the English understood the culinary benefits of expanding their control into other parts of the world.

Conclusion

As their diets and medical knowledge expanded, so too did their belief in an English empire.

Even more interesting is the chance these foreign foods offered women to engage with the burgeoning empire while remaining within the domestic sphere. Unlike their male counterparts, females were not afforded the same opportunities to participate in empire building activities. Ensconced within the home and its domestic activities, women were able to exercise control over their family's diets and health regiments. Thus, any physical consumption of foreign foods would have been at the direction of the female head of household. While women were not explicitly building the empire from the confines of their homes, they were implicitly encouraging expansion by reaping the benefits of it.

Texts detailing tobacco, chocolate, coffee, and tea usage also indicate that contemporary English men and women were consuming these four foreign products frequently and quite regularly. Whether authors sought to advertise their own business, convince the public of the virtues of the product, or steer naïve consumers away from the dangers of a foreign plant or drink, it is clear that tobacco, chocolate, coffee, and tea were available in England and being enjoyed quite regularly. Not only do such texts show the popularity of these four products, but they demonstrate how eager the English were to incorporate new goods into their culture and the impact they could make.

This duality in seventeenth century foreign food consumption is important to understanding England's culinary history and the role food played in the expansion of the British Empire. While the incorporation of foreign foods into English diets did continue to grow throughout the eighteenth century, it would be a mistake to diminish their presence in seventeenth century English culture.

Eaten and imagined, foreign foods had an undeniable place in the hearts, minds, and stomachs of contemporary English men and women. The proliferation of these products in seventeenth century culture demonstrates that both English men and women were eager to actively engage with products from outside of Europe. This illustrates that they understood the material goods they could gain if their country expanded and controlled foreign lands. Whether in mind or in body, foreign foods from England's expanding empire were clearly being consumed regularly and, by the end of the seventeenth century, quite frequently.

Appendix
English Plays Featuring Foreign Foods

• Denotes a play seen by Samuel Pepys.

Pumpkins in Seventeenth Century Plays

Playwright	*Play*	*Year*[1]
Otway, Thomas	Venice Preserv'd	1682
D'urfey, Thomas,	A Fool's Preferment	1688
Mountfort, William	The Successfull Straingers	1690
Powell, George	Alphonso	1691
Wilson, John	Belphegor	1691
Mountfort, William	The Life and Death of Doctor Faustus	1697

Potatoes in Seventeenth Century Plays

Playwright	*Play*	*Year*
Marston, John	Iacke Drums Entertainment	1601
Marston, John	Antonio and Mellida, Part I	1602
Dekker, Thomas	The Honest Whore, Part I	1604
Chapman, George	Byrons Conspiracie	1608
Shakespeare, William	Troylus and Cressida	1609
Chapman, George	May-Day	1611
Jonson, Ben	Cynthia's Revels	1616
Shakespeare, William	The Merry Wiues of Windsor •	1623
Massinger, Philip	The Pictvre	1630
Middleton, Thomas	A Chast Mayd in Cheape-Side	1630
Heywood, Thomas	The English Traveller	1633
Massinger, Philip	A New Way to Pay Old Debts	1633
Shirley, James	The Wittie Faire One	1633
Shirley, James	The Gamester	1637

Appendix

Playwright	Play	Year
Heywood, Thomas	The Rape of Lvcrece	1638
Shirley, James	The Royall Master	1638
Chamberlain, Robert	The Swaggering Damsel	1640
Beaumont, Francis	Loves Cure	1647
Fletcher, John	The Island Princesse •	1647
Fletcher, John	The Loyal Subject •	1647
Fletcher, John	The Sea Voyage •	1647
Anonymous	The Ghost	1653
Massinger, Philip	The Guardian	1655
Strode, William	The Floating Island	1655
Massinger, Philip	The City-Madam	1658
Cavendish, Margaret	Love's Adventures, Part I	1662
Duffett, Thomas	The Empress of Morocco	1674
Howard, Edward	The Man of Newmarket	1678
Dryden, John	Troilus and Cressida	1679
Fletcher, John	The Elder Brother •	1679
Mountfort, William	Greenwich-Park	1691
D'urfey, Thomas	The Intrigues at Versailles	1697
D'urfey, Thomas	The Campaigners	1698
Harris, Joseph	Love's a Lottery	1699
D'urfey, Thomas	The Rise and Fall of Massaniello, Part II	1700

Cinnamon in Seventeenth Century Plays

Playwright	Play	Year
Dekker, Thomas	West-Ward Hoe	1607
Middleton, Thomas	A Faire Quarrell	1617
Jonson, Ben	The Magnetick Lady	1640
Randolph, Thomas	Hey for Honesty, Down with Knavery	1651
Cartwright, William	The Ordinary	1651
Goldsmith, Francis	Sophompaneas	1652
Cokain, Aston	The Obstinate Lady	1658
Howard, Robert	The Committee •	1665
D'avenant, William	The Man's the Master •	1669
Dryden, John	An Evening's Love •	1671
D'avenant, William	The Distresses	1673
Dryden, John	Amboyna	1673
Beaumont, Francis	The Knight of the Burning Pestle •	1679
Congreve, William	The Way of the World	1700
D'urfey, Thomas	The Rise and Fall of Massaniello, Part II	1700

English Plays Featuring Foreign Foods

Nutmeg in Seventeenth Century Plays

Playwright	Play	Year
Dekker, Thomas	The Shomakers Holiday	1600
Middleton, Thomas	The Tryumphs of Honor and Industry	1617
Webster, John	The Dutchesse of Malfy •	1623
Anonymous	Wine, Beere, and Ale	1629
Randolph, Thomas	Amyntas	1638
Fletcher, John	The Pilgrim	1647
Brome, Richard	A Joviall Crew •	1652
Middleton, Thomas	The Widdow •	1652
Anonymous	Thomas Lord Cromwell	1664
D'avenant, William	The Tempest	1670
Shadwell, Thomas	The Miser	1672
Shadwell, Thomas	The Tempest	1674
Duffett, Thomas	The Mock-Tempest	1675
Shadwell, Thomas	The Virtuoso	1676
Duffett, Thomas	Psyche Debauch'd	1678
Howard, Edward	The Man of Newmarket	1678
Rawlins, Thomas	Tunbridge Wells	1678
Beaumont, Francis	The Woman-Hater	1679
Shadwell, Thomas	A True Widow	1679
Otway, Thomas	The Atheist	1684
Crown, John	Sir Courtly Nice	1685
D'urfey, Thomas	The Banditti	1686
Mountfort, William	The Successfull Straingers	1690
D'urfey, Thomas	Love for Money	1691
D'urfey, Thomas	The Marriage-Hater Match'd	1692
Higden, Henry	The Wary Widdow	1693
Congreve, William	Love for Love	1695
D'urfey, Thomas	The Campaigners	1698
Congreve, William	The Way of the World	1700
Vanbrugh, John	The Pilgrim	1700

Sugar in Seventeenth Century Plays

Playwright	Play	Year
Dekker, Thomas	The Shomakers Holiday	1600
Marston, John	Iacke Drums Entertainment	1601
Anonymous	Blurt Master-Constable	1602
Dekker, Thomas	Satiro-Mastix	1602
Marston, John	Antonio and Mellida, Part I	1602
Dekker, Thomas	The Honest Whore, Part I	1604
Heywood, Thomas	If You Know Not Me, You Know No Bodie, Part I •	1605

Appendix

Playwright	Play	Year
Anonymous	The Returne from Pernassus	1606
Anonymous	Wily Beguilde	1606
Barnes, Barnabe	The Divils Charter	1607
Dekker, Thomas	West-Ward Hoe	1607
Marston, John	What You Will	1607
Anonymous	Everie Woman in Her Humor	1609
Armin, Robert	The Two Maids of More-Clacke	1609
Chapman, George	May-Day	1611
Dekker, Thomas	If It Be Not Good, the Diuel is in It	1612
Fletcher, John	The Scornful Ladie	1616
Jonson, Ben	Cynthia's Revels	1616
Jonson, Ben	Mercurie Vindicated from the Alchemists	1616
Jonson, Ben	Volpone •	1616
Middleton, Thomas	A Faire Quarrell	1617
Dekker, Thomas	The Virgin Martir	1622
Hawkins, William	Apollo Shroving	1627
Anonymous	Wine, Beere, and Ale	1629
Anonymous	Pathomachia	1630
Middleton, Thomas	A Chast Mayd an Cheape-Side	1630
Chapman, George	Caesar and Pompey	1631
Fletcher, Phineas	Sicelides	1631
Heywood, Thomas	The Fair Maid of the West, Part I	1631
Field, Nathan	The Fatall Dowry	1632
Hausted, Peter	The Rivall Friends	1632
Marmion, Shackerley	Hollands Leaguer	1632
Ford, John	Perkin Warbeck	1634
D'avenant, William	The Wits •	1636
Dekker, Thomas	The Wonder of a Kingdome	1636
Massinger, Philip	The Great Duke of Florence	1636
Nabbes, Thomas	Microcosmus	1637
Heywood, Thomas	The Wise-Woman of Hogsdon	1638
Nabbes, Thomas	Covent Garden	1638
Nabbes, Thomas	Totenham Court	1638
Mayne, Jasper	The Citye Match •	1639
Anonymous	The Knave in Graine, New Vampt	1640
Brome, Richard	The Sparagvs Garden	1640
Chamberlain, Robert	The Swaggering Damsel	1640
Glapthorne, Henry	Wit in a Constable	1640
Jonson, Ben	The Magnetick Lady	1640
Jonson, Ben	The Staple of Newes	1640
L. S.	The Noble Stranger	1640

English Plays Featuring Foreign Foods

Playwright	Play	Year
Rawlins, Thomas	The Rebellion	1640
Richards, Nathaniel	Messallina	1640
Fanshawe, Richard	Il Pastor Fido	1647
Field, Nathan,	The Honest Mans Fortune	1647
Fletcher, John	The Beggars Bush •	1647
Fletcher, John	The Captaine	1647
Fletcher, John	The Chances •	1647
Fletcher, John	The Pilgrim	1647
Fletcher, John	The Maid in the Mill •	1647
Mayne, Jasper	The Amorovs Warre	1648
Randolph, Thomas	Hey for Honesty, Down with Knavery	1651
Anonymous	The Bastard	1652
Brome, Richard	A Joviall Crew • 1652	
Fletcher, John	The Wild-Goose Chase •	1652
Anonymous	The Ghost	1653
Massinger, Philip	A Very Woman	1655
Dekker, Thomas	The Sun's Darling	1656
Cokain, Aston, Sir	Trappolin Suppos'd a Prince	1658
Meriton, Thomas	Love and War	1658
Brome, Richard	The English Moor	1659
Brome, Richard	The New Academy	1659
Cavendish, Margaret	Love's Adventures, Part I	1662
Cavendish, Margaret	Matrimonial Trouble, Part I	1662
Cavendish, Margaret	The Unnatural Tragedie	1662
Cavendish, Margaret	Wits Cabal, Part II	1662
Cowley, Abraham	Cutter of Coleman Street •	1663
Porter, Thomas	The Villain •	1663
Killigrew, Thomas	Thomaso, Part II	1664
Dryden, John	Sr Martin Mar-All •	1668
Cavendish, Margaret	The Presence	1668
Howard, Edward	The Six Days Adventure	1671
Fane, Francis	Love in the Dark	1671
D'avenant, William	News from Plimouth	1673
D'avenant, William	The Play-House to Be Let	1673
D'avenant, William	The Siege	1673
Duffett, Thomas	The Amorous Old-Woman	1674
Anonymous	The Mistaken Husband	1675
Duffett, Thomas	The Mock-Tempest	1675
Cavendish, William	The Humorous Lovers	1677
Cavendish, William	The Triumphant Widow	1677
Duffett, Thomas	Psyche Debauch'd	1678
Beaumont, Francis	The Knight of the Burning Pestle •	1679

Appendix

Playwright	Play	Year
Behn, Aphra	The Feign'd Curtizans	1679
Fletcher, John	Monsieur Thomas • 1679	
Fletcher, John	Rule a Wife, and Have a Wife •	1679
Behn, Aphra	The Rover, Part II	1681
D'urfey, Thomas	Sir Barnaby Whigg	1681
Lacy, John	Hercules Buffoon	1684
Otway, Thomas	The Atheist	1684
D'urfey, Thomas	The Banditti	1686
Behn, Aphra	Emperor of the Moon	1687
Crown, John	The English Frier	1690
Mountfort, William	The Successfull Straingers	1690
D'urfey, Thomas	Love for Money	1691
Mountfort, William	Greenwich-Park	1691
D'urfey, Thomas	The Marriage-Hater Match'd	1692
Higden, Henry	The Wary Widdow	1693
Crown, John	The Married Beau	1694
Dilke, Thomas	The Lover's Luck	1696
Dogget, Thomas	The Country Wake	1696
Motteux, Peter Anthony	Love's a Jest	1696
Motteux, Peter Anthony	The Novelty	1697
D'urfey, Thomas	The Campaigners	1698
Harris, Joseph	Love's a Lottery	1699
Betterton, Thomas	Henry IV, Part I	1700
Congreve, William	The Way of the World	1700
D'urfey, Thomas	The Rise and Fall of Massaniello, Part I	1700
D'urfey, Thomas	The Rise and Fall of Massaniello, Part II	1700

Sugar-Loaf in Seventeenth Century Plays

Playwright	Play	Year
Dekker, Thomas	West-Ward Hoe	1607
Cavendish, Margaret	Matrimonial Trouble, Part I	1662
Duffett, Thomas	The Amorous Old-Woman	1674
Anonymous	The Mistaken Husband	1675
Mountfort, William	The Successfull Straingers	1690
Mountfort, William	Greenwich-Park	1691
Higden, Henry	The Wary Widdow	1693
Congreve, William	The Way of the World	1700

English Plays Featuring Foreign Foods

Cloves in Seventeenth Century Plays

Playwright	Play	Year
Munday, Anthony	The Trivmphes of Re-Vnited Britania	1605
Armin, Robert	The Two Maids of More-Clacke	1609
Barry, Lording	Ram-Alley	1611
Tomkis, Thomas	Albumazar	1615
Jonson, Ben	Poetaster	1616
Jonson, Ben	Volpone •	1616
Holyday, Barten	Technogamia	1618
Anonymous	The Two Merry Milke-Maids	1620
D'avenant, William	The Platonick Lovers	1636
Suckling, John, Sir	Aglaura •	1638
Jonson, Ben	Christmas, His Masque	1640
Cartwright, William	The Siedge	1651
Anonymous	Lady Alimony	1659
Cavendish, Margaret	Matrimonial Trouble, Part I	1662
Cavendish, Margaret	The Presence	1668
D'avenant, William	The Siege	1673
Dryden, John	Amboyna	1673
Duffett, Thomas	The Mock-Tempest	1675
Cavendish, William	The Triumphant Widow	1677
Duffett, Thomas	Psyche Debauch'd	1678
Beaumont, Francis	The Knight of the Burning Pestle •	1679
D'urfey, Thomas	The Royalist	1682
Motteux, Peter y Anthon	Love's a Jest	1696
Dilke, Thomas	The Pretenders	1698

Tobacco in Seventeenth Century Plays

Playwright	Play	Year
Anonymous	The Wisdome of Doctor Dodypoll	1600
Dekker, Thomas	The Shomakers Holiday	1600
Anonymous	Blurt Master-Constable	1602
Dekker, Thomas	Satiro-Mastix	1602
Marston, John	Antonio and Mellida, Part I	1602
Marston, John	Antonio's Revenge, Part II	1602
Chettle, Henry	Patient Grissill	1603
Dekker, Thomas	The Honest Whore, Part I	1604
Marston, John	The Malcontent	1604
Chapman, George	All Fooles	1605
Anonymous	The Returne from Pernassus	1606

Appendix

Playwright	Play	Year
Chapman, George	Monsieur D'olive	1606
Marston, John	The Fawne	1606
Anonymous	The Fayre Mayde of the Exchange	1607
Sharpham, Edward	The Fleire	1607
Dekker, Thomas	The Whore of Babylon	1607
Dekker, Thomas	West-Ward Hoe	1607
Marston, John	What You Will	1607
Middleton, Thomas	The Phoenix	1607
Sharpham, Edward	Cvpid's Whirligig	1607
Tomkis, Thomas	Lingva •	1607
Wilkins, George	The Miseries of Inforst Mariage	1607
Anonymous	The Merry Devill of Edmonton	1608
Day, John	Law-Trickes	1608
Middleton, Thomas	The Familie of Love	1608
Middleton, Thomas	A Mad World, My Masters	1608
Anonymous	Everie Woman in Her Humor	1609
Chapman, George	May-Day	1611
Dekker, Thomas	The Roaring Girle	1611
Dekker, Thomas	If it Be Not Good, the Diuel is in It	1612
Field, Nathan	A Woman is a Weather-Cocke	1612
Marston, John	The Insatiate Countesse	1613
Anonymous	The Maske of Flowers	1614
Cooke, Jo	Greenes Tu Quoque	1614
Tailor, Robert	The Hogge Hath Lost His Pearle	1614
Tomkis, Thomas	Albumazar	1615
Fletcher, John	The Scornful Ladie	1616
Jonson, Ben	Epicoene •	1616
Jonson, Ben	Mercurie Vindicated from the Alchemists	1616
Middleton, Thomas	A Faire Quarrell	1617
Field, Nathan	Amends for Ladies	1618
Holyday, Barten	Technogamia	1618
Anonymous	Two Wise Men and All the Rest Fooles	1619
Middleton, Thomas	A Game at Chess	1625
Hawkins, William	Apollo Shroving	1627
Anonymous	Wine, Beere, and Ale	1629
Ford, John	The Lovers Melancholy	1629
Shirley, James	The Wedding	1629
Dekker, Thomas	The Honest Whore, Part II	1630
Randolph, Thomas	Aristippus	1630
Dekker, Thomas	Match Mee in London	1631

English Plays Featuring Foreign Foods

Playwright	Play	Year
Jonson, Ben	The New Inne	1631
Brome, Richard	The Northern Lasse •	1632
Hausted, Peter	The Rivall Friends	1632
Marmion, Shackerley	Hollands Leaguer	1632
Rowley, William	A Woman Never Vext	1632
Marmion, Shackerley	A Fine Companion	1633
Massinger, Philip	A New Way to Pay Old Debts	1633
Rowley, William	A Match at Mid-Night	1633
Dekker, Thomas	The Noble Sovldier	1634
Heywood, Thomas	A Mayden-Head Well Lost	1634
D'avenant, William	The Triumphs of the Prince D'amour	1635
D'avenant, William	The Platonick Lovers	1636
Dekker, Thomas	The Wonder of a Kingdome	1636
Shirley, James	The Lady of Pleasvre	1637
Kirke, John	The Seven Champions of Christendome	1638
Randolph, Thomas	The Muses Looking Glasse	1638
Davenport, Robert	A New Tricke to Cheat the Divell	1639
Shirley, James	The Ball	1639
Zouch, Richard	The Sophister	1639
Anonymous	The Knave in Graine, New Vampt	1640
Glapthorne, Henry	The Hollander	1640
Jonson, Ben	Bartholmew Fayre •	1640
Jonson, Ben	The Fortunate Isles, and Their Union	1640
Jonson, Ben	The Gypsies Metamorphos'd	1640
Jonson, Ben	The Magnetick Lady	1640
Jonson, Ben	The Masque of Owles	1640
Nabbes, Thomas	The Bride	1640
Shirley, James	The Constant Maid	1640
Day, John	The Parliament of Bees	1641
Marmion, Shackerley	The Antiquary	1641
Beaumont, Francis	Loves Cure	1647
Field, Nathan	The Honest Mans Fortune	1647
Fletcher, John	The Captaine	1647
Fletcher, John	The Loyal Subject •	1647
Fletcher, John	The Pilgrim	1647
Fletcher, John	The Queene of Corinth	1647
Cowley, Abraham	The Guardian •	1650
Cartwright, William	The Ordinary	1651
Manuche, Cosmo	The Just General	1652
Anonymous	The Ghost	1653

Appendix

Playwright	Play	Year
Brome, Richard	The City Wit	1653
Brome, Richard	The Court Begger	1653
Brome, Richard	The Damoiselle	1653
Brome, Richard	Madd Couple Well Matcht	1653
Mead, Robert	The Combat of Love and Friendship	1654
Anonymous	The Gossips Braule	1655
Massinger, Philip	The Guardian	1655
Dekker, Thomas	The Sun's Darling	1656
Goffe, Thomas	The Careles Shepherdess	1656
Anonymous	Lust's Dominion	1657
Jordan, Thomas	The Walks of Islington	1657
Middleton, Thomas	No Wit/Help Like a Womans	1657
Brome, Richard	The Weeding of the Covent-Garden	1658
Cokain, Aston, Sir	Trappolin Suppos'd a Prince	1658
Dekker, Thomas	The Witch o Edmonton	1658
Shirley, James	Honoria and Mammon	1658
Anonymous	Lady Alimony	1659
Anonymous	The Marriage-Broaker	1662
Clark, William	Marciano	1663
Cowley, Abraham	Cutter of Coleman Street •	1663
Porter, Thomas	A Witty Combat	1663
Anonymous	The Puritan	1664
Killigrew, Thomas	The Princesse •	1664
Killigrew, Thomas	Thomaso, Part II	1664
Howard, Robert	The Committee •	1665
Dryden, John	Sr Martin Mar-All •	1668
Cavendish, Margaret	The Bridals	1668
Cavendish, Margaret	The Sociable Companions	1668
Shadwell, Thomas	The Sullen Lovers •	1668
Etherege, George	She Wou'd If She Cou'd	1671
Lacy, John	The Dumb Lady	1672
Ravenscroft, Edward	The Citizen Turn'd Gentleman	1672
D'avenant, William	News from Plimouth	1673
D'avenant, William	The Siege	1673
Dryden, John	Amboyna	1673
Payne, Henry Neville	The Morning Ramble	1673
Ravenscroft, Edward	The Careless Lovers	1673
Duffett, Thomas	The Empress of Morocco	1674
Anonymous	The Mistaken Husband	1675
Etherege, George	The Man of Mode •	1676
Shadwell, Thomas	The Virtuoso	1676
D'urfey, Thomas	Madam Fickle	1677

English Plays Featuring Foreign Foods

Playwright	Play	Year
Leanerd, John	The Country Innocence	1677
Cavendish, Margaret	The Humorous Lovers	1677
Cavendish, Margaret	The Triumphant Widow	1677
Wycherley, William	The Plain-Dealer	1677
D'urfey, Thomas	Trick for Trick	1678
Duffett, Thomas	Psyche Debauch'd	1678
Beaumont, Francis	The Knight of the Burning Pestle	1679
Fletcher, John	Wit Without Money •	1679
Shadwell, Thomas	A True Widow	1679
Behn, Aphra	The Revenge	1680
D'urfey, Thomas	The Virtuous Wife	1680
Behn, Aphra	The Rover, Part II	1681
D'urfey, Thomas	Sir Barnaby Whigg	1681
Otway, Thomas	The Souldiers Fortune	1681
D'urfey, Thomas	The Royalist	1682
Ravenscroft, Edward	The London Cuckolds	1682
Shadwell, Thomas	The Lancashire-Witches	1682
Otway, Thomas	The Atheist	1684
Southerne, Thomas	The Disappointment	1684
Crown, John	Sir Courtly Nice	1685
D'urfey, Thomas	A Common-Wealth of Women	1686
Sedley, Charles	Bellamira	1687
Shadwell, Thomas	Bury-Fair	1689
Wild, Robert	The Benefice	1689
Behn, Aphra	The Widdow Ranter	1690
Dryden, John	Don Sebastian	1690
Mountfort, William	The Successfull Straingers	1690
D'urfey, Thomas	Love for Money	1691
Mountfort, William	Greenwich-Park	1691
Southerne, Thomas	The Wives Excuse	1692
Congreve, William	The Old Batchelour	1693
Higden, Henry	The Wary Widdow	1693
Southerne, Thomas	The Maid's Last Prayer	1693
Southerne, Thomas	The Fatal Marriage	1694
Congreve, William	Love for Love	1695
Anonymous	The Cornish Comedy	1696
Cibber, Colley	Love's Last Shift	1696
Dogget, Thomas	The Country Wake	1696
Manley, Mrs.	The Lost Lover	1696
Motteux, Peter Anthony	Love's a Jest	1696
Dennis, John	A Plot and No Plot	1697
Dilke, Thomas	The City Lady	1697
Vanbrugh, John	Aesop	1697

Appendix

Playwright	Play	Year
Vanbrugh, John	The Provok'd Wife	1697
Vanbrugh, John	The Relapse	1697
Lacy, John	Sauny the Scott	1698
Pix, Mary	The Beau Defeated	1700
Vanbrugh, John	The Pilgrim	1700

Tortoises in Seventeenth Century Plays

Playwright	Play	Year
Dekker, Thomas	Satiro-Mastix	1602
Dekker, Thomas	The Honest Whore, Part I	1604
Marston, John	The Malcontent	1604
Dekker, Thomas	The Whore of Babylon	1607
Mason, John	The Turke	1610
Webster, John	The White Divel •	1612
Jonson, Ben	Catiline His Conspiracy •	1616
Jonson, Ben	Volpone • 1616	
Shakespeare, William	The Tempest • 1623	
Dekker, Thomas	The Honest Whore, Part II	1630
Dekker, Thomas	Match Mee in London	1631
Fletcher, Phineas	Sicelides	1631
Randolph, Thomas	The Jealous Lovers	1632
Shirley, James	The Lady of Pleasvre	1637
Heywood, Thomas	Porta Pietatis	1638
Mayne, Jasper	The Citye Match •	1639
Glapthorne, Henry	The Hollander	1640
D'avenant, William	The Unfortunate Lovers •	1643
Fletcher, John	The Lovers Progress	1647
Anonymous	The Bastard	1652
Shirley, James	The Brothers	1652
D'avenant, William	The Tempest	1670
D'avenant, William	The Siege	1673
Anonymous	The Mistaken Husband	1675
Cavendish, William	The Triumphant Widow	1677
Otway, Thomas	Caius Marius	1680
Sedley, Charles	Bellamira	1687
Dryden, John	Don Sebastian	1690
D'urfey, Thomas	Don Quixote, Part I	1694
D'urfey, Thomas	The Rise and Fall of Massaniello, Part I	1700

Turkeys in Seventeenth Century Plays

Playwright	Play	Year
Chettle, Henry	Patient Grissill	1603
Anonymous	The Returne from Pernassus	1606

English Plays Featuring Foreign Foods

Playwright	Play	Year
Armin, Robert	The Two Maids of More-Clacke	1609
Shakespeare, William	Twelfe Night •	1623
Massinger, Philip	A New Way to Pay Old Debts	1633
Brome, Richard	The Late Lancashire Witches	1634
Nabbes, Thomas	Microcosmus	1637
Jonson, Ben	Bartholmew Fayre •	1640
Jonson, Ben	The Gypsies Metamorphos'd	1640
Jonson, Ben	The Staple of Newes	1640
Fletcher, John	The Beggars Bush •	1647
Mayne, Jasper	The Amorovs Warre	1648
Quarles, Francis	The Virgin Widow	1649
Anonymous	Thorny-Abbey	1662
Lacy, John	The Old Troop •	1672
Dryden, John	The Assignation	1673
Cavendish, William	The Triumphant Widow	1677
Fletcher, John	The Elder Brother •	1679
Fletcher, John	The Bloody Brother •	1679
Dryden, John	The Spanish Fryar	1681
Mountfort, William	Greenwich-Park	1691
D'urfey, Thomas	The Marriage-Hater Match'd	1692
D'urfey, Thomas	The Richmond Heiress	1693
D'urfey, Thomas	Don Quixote, Part II	1694
D'urfey, Thomas	Don Quixote, Part III	1696
Vanbrugh, John	Aesop	1697
Ravenscroft, Edward	The Italian Husband	1698
Burnaby, William	The Reform'd Wife	1700
Pix, Mary	The Beau Defeated	1700
Vanbrugh, John	The Pilgrim	1700

Coffee in Seventeenth Century Plays

Playwright	Play	Year
D'avenant, William	The Siege of Rhodes, Part I •	1663
Porter, Thomas	A Witty Combat	1663
Sedley, Charles	The Mulberry-Garden •	1668
St. Serfe, Thomas	Tarugo's Wiles •	1668
Etherege, George	The Man of Mode •	1676
Behn, Aphra	The Debauchee	1677
Behn, Aphra	Sir Patient Fancy	1678
Behn, Aphra	The Rover, Part II	1681
Behn, Aphra	The City-Heiress	1682
Crown, John	City Politiques	1683
Lacy, John	Hercules Buffoon	1684
Crown, John	Sir Courtly Nice	1685
Behn, Aphra	Emperor of the Moon	1687

Appendix

Playwright	Play	Year
Behn, Aphra	The Luckey Chance	1687
D'urfey, Thomas	Love for Money	1691
Congreve, William	The Old Batchelour	1693
D'urfey, Thomas	The Richmond Heiress	1693
Congreve, William	Love for Love	1695
Anonymous	The Cornish Comedy	1696
Cibber, Colley	Love's Last Shift	1696
Motteux, Peter Anthony	Love's a Jest	1696
Dennis, John	A Plot and No Plot	1697
Vanbrugh, John	Aesop	1697
Dilke, Thomas	The Pretenders	1698
Lacy, John	Sauny the Scott	1698
Farquhar, George	Love and a Bottle	1699
Burnaby, William	The Reform'd Wife	1700
Centlivre, Susanna	The Perjur'd Husband	1700
Congreve, William	The Way of the World	1700
D'urfey, Thomas	The Rise and Fall of Massaniello, Part I	1700

Tea in Seventeenth Century Plays

Playwright	Play	Year
Sedley, Charles	The Mulberry-Garden •	1668
St. Serfe, Thomas	Tarugo's Wiles •	1668
Dryden, John	The Wild Gallant •	1669
Wycherley, William	The Country Wife	1675
D'urfey, Thomas	The Virtuous Wife	1680
D'urfey, Thomas	The Royalist	1682
D'urfey, Thomas	A Common-Wealth of Women	1686
Shadwell, Thomas	The Squire of Alsatia	1688
Shadwell, Thomas	Bury-Fair	1689
D'urfey, Thomas	Love for Money	1691
D'urfey, Thomas	The Marriage-Hater Match'd	1692
Southerne, Thomas	The Wives Excuse	1692
Shadwell, Thomas	The Volunteers	1693
Southerne, Thomas	The Maid's Last Prayer	1693
Congreve, William	The Double Dealer	1694
Dilke, Thomas	The Lover's Luck	1696
Hopkins, Charles	Neglected Virtue	1696
Granville, George	The She-Gallants	1696
Manley, Mrs.	The Lost Lover	1696
Motteux, Peter Anthony	Love's a Jest	1696
Dilke, Thomas	The City Lady	1697

English Plays Featuring Foreign Foods

Playwright	Play	Year
Motteux, Peter Anthony	Europe's Revels for the Peace, and His Majesties Happy Return	1697
Pix, Mary	The Innocent Mistress	1697
Vanbrugh, John	The Provok'd Wife	1697
Dilke, Thomas	The Pretenders	1698
Lacy, John	Sauny the Scott	1698
Burnaby, William	The Reform'd Wife	1700
Congreve, William	The Way of the World	1700
Farquhar, George	The Constant Couple	1700

Chocolate in Seventeenth Century Plays

Playwright	Play	Year
Tuke, Samuel	The Adventures of Five Hours •	1663
St. Serfe, Thomas	Tarugo's Wiles •	1668
Duffett, Thomas	The Empress of Morocco	1674
Ravenscroft, Edward	The London Cuckolds	1682
D'urfey, Thomas	The Banditti	1686
Crown, John	The English Frier	1690
Mountfort, William	The Successfull Straingers	1690
Mountfort, William	Greenwich-Park	1691
Dryden, John	King Arthur	1691
Southerne, Thomas	The Wives Excuse	1692
Southerne, Thomas	The Maid's Last Prayer	1693
Southerne, Thomas	The Fatal Marriage	1694
Congreve, William	Love for Love	1695
Anonymous	The Cornish Comedy	1696
Cibber, Colley	Love's Last Shift	1696
Dilke, Thomas	The Lover's Luck	1696
Granville, George	The She-Gallants	1696
Motteux, Peter Anthony	Love's a Jest	1696
Scott, Thomas	The Mock-Marriage	1696
Southerne, Thomas	Oroonoko	1696
Dennis, John	A Plot and No Plot	1697
Motteux, Peter Anthony	The Novelty	1697
Pix, Mary	The Innocent Mistress	1697
Settle, Elkanah	The World in the Moon	1697
Vanbrugh, John	The Relapse	1697
Dilke, Thomas	The Pretenders	1698
Farquhar, George	Love and a Bottle	1699
Burnaby, William	The Reform'd Wife	1700
Congreve, William	The Way of the World	1700

Appendix

Playwright	Play	Year
D'urfey, Thomas	The Rise and Fall of Massaniello, Part II	1700
Farquhar, George	The Constant Couple	1700
Pix, Mary	The Beau Defeated	1700

Cassia in Seventeenth Century Plays

Playwright	Play	Year
Webster, John	The White Divel •	1612
Webster, John	The Dutchesse of Malfy •	1623
Massinger, Philip	The Bond-Man •	1624
D'avenant, William	The Just Italian	1630
Heywood, Thomas	The English Traveller	1633
D'avenant, William	The Platonick Lovers	1636
Randolph, Thomas	The Muses Looking Glasse	1638
Shirley, James	The Coronation	1640
Shirley, James	St. Patrick for Ireland,	1640
Hemings, William	The Fatal Contract	1653
Middleton, Thomas	More Dissemblers Besides	1657
D'urfey, Thomas	The Siege of Memphis	1676
Cavendish, William	The Humorous Lovers	1677
Gould, Robert	The Rival Sisters	1696

Gingerbread in Seventeenth Century Plays

Playwright	Play	Year
Anonymous	Blurt Master-Constable	1602
Dekker, Thomas	Satiro-Mastix	1602
Anonymous	The History of the Tryall of Cheualry	1605
Chapman, George	Eastward Hoe	1605
Jonson, Ben	The Alchemist •	1616
Jonson, Ben	Poetaster	1616
Jonson, Ben	Volpone •	1616
Markham, Gervase	Herod and Antipater	1622
Ford, John	The Lovers Melancholy	1629
Rowley, William	A Woman Never Vext	1632
Mayne, Jasper	The Citye Match •	1639
Brome, Richard	The Sparagvs Garden	1640
Glapthorne, Henry	Wit in a Constable	1640
Jonson, Ben	Bartholmew Fayre •	1640
Shirley, James	The Hvmorovs Covrtier	1640
D'avenant, William	The Unfortunate Lovers •	1643
Fletcher, John	The Chances •	1647
Fletcher, John	The Faire Maide of the Inne	1647
Fletcher, John	The Custome of the Countrey •	1647

English Plays Featuring Foreign Foods

Playwright	Play	Year
Fletcher, John	The Spanish Curat ◆	1647
Cowley, Abraham	The Guardian ◆	1650
Cartwright, William	The Lady-Errant	1651
Ford, John	The Queen	1653
Hemings, William	The Fatal Contract	1653
Brome, Alexander	The Cunning Lovers	1654
Dekker, Thomas	The Sun's Darling	1656
Porter, Thomas	The Villain ◆	1663
Wilson, John	The Cheats	1664
Shadwell, Thomas	Epsom Wells	1673
Crown, John	The Countrey Wit	1675
Duffett, Thomas	The Mock-Tempest	1675
Etherege, George	The Man of Mode ◆	1676
Duffett, Thomas	Psyche Debauch'd	1678
Fletcher, John	The Elder Brother ◆	1679
Shadwell, Thomas	Bury-Fair	1689
Crown, John	The English Frier	1690
D'urfey, Thomas	The Richmond Heiress	1693
D'urfey, Thomas	The Campaigners	1698
Dilke, Thomas	The Pretenders	1698
Pix, Mary	The Beau Defeated	1700

Plantains in Seventeenth Century Plays

Playwright	Play	Year
Shakespeare, William	The Two Noble Kinsmen	1634
Fanshawe, Richard	Il Pastor Fido	1647
Howard, Robert	The Indian-Queen ◆	1665
D'urfey, Thomas	The Campaigners	1698
Oldmixon, John	Amintas	1698

Chapter Notes

Preface

1. Katharina Vester, *A Taste of Power: Food and American Identities* (Oakland: University of California Press, 2015), 3.
2. Alfred W. Crosby Jr., *The Columbian Exchange: Biological and Cultural Consequences of 1492* (Westport, Connecticut: Praeger, 1973); Alfred W. Crosby Jr., *Ecological Imperialism: The Biological Expansion of Europe, 900–1900* (Cambridge: Cambridge University Press, 1986).
3. Troy Bickham, "Eating the Empire: Intersections of Food, Cookery, and Imperialism in Eighteenth-Century Britain," in *Past and Present* no. 198 (Oxford: Oxford University Press, February 2008), 71–109.
4. Carole Shammas, "The Revolutionary Impact of European Demand for Tropical Goods," in *The Early Modern Atlantic Economy*, ed. John J. McCusker and Kenneth Morgan (Cambridge: Cambridge University Press, 2000), 163–185.
5. Ken Albala, "Cookbooks as Sources for Food History" in *Handbook of Food History*, ed. Jeffrey Pilcher (Oxford: Oxford University Press, 2017).
6. Ken Albala, *The Banquet: Dining in the Great Courts of Late Renaissance Europe* (Urbana: University of Illinois Press, 2007).
7. Susan Dwyer Amussen, *Caribbean Exchanges: Slavery and the Transformation of English Society 1640–1700* (Chapel Hill: University of North Carolina Press, 2007).
8. Ibid., 191.
9. Andrew Wear, *Knowledge and Practice in English Medicine, 1550–1680* (Cambridge: Cambridge University Press, 2000).
10. Ibid.
11. Jennifer Kay Stine, "Opening Closets: The Discovery of Household Medicine in Early Modern England" (PhD diss.: Stanford University, 1996), 216.
12. Ibid., 6–31.

Introduction

1. Anonymous, *The Queens Closet Opened* (1661) Wing M99A, 36–38.
2. Joan Thirsk, *Food in Early Modern England: Phases, Fads, Fashions 1500–1760* (London: Hambledon Continuum, 2007), 1–10.
3. Paul Freedman, *Out of the East: Spices and the Medieval Imagination* (New Haven: Yale University Press, 2008), 3.
4. Erik Gilbert and Jonathan T. Reynolds, *Trading Tastes: Commodity and Cultural Exchange to 1750* (Upper Saddle River: Pearson Prentice Hall, 2006), 12–13.
5. Ken Albala, *The Banquet: Dining in the Great Courts of Late Renaissance Europe* (Urbana: University of Illinois Press, 2007).
6. Turner, 103.
7. William Langland, *Piers Plowman: A New Translation from the B-*

Chapter Notes—Introduction

Text, trans. A.V.C. Schmidt (Oxford: Oxford University Press, 1992.)

8. Freedman, 52.

9. *Ibid.*, 54; Ken Albala, *Eating Right in the Renaissance* (Berkeley: University of California Press, 2002); Andrew Wear, *Knowledge and Practice in English Medicine, 1550–1680* (Cambridge: Cambridge University Press, 2000), 169–178.

10. Wear, 39.

11. Albala, *The Banquet.*

12. *Ibid.*, 56.

13. Gilbert and Reynolds, 39.

14. Anthony Pagden, *Peoples and Empires: A Short History of European Migration, Exploration, and Conquest, from Greece to Present* (New York: The Modern Library, 2001), 85–86.

15. Susan Dwyer Amussen, *Caribbean Exchanges: Slavery and the Transformation of English Society 1640–1700* (Chapel Hill: University of North Carolina Press, 2007), 16.

16. Pagden, 100.

17. Amussen, 25–35.

18. Ken Albala, *Food in Early Modern Europe* (Westport, Connecticut: Greenwood Press, 2003); Turner, 11.

19. Ken Albala, *Food in Early Modern Europe*, 20

20. Amussen, 40.

21. Sidney W. Mintz, *Sweetness and Power: The Place of Sugar in the Modern World* (New York: Penguin Books, 1985); Paul Freedman, *Out of the East*, 11.

22. G.R. Elton, *England Under the Tudors* (London: Routledge, 1955), 330–356; Daniel Goffman, *The Ottoman Empire and Early Modern Europe* (Cambridge: Cambridge University Press, 2002), 193–196.

23. Albala, *Food in Early Modern Europe*; E. Ashtor, "Profits from Trade with the Levant in the Fifteenth Century," in *Bulletin of the School on Oriental and African Studies, University of London*, vol. 38, no. 2 (Cambridge: Cambridge University Press, 1975), 250–275.

24. John E. Willis Jr., "European Consumption and Asian Production in the 17th and 18th centuries," in *Consumption and the World of* Goods, John Brewer and Roy Porter, eds. (London: Routledge, 1993); Brian Cowan, *The Social Life of Coffee: The Emergence of the British Coffeehouse* (New Haven: Yale University Press, 2005), 1–10.

25. Arnold A. Sherman, "Pressures from Leadenhall: The East India Company Lobby, 1660–1678" in *The Business History Review* vol. 50, no. 3 (Cambridge: The President and Fellows of Harvard College, 1976), 332.

26. Elton, *England Under the Tudors*; Roland Oliver and Anthony Atmore, *The African Middle Ages, 1400–1800* (Cambridge: Cambridge University Press, 1981), 88–91.

27. Ernst Van Den Boogaart, "The Trade between Western Africa and the Atlantic World, 1600–90: Estimates of Trends in Composition and Value," in *The Journal of African History*, vol. 33, no. 3 (Cambridge: Cambridge University Press, 1992), 369–385.

28. Amussen; Sherman.

29. Adam Jones, ed. *West Africa in the Mid-Seventeenth Century: An Anonymous Dutch Manuscript* (New Brunswick, NJ: African Studies Association Press, 1995), 182–195.

30. Joyce Appleby, "Consumption in Early Modern Social Thought," in *Consumption and the World of Goods*, ed. John Brewer and Ray Porter (Routledge: London and New York, 1993), 162.

31. Sidney W. Mintz, "The Changing Roles of Food in the Study of Consumption," in *Consumption and the World of Goods*, ed. John Brewer and Ray Porter (Routledge: London and New York, 1993), 262.

32. William Dampier, *A New Voyage Round the World* (1697) Wing D162.

33. Francis Beaumont, *The Knight of the Burning Pestle* (1679) Act I, Scene I.

34. Ken Albala, "Cookbooks as Sources for Food History" in *The Oxford Handbook of Food History*, ed. Jeffrey Pilcher (Oxford University Press, 2017.)

Chapter 1

1. Joel H. Baer, 'Dampier, William (1651–1715),' *Oxford Dictionary of National Biography* (hereafter *ODNB*) (Oxford: Oxford University Press, 2004); Anonymous, *Prince Giolo Son to the King of Moangis or Gilol* (1692) Wing P3484.
2. Anonymous, *Prince Giolo*.
3. Anita McConnell, 'Exotic visitors (act. c. 1500-c. 1855),' *ODNB* (Oxford: Oxford University Press, 2004).
4. Baer, "Dampier, William (1651–1715)," *ODNB*.
5. William Dampier, *A New Voyage Round the World* (1697) Wing D162, A3.
6. *Ibid.*; Baer, "Dampier, William (1651–1715)," *ODNB*.
7. Susan Dwyer Amussen, *Caribbean Exchanges: Slavery and the Transformation of English Society 1640–1700* (Chapel Hill: University of North Carolina Press, 2007), 20.
8. John Smith, *A Map of Virginia* (Oxford: 1612) STC 22791.
9. *Ibid.*, 2.
10. *Ibid.*, 12.
11. *Ibid.*, 13.
12. John Smith, *The True Travels, Adventvres, and Observations of Captaine Iohn Smith* (1630) STC 22796.
13. *Ibid.*, 51.
14. *Ibid.*, 51–52.
15. *Ibid.*, 54.
16. *Ibid.*
17. Alan Davidson, *The Oxford Companion to Food*, Tom Jaines, ed. (Oxford: Oxford University Press, 2006), 23.
18. John Josselyn, *New Englands Rarities Discovered* (1675) Wing J1094, 8–9.
19. Gordon Goodwin, "John Josselyn (c. 1608–1700)," *ODNB* (Oxford: Oxford University Press, 2004.)
20. Josselyn, *New Englands Rarities Discovered*.
21. *Ibid.*, 57.
22. *Ibid.*, 65.
23. Smith, *The True Travels, Adventvres, and Observations of Captaine Iohn Smith*, 51–52; Christopher Levett, *A Voyage Into New England* (1624) STC 15553.5, 28; Sir William Alexander, *The Mapp and Description of New England* (1630) STC 342, 29 & 37; Anonymous, *A Perfect Description of Virginia*, 3; and Clarke, *A True and Faithful Account*, 5.
24. Josselyn, *New Englands Rarities Discovered*, 54.
25. John Brereton, *A Briefe and True Relation of the Discoverie of the North Part of Virginia* (1602) STC 3611, 6.
26. Jason McElligott, "Crouch, Nathaniel [Robert Burton] (c. 1640–1725?)," *ODNB* (Oxford: Oxford University Press, 2004).
27. Nathaniel Crouch, *The English Empire in America* (1685) Wing B5358, 53.
28. *Ibid.*, 90.
29. *Ibid.*, 114.
30. *Ibid.*, 100.
31. Pietro Martire d'Anghiera, *The Decades of the Newe Worlde or West India* (1555), STC 645; Pietro Martire d'Anghiera, *The History of Trauayle in the VVest and East Indies* (1577), STC 649; Pietro Martire d'Anghiera, *De nouo orbe, or the Historie of the West Indies* (1612), STC 650; Pietro Martire d'Anghiera, *The Historie of the VVest Indies* (1625), STC 651; and Pietro Martire d'Anghiera, *The Famous Historie of the Indies* (1628), STC 652.
32. d'Anghiera, *De nuou orbe*, 11.
33. *Ibid.*, 88.
34. Dampier, *A New Voyage Round the World*, 37.
35. Sir Francis Drake, *Sir Francis Drake Revived* (1652) Wing D84, 86.
36. Charles-Cesar Rochefort, *The History of the Caribby-Islands* (1666) Wing R1740, 134–135.
37. Richard Blome, *The Present State of His Majesties Isles and Territories in America* (1687) Wing B3215, 14.
38. Richard Ligon, *A True & Exact History of the Island of Barbados* (1657) Wing L2075, 31.

Chapter Notes—1

39. William Hughes, *The American Physitian* (1672) Wing H3332, 14.
40. John Poyntz, *The Present Prospect of the Famous and Fertile Island of Tobago* (1695) Wing P3131, 11–12.
41. Amy Stewart, *The Drunken Botanist: The Plants That Create the World's Great Drinks* (Chapel Hill: Algonquin Books of Chapel Hill, 2013), 73.
42. Dampier, *A New Voyage Round the World*, 9, 12, 14, 18, 19, and 75.
43. *Ibid.*, 16.
44. *Ibid.*, 203
45. *Ibid.*, 222.
46. *Ibid.*, 202.
47. Sir Francis Drake, *The World Encompassed* (1628) STC 7161.3, 8.
48. Ligon, *A True & Exact History of the Island of Barbados*, 81.
49. *Ibid.*, 82.
50. Poyntz, *The Present Prospect of the Famous and Fertile Island of Tobago*, 9.
51. George Gardyner, *A Description of the New World* (1651) Wing G221, 59–60.
52. Ligon, *A True & Exact History of the Island of Barbados*, 82.
53. Poyntz, *The Present Prospect of the Famous and Fertile Island of Tobago*, 8.
54. Thomas Gage, *The English-American His Travail by Sea and Land* (1648) Wing G109; Drake, *Sir Francis Drake Revived*; Samuel Clarke, *The Life and Death of the Valiant and Renowned Sir Francis Drake* (1671) Wing C4533; Blome, *The Present State of His Majesties Isles and Territories in America*; Thomas Dalby, *An Historical Account of the Rise and Growth of the West-India Collonies* (1690) Wing T961; West-India Merchant, *A Brief Account of the Present Declining State of the West-Indies in Reference to its Trade, and in Particular, That of Barbadoes* (1695) Wing B4514; and Merchant, *A State of the Present Condition of the Island of Barbadoes* (1698) Wing S5323A.
55. Karen Ordahl Kupperman, "Ligon, Richard (c. 1588–1662)," *ODNB* (Oxford: Oxford University Press, 2004).
56. Ligon, *A True & Exact History of the Island of Barbados*, 85.
57. *Ibid.*, 96.
58. *Ibid.*, 86.
59. *Ibid.*, 92.
60. *Ibid.*, 93.
61. *Ibid.*, 92.
62. Jose de Acosta, *The Natvrall and Morall Historie of the East and West Indies* (1604) STC 94; Sir Francis Drake, *The VVorld Encompassed* (1628) STC 7161.3; Richard Blome, *A Description of the Island of Jamaica* (1672) Wing B3208B; Philip Ayers, *The Voyages and Adventures of Capt. Barth. Sharp* (1684) Wing A4315, Alexandre Olivier, *Bucaniers of America* (1684) Wing E3894; Blome, *The Present State of His Majesties Isles and Territories in America*; and Dalby.
63. Gage, *The English-American His Travail by Sea and Land* 106.
64. *Ibid.*, 108.
65. *Ibid.*, 109.
66. *Ibid*.
67. Hughes, *The American Physitian*, 112.
68. *Ibid.*, 109.
69. *Ibid.*, 111.
70. *Ibid.*, 115.
71. *Ibid.*, 134.
72. *Ibid.*, 119.
73. *Ibid.*, 134.
74. *Ibid.*, 51–52.
75. W. Glanius, *A New Account of East-India and Persia* (1682) Wing G793, 77–78.
76. Dampier, *A New Voyage Round the World*, 391.
77. *Ibid.*, 409.
78. Nathaniel Crouch, *A View of the English Acquisitions in Guinea and the East-Indies* (1686) Wing C7356, 130.
79. Dampier, *A New Voyage Round the World*, 316–317.
80. *Ibid.*, 392 and 513.
81. Anonymous, *An Historicall and True Discourse of a Voyage Made by the Admirall Cornelis Matelife the Yonger into the East Indies* (1608) STC 17651, 18;

Henri de Feyens, *An Exact and Cvriovs Svrey of All the East Indies* (1615) STC 10840, 20; and William Bruton, *Newes from the East-Indies* (1638) STC 3946, 5.

82. Richard Boothby, *A Breife Discovery or Description of the Most Famous Island of Madagascar or St. Laurence in Asia* (1646) Wing B3743, 33.

83. Edward Terry, *A Voyage to East-India* (1655) Wing T782, 206–211; Josiah Child, *A Treatise* (1681) Wing C3866, 7; and Josiah Child, *A Discourse Concerning Trade* (1689) Wing D1590, 3.

84. George White, *An Account of the Trade to the East Indies Together with the State of the Present* (1691) Wing W1768, 3.

85. Anonymous, *The East-India Trade* (1693) Wing E101A, 7–8.

86. *Ibid.*

87. *Ibid.*, 14–15.

88. Abraham Du Quesne, *A New Voyage to the East-Indies* (1696) Wing D2669, 65; Gabriel Dellon, *A Voyage to the East-Indies* (1698) Wing D943A, 39, 66–67; and John Fryer, *A New Account of East-India and Persia* (1698) F2257, 51, 163, 179.

89. Fryer, *A New Account of East-India and Persia*, 163.

90. Pietro Della Valle, *The Travels of Sig. Pietro della Valle, a Noble Roman* (1665) Wing V47, 106.

91. John Ogilby, *Asia* (1673) Wing O166, 54.

92. Jean-Baptiste Tavernier, *Collections of Travel Through Turky into Persia* (1684) Wing T251, 241–242 and Sir John Chardin, *The Travels of Sir John Chardin into Persia and the East-Indies the First Volume* (1686) Wing C2043, 23.

93. Ogilby, *Asia*, 54.

94. Baer, "Dampier, William (1651–1715)," *ODNB*.

Chapter 2

1. William Shakespeare, *The Merry Wives of Windsor* (1623) Act 5, Scene 5; According to Alan Davidson's *The Oxford Companion to Food*, ed. Tom Jaine (Oxford: Oxford University Press, 2006), a comfit is a sugar coated nut or seed often used to sweeten one's breath and an eringo is the root of sea holly, which in seventeenth and eighteenth century England was frequently pickled or candied and was considered an aphrodisiac.

2. Davidson, *The Oxford Companion to Food*, 627.

3. George Chapman, *Byron's Conspiracie* (1608) Act 3, Scene 1.

4. James Shirley, *The Gamester* (1637) Act 3, Scene 1.

5. Thomas D'Urfey, *The Campaigners* (1698) Act 1, Scene 1.

6. Katherine Eisaman Maus and David Bevington, "Genral Introduction," in David Bevington et al., *English Renaissance Drama: A Norton Anthology* (New York: W.W. Norton & Company, Inc., 2002), xxxii.

7. See Appendix for a full list of English plays that reference foreign foods.

8. Maus and Bevington, "Genral Introduction," xiii.

9. *Ibid.*, xiv.

10. Andrew Gurr, *Playgoing in Shakespeare's London*, 3rd ed (Cambridge: Cambridge University Press, 2004), 4.

11. *Ibid.*, 21–22.

12. *Ibid.*, 26.

13. *Ibid.*, 32.

14. *Ibid.*, 90.

15. Maus and Bevington, "Genral Introduction," lv.

16. John Brewer, *The Pleasures of the Imagination: English Culture in the Eighteenth Century* (New York: Farrar, Straus, and Giroux, 1997), 351.

17. Gurr, *Playgoing in Shakespeare's London*, 58.

18. *Ibid.*

19. *Ibid.*, 58 and 71.

20. *Ibid.*, 67.

21. Brewer, *The Pleasures of the Imagination*, 348.

22. *Ibid.*, 350.

23. *Ibid.*, 333.

Chapter Notes—2

24. Gurr, *Playgoing in Shakespeare's London*, 11.
25. Brewer, *The Pleasures of the Imagination*, 357.
26. D'Urfey, *A Fool's Preferment* (1688) Act 1, Scene 1.
27. William Mountfort, *The Life and Death of Doctor Faustus* (1697) Act 1, Scene 1; John Wilson, *Belphegor: or The Marriage of the Devil* (1691) Act 5, Scene 1.
28. Mark McWilliams, "The American Pumpkin" in *Vegetables: Proceedings of the Oxford Symposium on Food and Cookery 2008*, ed. Susan R. Friedland (Blackawton: Prospect Books, 2009), 132.
29. John Dryden, *Troilus and Cressida* (1679) Act 4, Scene 2.
30. Mountfort, *Greenwich-Park* (1691) Act 3, Scene 3.
31. Joseph Harris, *Love's a Lottery, and a Woman the Prize* (1699) Act 2, Scene 2.
32. Davidson contends that while potatoes were introduced to all of the British Isles in the sixteenth century, the Irish tended to grow them more than the English. He notes that it was a common Irish Catholic practice to sprinkle potato seeds with Holy Water before planting them.
33. Sir Robery Howard, *The Committee: A Comedy* (1665) Act 3, Scene 1.
34. Sir William D'Avenant, *The Distresses* (1673) Act 2, Scene 1.
35. Thomas Middleton, *The Widow: A Comedie* (1652) Act 2, Scene 1.
36. Middleton, *Anything for a Quiet Life: A Comedy* (1662), Act II.
37. Edward Howard, *The Man of Newmarket* (1678) Act 4, Scene 1.
38. Davidson, *The Oxford Companion to Food*, 546.
39. John Webster, *The Tragedy of the Dutchesse of Malfy* (1623) Act 2, Scene 1.
40. Henry Higden, *The Wary Widdow: Or, Sir Noisy Parrat* (1693) Act 3, Scene 1.
41. Davidson, *The Oxford Companion to Food*, 767.
42. Mountfort, *The Successful Straingers* (1690) Act 3, Scene 1; William Congreve, *The Way of the World* (1700) Act 4, Scene 1.
43. Sir John Suckling, *Aglaura* (1638) Act 1, Scene 1.
44. Thomas Dekker, *North-Ward Hoe* (1607) Act 1, Scene 1; Peter Anthony Motteux, *Love's a Jest* (1696) Act 4, Scene 1.
45. William Cartwright, *The Siedge* (1651) Act 2, Scene 5.
46. D'Urfey, *The Royalist* (1682) Act 4, Scene 1.
47. Sir George Etherege, *The Man of Mode* (1676) Act 3, Scene 3.
48. Mrs. Manley, *The Lost Lover* (1696) Act 3, Scene 2.
49. D'Urfey, *Trick for Trick* (1678) Act 1, Scene 1.
50. Congreve, *The Old Batchelour* (1693) Act 4, Scene 1.
51. Ben Johnson, *Catiline His Conspiracy* (1616) Act 1, Scene 1.
52. Henry Glapthorne, *The Hollander* (1640) Act 3, Scene 1; John Dryden, *Don Sebastian* (1690) Act 3, Scene 1.
53. Thomas Randolph, *The Jealous Lovers* (1632) Act 3, Scene 7.
54. D'Urfey, *The Comical History of Don Quixote, Part I* (1694) Act 1, Scene 2.
55. Shakespeare, *Twelfth Night* (1623) Act 2, Scene 5; William Shakespeare and John Fletcher, *The Two Noble Kinsmen* (1634) Act 2, Scene 3.
56. Dryden, *The Assignation* (1673) Act 3, Scene 1.
57. Davidson, *The Oxford Companion to Food*, 813.
58. Peter Anthony Motteux, *Love's a Jest* (1696) Act 1, Scene 3.
59. For more about contemporary consumption habits of chocolate, coffee, and tea, see Chapter 5.
60. Brian Cowan, *The Social Life of Coffee: The Emergence of the British Coffeehouse* (New Haven: Yale University Press, 2005).

Chapter Notes—2

61. Aphra Behn, *The City-Heiress* (1682) Act 1, Scene 1.
62. John Crown, *City Politiques* (1683) Act 2, Scene 2.
63. Thomas Porter, *A Witty Combat* (1663) Act 1, Scene 1; William Congreve, *Love for Love* (1695) Act 1, Scene 1.
64. D'Urfey, *The Richmond Heiress* (1693) Act 4, Scene 1.
65. D'Urfey, *The Famous History of the Rise and Fall of Massaniello, Part I* (1700) Act 5, Scene 1.
66. Sir Charles Sedley, *The Mulberry-Garden* (1700) Act 2, Scene 2.
67. Mrs. Manley (Mary de la Rivière) *The Lost Lover* (1696) Prologue.
68. Colley Cibber, *Love Makes a Man* (1700) Act 4, Scene 1.
69. Congreve, *The Double-Dealer* (1694) Act 1, Scene 1.
70. Thomas Southerne, *The Wives Excuse* (1692) Act 4, Scene 1; Thomas Shadwell, *Bury-Fair* (1689) Act 3, Scene 1.
71. Sedley, *The Mulberry-Garden* (1668) Act 4, Scene 1.
72. Thomas Dilke, *The Lover's Luck* (1698) Act 3, Scene 1.
73. D'Urfey, *A Common-Wealth of Women* (1686) Act 1, Scene 1.
74. Dilke, *The Pretenders* (1698) Act 1, Scene 1.
75. Congreve, *The Way of the World* (1700) Act 1, Scene 1.
76. Elkanah Settle, *The World in the Moon* (1697) Act 5, Scene 1.
77. Mountfort, Greenwich-Park (1691) Act 1, Scene 1.
78. Samuel Tuke, *The Adventures of Five Hours* (1663) Act 1, Scene 1; Sir Thomas St. Serfe, *Tarugo's Wiles* (1668) Act 3, Scene 1; John Crown, *The English Frier* (1690) Act 3 Scene 1; William Mountfort, *The Successfull Straingers* (1690) Act 1, Scene 1; Thomas Scott, *The Mock-Marriage* (1696) Act 1, Scene 1; William Burnaby, *The Reformed Wife* (1700) Act 3, Scene 1.
79. Davidson, *The Oxford Companion to Food*, 145–146.
80. Webster, *The Tragedy of the Dutchesse of Malfy* (1623) Act 3, Scene 5.
81. Ibid. Act 4, Scene 2.
82. Thomas Randolph, *The Mvses Looking-Glasse* (1638) Act 3, Scene 1.
83. Cowan, *The Social Life of Coffee*, 34.
84. Margaret Cavendish, Duchess of Newcastle, *Matrimonial Trouble, part 1* (1662) Act 4, Scene 32
85. Thomas D'Urfey, *The Banditti* (1686) Act 5, Scene 2; Thomas D'Urfey, *Love for Money* (1691) Act 2, Scene 2; Thomas D'Urfey, *The Marriage-hater Match'd* (1692) Act 2, Scene 1.
86. Thomas Dekker, *West-ward Hoe* (1607) Act 2, Scene 2.
87. Ibid. Act 4, Scene 2.
88. Ben Jonson, *The Magnetick Lady* (1640) Act 3, Scene 2.
89. Davidson, *The Oxford Companion to Food*, 339–340.
90. Richard Brome, *The Sparagvs Garden* (1652) Act 4, Scene 4.
91. D'Urfey, *The Campaigners* (1698) Act 5, Scene 3.
92. Ben Johnson, *Volpone, or The Foxe* (1616) Act 2, Scene 2.
93. Barten Holyday, *Technogamia* (1618) Act 2, Scene 3.
94. Anonymous, *The Gossips Braule* (1655) Main Text.
95. For more about the debate surrounding tobacco consumption, see Chapter 5.
96. Walter Mountfort, *The Launching of the Mary* (1632) Act 1, Scene 1.
97. For more information about plantains, see Chapter 4.
98. Shakespeare and Fletcher, *The Two Noble Kinsmen* (1634) Act 1, Scene 2.
99. Sir Richard Fanshawe's, *The Faithfull Shepherd* (1647) Act 5, Scene 7. Translated from the original: Battista Guarini, *Il Pastor Fido*.
100. Edward Ravenscroft, *The London Cuckolds* (1682) Act 1, Scene 1.
101. Dilke, *The Lover's Luck* (1696) Act 5, Scene 1.

102. D'Urfey, *The Famous History and Fall of Massaniello, Part II* (1700) Act 1, Scene 2.

Chapter 3

1. Anonymous, *The Court & Kitchin of Elizabeth, commonly called Joan Cromwel* (1664) Wing C6584D, 37–38.
2. John Morrill, "Cromwell, Oliver (1599–1658)," *ODNB* (Oxford University Press, 2004).
3. Anonymous, *The Court & Kitchin of Elizabeth, commonly called Joan Cromwel* (1664) Wing C6584D, 37–38.
4. Robert Appelbaum, *Aguecheek's Beef, Belch's Hiccup, and Other Gastronomic Interjections: Literature, Culture, and Food Among the Early Moderns* (Chicago: The University of Chicago Press, 2006), 85.
5. Sara Pennell, *The Birth of the English Kitchen 1600–1850* (London: Bloomsbury Academic, 2016), 18.
6. The only exception to this was in the elitist of households, where professional male chefs controlled the cuisine.
7. Jennifer K. Stine "Opening Closests: The Discovery of Household Medicine in Early Modern England" (PhD diss.: Stanford University, 1996), 21–22.
8. Ken Albala, "Cookbooks as Sources for Food History" in *The Oxford Handbook of Food History*, ed. Jeffrey Pilcher (Oxford University Press, 2012.)
9. Wendy Wall, *Recipes for Thought: Knowledge and Taste in the Early Modern English Kitchen* (Philadelphia: University of Pennsylvania Press, 2016), 5.
10. Sara Mendelson and Patricia Crawford, *Women in Early Modern England 1550–1720* (Oxford: Oxford University Press, 1998), 304.
11. Amanda Vickery, *The Gentleman's Daughter: Women's Lives in Gregorian England* (New Haven: Yale University Press, 1998), 151–156.
12. Gilly Lehmann, *The British Housewife: Cookery Books, Cooking and Society in Eighteenth-Century Britain* (Blackawton: Prospect Books, 2003), 101–102.
13. Ibid.; Albala, *The Banquet*, 64.
14. Wall, *Recipes for Thought*, 7
15. Anonymous, *The Ladies Cabinet Opened VVherein Is Found Hidden Severall Experiments in Preserving and Conserving, Physicke, and Surgery, Cookery and Huswifery* (1639) STC 15119; Earl of Forth and Brentford Patrick Ruthven, *The Ladies Cabinet Enlarged and Opened Containing Many Rare Secrets* (1654) Wing B135; J.S., *The Accomplished Ladies Rich Closet of Rarities* (1687) Wing S3498A; Anonymous, *The Ladies Companion* (1653) Wing L152; and Hannah Woolley, *The Accomplish'd Ladies Delight in Preserving, Physick, Beautifying, and Cookery* (1683) Wing W3270.
16. Anonymous, *The Gentlewomans Delight in Cookery* (1690) Wing G523eA; Anonymous, *The Gentlewomans Cabinet Unlocked.* (1688) Wing G523dA; and Countess of Kent Elizabeth Grey, *A True Gentlewomans Delight* (1653) Wing K317A.
17. Thomas Dawson, *The Good Husvvifes Iewell* (1610) STC 6393; Thomas Dawson, *The Second Part of The Good Hus-wiues Iewell* (1606) STC 6396; and Gervase Markham, *The English House-vvife* (1631) STC 17353.
18. "Cookery and Medical Recipe Book," Late 17th century-18th century, Wellcome Institute Library (hereafter WI), MS.7892, 65.
19. J.S., *The Sccomplished Ladies Rich Closet of Rarities.*
20. Anonymous, *The Compleat Cook* (1694) Wing C5638AC.
21. David Cressy, *Literacy and Social Order: Reading & Writing in Tudor & Stuart England* (Cambridge: Cambridge University Press, 1980), 144–145.
22. Ibid., 143.
23. Wall, *Recipes for Thought*, 117.
24. Tessa Watt, *Cheap Print and Popular Piety, 1550–1640* (Cambridge: Cambridge University Press, 1991), 1.

Chapter Notes—3

25. Ken Albala, *The Banquet: Dining in the Great Courts of Late Renaissance Europe* (Urbaba: University of Illinois Press, 2007), 92.
26. Alan Davidson, *The Oxford Companion to Food*, ed. Tom Jaine (Oxford: Oxford University Press, 2006), 764–767.
27. Mintz, *Sweetness and Power*, xxix.
28. Hugh Plat, *Delightes for Ladies* (1608) STC 19980; John Murrell, *A Nevv Booke of Cookerie* (1615) STC 18299; John Murrell, *A Daily Exercise for Ladies and Gentlewomen* (1617) STC 18301; John Partridge, *The Widdowes Treasure* (1631) STC 19437; John Murrell, *Murrels Two Books of Cookerie and Carving* (1638) STC 18303; Anonymous, *The Ladies Cabinet Opened* (1639) STC 15119; Thomas Dawson, *A Book of Cookery* (1650) Wing B3705; Anonymous, *The Ladies Companion*; Countess of Kent Elizabeth Grey, *A Choice Manual of Rare and Select Secrets in Physick and Chyrurgery* (1653) Wing K310A; Countess of Kent Elizabeth Grey, *A True Gentlewomans Delight* (1653) Wing K317A; Anonymous, *A Book of Fruits and Flowers* (1653) Wing 3708; Joseph Cooper, *The Art of Cookery Refin'd and Augmented* (1654) Wing C6055; Earl of Forth and Brentford; Patrick Ruthven, *The Ladies Cabinet Enlarged and Opened* (1654) Wing B135; Gervase Markham, *The English Hous-wife* (1656) Wing M631; Monsieur Marnettè, *The Perfect Cook* (1656) M706 ; Sir Théodore Turquet de Mayerne, *Archimagirus Anglo-Gallicus* (1658) Wing M1427; William Rabisha, *The VVhole Body of Cookery Dissected* (1661) Wing R114; Anonymous, *The Queens Closet Opened* (1661) Wing M99A; W.M., *The Compleat Cook* (1663) Wing M92A; Anonymous, *The Court and Kitchin of Elizabeth, Commonly Called Joan Cromwell*; Anonymous, *The Ladies Cabinet Enlarged and Opened* (1667) Wing B137; Sir Digby Kenelm, *The Closet of the Eminently Learned Sir Kenelme Digbie* (1669) Wing D1427; François Pierre de La Varenne, *The French Cook* (1673) Wing L625A; Anonymous, *A Queens Delight* (1675) Wing Q157A; Thomas Cock, *Kitchin-Physick* (1676) Wing C4792; Robert May, *The Accomplisht Cook* (1678) Wing M1393A; Anonymous, *The True Way of Preserving and Candying* (1681) Wing T3126A; Denis Papin, *A New Digester or Engine for Softning Bones* (1681) Wing P309; John Collins, *Salt and Fishery* (1682) Wing C5380B; G. Hartman, *The True Preserver and Restorer of Health* (1682) Wing H1004; M.H., *The Young Cooks Monitor* (1683) Wing H95; Woolley, *The Accomplish'd Ladies Delight in Preserving*; Hannah Woolley, *The Compleat Servant-Maid* (1683) Wing W3273B; Anonymous, *The Court of Curiosities* (1685) Wing C6588; J.S., *The Accomplished Ladies Rich Closet of Rarities*; Anonymous, *The Gentlewomans Cabinet Unlocked*; Anonymous, *The Compleat English and French Cook* (1690) Wing C5638B; Anonymous, *The Gentlewoman's Delight in Cookery*; Mary Tillinghast, *Rare and Excellent Receipts* (1690) Wing T1183; Anonymous, *The Genteel House-Keepers Pastime* (1693) Wing G521; Thomas Tryon, *A Pocket-Companion* (1693) Wing T3192; Anonymous, *The Compleat Cook* (1694) Wing C5638AC; Lady, *The Whole Duty of a Woman: or a Guide to the Female Sex* (1696) Wing W2054A.
29. Murrell, *A Daily Exercise for Ladies and Gentlewomen*, 35–36.
30. Anonymous, *The Queens Closet Opened*, 218.
31. Anonymous, *The Gentlewomans Cabinet Unlocked*, 2.
32. Dawson, *A book of cookery*.
33. Anonymous, *The compleat cook*, 37–38.
34. "Jane Baber," c. 1625, WI, MS.108; "Anne Brumwich & others," c. 1625–1700, WI, MS.160; "Townshend Family," 1636–1647, WI MS.774; "Elizabeth Sleigh & Felicia Whitfield," 1647–1772, WI, MS.751; "A Book of Receites," c. 1650–

1739, WI, MS.144; "Jane Parker," 1651, WI, MS.3769; "Mrs. Mary Miller," 1660, WI, MS.3547; "Mary Bent," 1664–1729, WI, MS.1127; "Sir Thomas Osborne," 1670–1695, WI, MS.3724; "A Book of Receipts," c. 1675–1725, WI, MS.1321; "Receipt-Book, 17th century," c. 1675, WI, MS.4050; "Bridget Hyde," 1676–1690, WI, MS.2990; "Sarah Hudson," 1678, WI, MS.2954; "Mrs. Carr," 1682, WI, MS.1511; "Mary Chantrell & others," 1682, WI, MS.1548; "Amy Eyton & others," 1691–1738, WI, MS.2323; "Hannah Bisaker," 1692, WI, MS.1176; "Mary Perrott," 1695, WI, MS.3834; "Edward Kidder & Katherine Kidder," 1699, WI, MS.3107; "Cookery and Medical Recipe Book," late 17th century, WI, MS.7892; "English Receipt Book, late 17th century," late 17th century, WI, MS.7787; "Family Receipts," late 17th century, WI, MS.2330; "Lowther Family," late 17th century, WI, MS.3341; "Heppington Receipts Volume 2," late 17th century to mid 18th century, WI, MS.7998; "Heppington Receipts Volume 3," late 17th century to mid 18th century, MS.7999, Wellcome Library, London.

35. "Townshend Family," 1636–1647, WI, MS.774, 5–7.

36. The book is labeled "Family Receipts" on the spine of the text; "Family Receipts," late 17th century, WI, MS.2330, 2–21.

37. *Ibid.*, 26.

38. *Ibid.*, 11.

39. For more on this and the eighteenth century sugar boycott, see J.R. Oldfield's *Popular Politics and British Anti-Slavery: The Mobilisation of Public Opinion Against the Slave Trade, 1787–1807* (London: Routledge, 1998).

40. Dawson, *A Book of Cookery*, 5–10.

41. Anonymous, *A Gentlewoman's Delight in Cookery*, 3.

42. *Ibid.*, 4–8.

43. *Ibid.*, A2v.

44. *Ibid.*, A6.

45. Anonymous, *The Compleat Cook*, 319–345.

46. Cooper, *The Art of Cookery Refin'd and Augmented*, 82–83.

47. "Elizabeth Sleigh & Felicia Whitfield," 1647–1722, WI, MS.751; "Mary Bent," 1664–1729, WI, MS.1127; "A Book of Receipts," c. 1675–1725, WI, MS.1321; "Receipt-Book, 17th Century," c. 1675, WI, MS.4050; "Hannah Bisaker," 1692, WI, MS.1176; "Mary Perrott," 1695, WI, MS.3834; "Edward Kidder & Katherine Kidder," 1699, WI, MS.3107; "Cookery and Medical Recipe Book," late 17th century, WI, MS.7892; "Heppington Receipts Volume 3," late 17th century to mid 18th century, WI, MS.7999.

48. "Heppington Receipts Volume 3," MS.7999, 38.

49. "Jane Parker," 1651, WI, MS.3769, fol. 8v, 13, 20, 43.

50. "Hannah Bisaker," 1692, WI, MS.1176, no foliation or pagination.

51. "Bridget Hyde," 1676–1690, WI, MS.2990, fol. 4, 11v, 16, 22v, and 50.

52. "Amy Eyton & others," 1691–1738, WI, MS.2323, fol. 2, 17, and 19.

53. "Bridget Hyde," 1676–1690, WI, MS.2990; "Sarah Hudson," 1678, WI, MS.2954; "Edward Kidder & Katherine Kidder," 1699, WI, MS.3107; "Lowther Family," late 17th century, WI, MS.3341; "Cookery and Medical Recipe Book," late 17th century to 18th century, WI, MS.7892; "Heppington Receipts Volume 2," late 17th century to mid 18th century, WI, MS.7998; "Heppington Receipts Volume 3," late 17th century to mid eighteenth century, WI, MS.7999.

54. "Cookery and Medical Recipe Book," late 17th century to 18th century, WI, MS.7892, fol. 73 and 80.

55. "A Book of Receipts," 1675–1725, WI, MS.1321; "Cookery and Medical Recipe Book," late 17th century to 18th century, WI, MS.7892; "Heppington Receipts Volume 3," late 17th century to mid eighteenth century, WI, MS.7999.

56. "Cookery and Medical Recipe Book," late 17th century to 18th century, WI, MS.7892, fol. 100.

Chapter Notes—3

57. Davidson, *The Oxford Companion to Food*.
58. Collins, *Salt and Fishery*, 116–117 and 120.
59. *Ibid.*, 117.
60. Hartman, *The True Preserver and Restorer of Health*, 14–15.
61. "A Book of receits," 1675–1725, WI, MS.1321, fol. 8.
62. "Mary Perrott," 1695, WI, MS.3834, fol. 18v.
63. Davidson, *The Oxford Companion to Food*, 812–813.
64. Dawson, *The Good Husvvifes Ievvell*, 14–15.
65. Anonymous, *A Good Huswifes Handmaide for the Kitchin*, 13–14.
66. Markham, 43–45 and 58–59.
67. Anonymous, *The Compleat Cook*, 95–96, 150, 186, and 188.
68. "A Book of Receits," 1650–1739, WI, MS.144; "Mary Bent," 1644–1729, WI, MS.1127; "A Book of Receits," 1675–1725, WI, MS.1321; "Hanah Bisaker," 1692, WI, MS.1176; "Edward Kidder & Katherine Kidder," 1699, WI, MS.3107; "Cookery and Medical Recipe Book," late 17th century, WI, MS.7892; "Heppington Receipts Volume 2," late 17th century to mid 18th century, WI, MS.7998; "Heppington Receipts Volume 3," late 17th century to mid 18th century, WI, MS.7999.
69. "A Book of Receits," 1675–1725, WI, MS.1321, 41.
70. *Ibid.*, 47.
71. "Heppington Receipts Volume 3," late 17th century to mid 18th century, WI, MS.7999, 34.
72. Because it was acceptable to eat tortoise on Friday Fasts and during Lent, I have decided to categorize them here as fish. Most modern sources, however, would have them labeled as meat.
73. Archie Carr, *So Excellent a Fish* (New York: Charles Scribner's, 1967).
74. Davidson, *The Oxford Companion to Food*, 710.
75. La Varenne, *The French Cook*; Papin; Hartman, *The True Preserver and Restorer of Health*; M.H.; Anonymous, *The Compleat English and French Cook*; Anonymous, *The Compleat Cook: or, the Whole Art of Cookery*.
76. La Varenne, *The French Cook*, 27 and 148–149.
77. *Ibid.*, 149.
78. Davidson, *The Oxford Companion to Food*, 608–609; Maguelonne Toussaint-Samat, *A History of Food* (Oxford: Wiley-Blackwell, 1992) 608–609; Gary Okihiro, *Pineapple Culture: A History of the Tropical and Temperate Zones* (Berkeley and Los Angeles: University of California Press, 2009.
79. Grey, *A Choice Manual of Rare and Select Secrets in Physick and Chyrurgery*; Ruthven; Marnettè; Mayerne,; W.M.; Anonymous, *The Ladies Cabinet Enlarged and Opened*; La Varenne, *The French Cook*; Rabisha, *The VVhole Body of Cookery Dissected*; May, *The Accomplisht Cook*; Anonymous, *The Compleat English and French Cook*; Anonymous, *The Compleat Cook: or, The Whole Art of Cookery*; Tryon.**
80. W.M., 32–33.
81. Rabisha, *The VVhole Body of Cookery Dissected,* 181, 208–209, 244, 270, 281.
82. May, *The Accomplisht Cook,* 2.
83. Rabisha, *The VVhole Body of Cookery Dissected*, 74–75.
84. Dawson, *The Good Husvvifes Ievvel*; Anonymous, *A Good Huswifes Handmaide for the Kitchin*; Murrell, *A Nevv Booke of Cookerie*; Dawson, *A Book of Cookery, and the Order of Meates to be Served to the Table, Both from Flesh and Fish Days*; Murrell, *Murrels Two Books of Cookerie and Carving*; Grey, *A Choice Manual of Rare and Select Secrets in Physick and Chyrurgery*; Grey, *A True Gentlewomans Delight*; Cooper; Markham; Marnettè; Rabisha; La Varenne, *The French Cook* ; May; Anonymous, *The Compleat English and French Cook*; Tillinghhast; Anonymous, *The Compleat Cook: or, The Whole Art of Cookery*; J.S.**
85. Davidson, *The Oxford Companion to Food*, 627.

86. Murrell, *A Nevv Booke of Cookerie*, 40–41; Murrell, *Murrels Two Books of Cookerie and Carving*, 63–64.
87. Cooper, *The Art of Cookery Refin'd and Augmented*, 22.
88. Tillinghast, *Rare and Excellent Receipts*, 14–15.
89. Anonymous, *The Compleat Cook*, 432–446.
90. "Elizabeth Sleigh and Felicia Whitfield," 1647–1772, WI, MS.751, fol. 78v.
91. "Mary Bent," 1664–1729, WI MS. 1127, 134.
92. "Heppington Receipts Volume 2," late 17th century to mid 18th century, WI, MS.7998, 79; "Heppington Receipts Volume 3," late 17th century to mid 18th century, WI, MS.7999, 36.
93. Marnettè; La Varenne, *The French Cook*; Anonymous, *The Compleat Cook: or, The Whole Art of Cookery*; Anonymous, *The Compleat English and French Cook*.
94. Marnettè, *The Perfect Cook*, 125–126 and 238–239.
95. La Varenne, *The French Cook*, 39, 48, 257.
96. Anonymous, *The Compleat English and French Cook*, 382–383 and 401.
97. J.S., *The Accomplished Ladies Rich Closet of Rarities*, 18.
98. Anonymous, *The True Way of Preserving and Candying*, 142–143.
99. "Mary Bent," 1664–1729, WI, MS.1127; "Mrs. Carr," 1682, WI, MS.1511; "Lowther Family," late 17th century, WI, MS.3341.
100. "Mrs. Carr, " 1682, WI, MS.1511, fol. 16v.
101. "Mary Bent," 1664–1729, WI, MS.1127, 157.

Chapter 4

1. Nicholas Culpeper, *The English Physician* (1652) Wing C7500, sig. A4v-A5.
2. Patrick Curry, "Culpeper, Nicholas (1616–1654)," *ODNB* (Oxford: Oxford University Press, 2004).
3. Joseph Blagrave, *Supplement or Enlargement to Mr. Nich. Culpepper's The English Physitian* (1674) Wing B3121, A2.
4. Patrick Curry, "Blagrave, Joseph (b. 1610, d. in or before 1682)," *ODNB* (Oxford: Oxford University Press, 2004).
5. Andrew Wear, *Knowledge and Practice in English Medicine, 1550–1680* (Cambridge: Cambridge University Press, 2000), 21–22.
6. Ibid., 47.
7. Ibid., 40–41.
8. Ibid., 42.
9. Ibid., 44.
10. Jennifer K. Stine "Opening Closets: The Discovery of Household Medicine in Early Modern England" (PhD diss.: Stanford University, 1996), 14.
11. Alun Withey, "Crossing the Boundaries: Domestic Recipe Collections in Early Modern Wales" in *Reading and Writing Recipe Books 1550–1800*, ed. Michelle DiMeo and Sara Pennell (Manchester: Manchester University Press, 2013), 179.
12. Michelle DiMeo and Rebecca Laroche "On Elizabeth Isham's 'Oil of Swallows': Animal Slaughter and Early Modern Women's Medical Recipes" in *Ecofeminist Approaches to Early Modernity*, ed. Jennifer Munroe and Rebecca Laroche (New York: Palgrave Macmillan, 2011), 89.
13. Stine, "Opening Closets," 62.
14. Ibid., 63.
15. Wear, *Knowledge and Practice in English Medicine*, 35.
16. Wear, *Knowledge and Practice in English Medicine*, 37.
17. Sara Mendelson and Patricia Crawford, *Women in Early Modern England 1550–1720* (Oxford: Clarendon Press, 1998), 19–20.
18. Wear, *Knowledge and Practice in English Medicine*, 38.
19. Ibid., 174.

Chapter Notes—4

20. *Ibid.*, 174.
21. Paul Freedman, *Out of the East: Spice and the Medieval Imagination* (New Haven: Yale University Press, 2009), 5.
22. *Ibid.*, 72.
23. *Ibid.*, 14.
24. Wear, *Knowledge and Practice in English Medicine*, 46.
25. Nicholas Culpepper, *Culpeper's Complete Herbal* (1653; repr., Bedford: Applewood Books), 376.
26. Wear, *Knowledge and Practice in English Medicine*, 48.
27. Freedman, *Out of the East*, 54.
28. *Ibid.*, 52.
29. Thomas Brugis, *The Marrow of Physicke* (1640) STC 3931, 75; Anonymous, *The Ladies Cabinet Enlarged and Opened* (1667) Wing B137, 55; Anonymous, *The Queens Closet Opened* (1696) Wing M105, 255.
30. "English Medical Notebook, 17th century," 1575–1663, WI, MS.6812; "A Book of Receites," 1650–1739, WI, MS.144; "Jacob, Elizabeth (& others)," 1654-c.1685, WI, MS.3009; "A Booke of divers receipts," c.1660-c.1750, WI, MS.1322; "Boyle Family," c.1675-c.1710, WI, MS.1340; Mary Glover, "Cookery and Medical Receipts," 1688, British Library (hereafter BL), Add MS.57944; Sir Peter Temple of Stanton Barry, "Medical, cookery and other recipes," 17th century, BL, Stowe MS.1077–1078; "Family Receipts," late 17th century, WI, MS.2330; and "Receipt-Book, 17th century," late 17th century, WI, MS.4051.
31. Brugis, *Marrow of Physicke*, 75.
32. *Ibid.*, 79; Anonymous, *The Ladies Cabinet Enlarged*, 53; Anonymous, *The Queens Closet Opened*, 19; Thomas Dawson, *A Book of Cookery* (1650) Wing B3705, 82; J.S., *The Accomplished Ladies Rich Closet of Rarities* (1687) Wing S3498A, 3; and G. Hartman, *The True Preserver and Restorer of Health* (1695) Wing H1006, 139.
33. "A Book of Receites," c. 1650–1739, WI, MS.144; "A Booke of divers receipts," c. 1660-c. 1750, WI, MS.1322; "Hyde, Bridget," 1676–1690, WI, MS.2990; "Saint John, Johanna," 1680, WI, MS.4338; "English Recipe Book," late 17th century, WI, MS.7849; and "Cookery and Medical Recipe Book," late 17th century-early 18th century, WI, MS.7892.
34. Anonymous, *The Ladies Cabinet Enlarged and Opened*, 54.
35. Blagrave, *Supplement or Enlargement to Mr. Nich. Culpepper's The English Physitian*, 140.
36. *Ibid.*, 140.
37. Brugis, *Marrow of Physicke*, 25, 62, 65, 75, 79, 97, and 111.
38. A.M., *Queen Elizabeths Closet of Physical Secrets* (1656) Wing M5B, 39 and 131.
39. Hartman, *The True Preserver and Restorer of Health*, 40.
40. Thomas Brugis, *Vade Mecum* (1651) Wing B5225, 56.
41. "English Recipe Book," mid 17th century, WI, MS.7391, 11.
42. Brugis, *The Marrow of Physicke*, 50, 74, 75, 79, and 106.
43. Thomas Cock, *Miscelanea Medica* (1675) Wing C4793, 35.
44. Anonymous, *The Queens Closet Opened*, 101.
45. Blagrave, *Supplement or Enlargement to Mr. Nich. Culpepper's The English Physitian*, 35.
46. Burgis, *The Marrow of Physick*, 25, 23, and 63.
47. Michael Foster, 'Digby, Sir Kenelm (1603–1665),' *ODNB* (Oxford: Oxford University Press, 2004).
48. Sir Kenelm Digby, *Choice and Experimental Receipts in Physick and Chirurgery* (1668) Wing D1424, 15 and 122.
49. Sir Kenelm Digby, *The Closet of the Eminently Learned Sir Kenelme Digbie* (1669) Wing D1427, 9, 12, 25, 36, 69, and 84.
50. Blagrave, *Supplement or Enlargement to Mr. Nich. Culpepper's The English Physitian*, 37.
51. Anonymous, *The Ladies Companion* (1653) Wing L152, 60–61.

Chapter Notes—4

52. "Bridget Hyde," 1676–1690, WI, MS.2990; "Hirst, Mrs. Elizabeth (& others)," 1684–c.1725, WI, MS.2840; "Chantrell, Mary (& others)," 1690, WI, MS.1548; "Kidder, Edward & Kidder, Katherine," 1699, WI, MS.3107; and "English Recipe Book," MS.7849.
53. A.M., *A Rich Closet of Physical Secrets* (1652) Wing M7, 22 and A.M., *Queen Elizabeths Closset of Physical Secrets*, 3–4.
54. Thomas Chamberlayne, *The Compleat Midvvifes Practice* (1653) Wing C1817E, 113.
55. John Hester, *The Secrets of Physick and Philosophy* (1633) STC 19182, 44–45.
56. *Ibid.*,, 46.
57. *Ibid.*, 46.
58. "English Recipe Book," mid 17th century, WI, MS.7391; "Saint John, Johanna," 1680, WI, MS.4338.
59. Seventeenth century English texts do not discern between plantain the fruit and plantain the plant. Davidson explains that "plantain (fruit) [is] the name given to varieties of the banana" and "plantain (plant) [is] a name given to a group of small leafy plants, of the genus Plantago, long before it was applied to the banana," 612–613.
60. John Partridge, *The Widows Treasure* (1631) STC 19437, 18, 28, and 31.
61. Anonymous, *A Book of Fruits and Flowers* (1653) Wing B3708, 11 and 18; and Patrick Ruthven, Earl of Forth and Brentford, *The Ladies Cabinet Enlarged and Opened* (1654) Wing B135, 53, 88, 106, 113, 127, and 147.
62. Burgis, *The Marrow of Physick*, 12,13, 32, 55, 60, 74, and 92.
63. Gervase Markham, *The English Hous-wife* (1656) Wing M631, 13, 14, 17, 20, 21, 22, 23, 26, 27, and 62.
64. J.S., *The accomplished ladies rich closet of rarities*, 8 and 28.
65. Anonymous, *The Queen's Closet Opened*, 109.
66. "A Large Collection of Quaint Medical and Other Receipts," c.1625–c.1725, WI, MS.400, no foliation or pagination.
67. "Brumwich, Anne," c.1625–1700, WI, MS.160, no foliation or pagination.
68. "English Recipe Book," mid 17th century, WI, MS.7391, 44.
69. Nicholas Culpeper, *A directory for Midvvives* (1651) Wing C7488, 145.
70. Anonymous, *The English Midwife Enlarged* (1682) Wing E3104A, 241–242.
71. "Hirst, Mrs. Elizabeth," 1684–c.1725, WI, MS.2840, 53.
72. G.L., *The Gentleman's New Jockey* (1691) Wing L20aA, 67–68.
73. Blagrave, *Supplement or Enlargement to Mr. Nich. Culpepper's The English Physitian*, 89–90.
74. Partridge, *The Widdowes Treasure*, 14–15;
75. Ruthven, *The Ladies Cabinet Enlarged and Opened*, 142–143.
76. "Saint John, Johanna," 1680, WI, MS.4338, fol. 26.
77. "Family Receipts," late 17th century, WI, MS.2330, fol. 44.
78. Blagrave, *Supplement or Enlargement to Mr. Nich. Culpepper's The English Physitian*, 197–198.
79. *Ibid.*, 198.
80. A.M., *Queen Elizabeths Closset of Physical Secrets*, 58.
81. William Drage, *A Physical Nosonomy* (1665) Wing D2117, 171.
82. Hartman, *The True Preserver and Restorer of Health*, 68, 100–109, and 135.
83. "Hyde, Bridget," 1676–1690, WI, MS.2990, fol. 88v and 89v.
84. "Jacob, Elizabeth," 1654-c.1685, WI, MS.3009, 15.
85. Blagrave, *Supplement or Enlargement to Mr. Nich. Culpepper's The English Physitian*, 199–200.
86. A.M., *Queen Elizabeths Closset of Physical Secrets*, 28 and 60.
87. Digby, *Choice and Experiment Receipts in Physick and Chirurgery*, 31 and 226; and Digby, *The Closet of the Eminently Learned Sir Kenelme Digbie*, 9 and 69.
88. "Saint John, Johanna," 1680, WI,

MS.4338, 7; "Family Receipts," late 17th century, WI, MS.2330, fol. 54; and Sir Peter Temple of Stanton Barry, "Medical, cookery and other recipes," 17th century, BL, Stowe 1078, fol. 6.
   89. A.M., *Queen Elizabeths Closset of Physical Secrets*, 26 and 41.
   90. William Rabisha, *The Whole Body of Cookery Dissected* (1661) Wing R114, 110–11.
   91. Ruthven, *The Ladies Cabinet Enlarged and Opened*, 119.
   92. "Saint John, Johanna," 1680, WI, MS.4338, fol. 27.
   93. "Kidder, Edward & Kidder, Katherine," 1699, WI, MS.3107, 267; "Family Receipts," late 17th century, WI, MS.2330, fol. 52; and "Harrow-upon-the-Hill. co. Middl. Medical receipts collected by an inhabitant," 17th century, BL, Sloane 566, 20.
   94. Blagrave, *Supplement or Enlargement to Mr. Nich. Culpepper's The English Physitian*, 217–218.
   95. John Chamberlayne, *The Natural History of Coffee, Thee, Chocolate, Tobacco* (1682) Wing C1860, 21.
   96. *Ibid.*, 23.
   97. *Ibid.*, 24.
   98. Ruthven, *The Ladies Cabinet Enlarged and Opened*,142.
   99. Brugis, *The Marrow of Physicke*, 58.
   100. Anonymous, *The Ladies Cabinet Enlarged and Opened*, 77.
   101. A.M., *Queen Elizabeths Closset of Physical Secrets* 111.
   102. "English Medical Notebook," 1575–1663, WI, MS. 6812, 74 and 81.
   103. "Harrow-upon-the-Hill. co. Middl. Medical receipts collected by an inhabitant," 17th century, BL Sloane 566, fol. 20; and "A large collection of quaint medical and other receipts," c.1625-c.1725, WI, MS.400, no foliation or pagination.
   104. "Jacob, Elizabeth (& others)," 1654-c.1685, WI, MS.3009, 41.
   105. G.L., *The Gentleman's New Jockey.*

106. J. Chamberlayne, *The Natural History of Coffee, Thee, Chocolate, Tobacco*, 17.
   107. Blagrave, *Supplement or Enlargement to Mr. Nich. Culpepper's The English Physitian*, 42–43.
   108. *Ibid.*, 45.
   109. J. Chamberlayne, *The Natural History of Coffee, Thee, Chocolate, Tobacco*, 4.
   110. *Ibid.*, 6.
   111. *Ibid.*, 5.

Chapter 5

   1. Anonymous, *Rebellions Antidote: or a Dialogue Between Coffee and Tea* (1685) Wing B131A.
   2. *Ibid.*
   3. Iain Gately, *Tobacco: A Cultural History of How an Exotic Plant Seduced Civilization* (New York: Grove Press, 2001), 45.
   4. *Ibid.*, 47.
   5. *Ibid.*, 51.
   6. *Ibid.*, 78.
   7. *Ibid.*, 72.
   8. Carole Shammas, *The Pre-Industrial Consumer in England and America* (Oxford: Oxford University Press, 1990), 78.
   9. Jordan Goodman, *Tobacco in History: The Cultures of Dependence* (London: Routledge, 1993),65.
   10. Kate Loveman, "The Introduction of Chocolate into England: Retailers, Researchers, and Consumers, 1640–1730," *Journal of Social History* vol. 47 no. 1 (2013), 29.
   11. Marcy Norton, *Sacred Gifts, Profane Pleasures: A History of Tobacco and Chocolate in the Atlantic World* (Ithaca: Cornell University Press, 2008), 260.
   12. *Ibid.*, 261.
   13. Loveman, "The Introduction of Chocolate into England," 31.
   14. *Ibid.*
   15. *Ibid.*, 38.
   16. *Ibid.*, 39.

17. Brian Cowan, *The Social Life of Coffee: The Emergence of the British Coffeehouse* (New Haven: Yale University Press, 2005), 25; William H. Ukers, *All About Coffee*, 2nd ed. (Mansfield Centre, CT: Martino Publishing, 2011), 37.
18. Ukers, *All About Coffee*, 38; Cowan, *The Social Life of Coffee*, 25.
19. Cowan, *The Social Life of Coffee*, 60.
20. *Ibid.*, 64.
21. *Ibid.*, 87.
22. *Ibid.*, 95.
23. *Ibid.*, 109 and 154.
24. Ukers, *All About Coffee*, 625.
25. *Ibid.*, 576–577.
26. Cowan, *The Social Life of Coffee*, 75.
27. Jane Pettigrew and Bruce Richardson, *A Social History of Tea: Tea's Influence on Commerce, Culture & Community* (Danville: Benjamin Press, 2014), 13.
28. *Ibid.*, 19; Kate Colquhoun, *Taste: The Story of Britain Through Its Cooking* (New York: Bloomsbury, 2007), 148.
29. Pettigrew and Richardson, *A Social History of Tea*, 19.
30. Colquhoun, *Taste*, 148.
31. Pettigrew and Richardson, *A Social History of Tea*, 21 and 26.
32. *Ibid.*, 26.
33. *Ibid.*, 28.
34. Reay Tannahill, *Food in History* (New York: Three Rivers Press, 1988), 268.
35. Doctor Bellamy, *A New and Short Defense of Tabacco* (1602) STC 6468.5, A3.
36. *Ibid.*, C4.
37. James I, King of England, *A Counterblaste to Tobacco* (1604) STC 14363, B2.
38. Gately, *Tobacco*, 66.
39. James I, *A Counterblaste to Tobacco*, B4.
40. *Ibid.*, D2.
41. Edmund Gardiner, *The Triall of Tabacco* (1610) STC 11564, 9.
42. *Ibid.*, 13
43. *Ibid.*
44. C.T., *An Advice How to Plant Tobacco in England* (1615) STC 23612, A2v.
45. *Ibid.*, B.
46. *Ibid.*, A3.
47. C.T., *An Advice How to Plant Tobacco in England*, A3
48. *Ibid.*, B2-B3.
49. *Ibid.*, C.
50. Tobias Venner, *A Briefe and Accurate Treatise, Concerning, the Taking of the Fume Tobacco* (1621) STC 24642, B2.
51. Venner, B2v.
52. John Lacy, *Tobacco, A Poem* (1669) Wing L148A.
53. *Ibid.*
54. Ken Albala, *Food in Early Modern Europe* (Westport: Greenwood Press, 2003), 85.
55. Antonio Colmenero de Ledesma, *A Curious Treatise of the Nature and Quality of Chocolate* (1640) STC 5570, 1.
56. Colmenero de Ledesma, *A Curious Treatise of the Nature and Quality of Chocolate*, 13.
57. *Ibid.*, 14.
58. *Ibid.*
59. Colmenero de Ledesma, *A Curious Treatise of the Nature and Quality of Chocolate*, 14.
60. Antonio Colmenero de Ledesma, *Chocolate: or, An Indian Drinke* (1652) Wing C5400.
61. *Ibid.*, A3.
62. *Ibid.*, A4.
63. *Ibid.*, A5-A7.
64. Anonymous, *The Vertues of Chocolate East India Drink* (1660) Wing V648.
65. *Ibid.*
66. *Ibid.*
67. Philippe Sylvestre Dufour, *The Manner of Making Coffee, Tea, and Chocolate* (1685) Wing D2455, A4.
68. *Ibid.*, 71–72.
69. *Ibid.*, 74–75.
70. Anonymous, *The Vertues of Coffee, Chocolette, and Thee or Tea* (1690) Wing P3398A.

71. *Ibid.*
72. *Ibid.*
73. Anonymous, *The Vertue of the Coffee Drink* (1652) Wing V645B; and Anonymous, *The Vertue of the Coffee Drink* (1660) Wing V646.
74. Anonymous, *The Vertue of the Coffee Drink* (1652); and Anonymous, *The Vertue of the Coffee Drink* (1660).
75. Anonymous, *The Vertue of the Coffee Drink* (1660).
76. N.D., *The Vertues of the Coffee* (1663) Wing D72aA, 3.
77. N.D., 4.**
78. *Ibid.*, 8.
79. Anonymous, *The Nature, Quality, and Most Excellent Vertues of Coffee* (1670) Wing V646A.
80. *Ibid.*
81. Anonymous, *The Nature, Quality, and Most Excellent Vertues of Coffee.*
82. *Ibid.*
83. Anonymous, *A Broad-side Against Coffee; or, The Marriage of the Turk* (1672) Wing B4830.
84. *Ibid.*
85. Anonymous, *A Broad-side Against Coffee.*
86. Anonymous, *A Satyr Against Coffee* (1674) Wing S709.
87. *Ibid.*
88. Anonymous, *A Satyr Against Coffee.*
89. Anonymous, *A Description of the Excellent Vertues of that Sober and Wholesome Drink, Called Coffee* (1674) Wing B4568.
90. *Ibid.*
91. *Ibid.*
92. Anonymous, *A Description of the Excellent Vertues of that Sober and Wholesome Drink, Called Coffee.*
93. Dufour, *The Manner of Making Coffee, Tea, and Chocolate*, 13–14.
94. Anonymous, *The Virtues of Coffee, Chocolette, and Thee or Tea.*
95. *Ibid.*
96. Albala, *Food in Early Modern Europe*, 84.
97. Thomas Garway, *An Exact Description of the Growth, Quality, and Vertues of the Leaf Tea* (1660) Wing G282.
98. Garway.
99. Garway.
100. Anonymous, *Rebellions Antidote: or a Dialogue Between Coffee and Tea.*
101. Dufour, *The Manner of Making Coffee, Tea, and Chocolate*, 42.
102. *Ibid.*, 43–44.
103. *Ibid.*, 43.
104. Samuel Price, *The Virtues of Coffee, Chocolette, and Thee or Tea, Experimentally Known in this Our Climate* (1690) Wing P3398A.
105. J. Ovington, *An Essay Upon the Nature and Qualities of Tea* (1699) Wing O700 2–3.
106. *Ibid.*, 30.

Conclusion

1. Jean Anthelme Brillat-Savarin, *Physiology of Taste* (1825.; repr., Ontario: General Publishing Company, 2002), 3.
2. Robert Latham, "The Diary as a History" in *The Diary of Samuel Pepys*, ed. Robert Latham and William Matthews (Berkeley: University of California Press, 2000), cxv-cxvi.
3. Samuel Pepys, *The Diary of Samuel Pepys*, ed. Robert Latham and William Matthews, Vols. I–XI(Berkeley: University of California Press, 2000), 3.
4. Pepys, vol. I, 8–9 and 11.
5. *Ibid.*, 23, 41, and 43.
6. Pepys, vol. I, 321; vol. II, 239; vol. IV, 427 and 428; vol. V, 354; vol. VI, 1 and 338.
7. Latham, cxiv-cxvii.
8. Pepys, vol. IV, 179.
9. Pepys, vol. I, 167; vol. II, 38; vol. III, 91; vol. IX, 477.
10. Pepys, vol IV, 242, 332, and 377; vol. V, 222.
11. Pepys, vol. IV, 332.
12. Pepys, vol. VI, 230, 240, and 241; vol. VII, 6.

13. Pepys, vol. I, 85.
14. Pepys, vol. I, 117; vol. IX, 127.
15. Pepys, vol. VI, 120.
16. Pepys, vol. I, 125; vol. VIII, 390.
17. Pepys, vol. II, 88.
18. *Ibid.*; Pepys, vol. III, 226–227; Pepys, vol. IV, 5; Pepys, vol. V, 64.
19. Kate Loveman, "The Introduction of Chocolate into England: Retailers, Researchers, and Consumers, 1640–1730," *Journal of Social History* vol. 47 no. 1 (2013), 31.
20. *Ibid.*
21. Pepys, vol. V, 329.
22. Pepys, vols. I–IX.
23. Pepys, vol. V, 105.
24. Loveman, 31.
25. Pepys, vol. II, 242.

Appendix

1. This refers to the year the play was first published.

Bibliography

Manuscripts
Wellcome Institute Library, London
MS.108 "Jane Baber." c. 1625.
MS.144 "A Book of Receites." c. 1650–1739.
MS.160 "Anne Brumwich & Others." c. 1625–1700.
MS.400 "A Large Collection of Quaint Medical and Other Receipts." c.1625–1725.
MS.751 "Elizabeth Sleigh & Felicia Whitfield." 1647–1772.
MS.774 "Townshend Family." 1636–1647.
MS.1127 "Mary Bent." 1664–1729.
MS.1176 "Hannah Bisaker." 1692.
MS.1321 "A Book of Receits." c. 1675–1725.
MS.1322 "A Booke of Divers Receipts." c.1660-c.1750.
MS.1340 "Boyle Family," c.1675-c.1710.
MS.1511 "Mrs. Carr." 1682.
MS.1548 "Chantrell, Mary (& others)." 1690.
MS.2323 "Amy Eyton & Others." 1691–1738.
MS.2330 "Family Receipts." Late 17th century.
MS.2840 "Hirst, Mrs. Elizabeth (& others)." 1684-c.1725.
MS.2954 "Sarah Hudson." 1678.
MS.2990 "Bridget Hyde." 1676–1690.
MS.3009 "Jacob, Elizabeth (& others)." 1654-c.1685.
MS.3107 "Kidder, Edward & Kidder, Katherine." 1699.
MS.3341 "Lowther Family." Late 17th century.
MS.3547 "Mrs. Mary Miller." 1660.
MS.3724 "Sir Thomas Osborne." 1670–1695.
MS.3769 "Jane Parker." 1651.
MS.3834 "Mary Perrott." 1695.
MS.4050 "Receipt-Book, 17th century." c. 1675.
MS.4051 "Receipt-Book, 17th century." Late 17th century.
MS.4338 "Saint John, Johanna." 1680
MS.6812 "English Medical Notebook, 17th century," 1575–1663.
MS.7391. "English Recipe Book." Mid 17th century.
MS.7787 "English Receipt Book, Late 17th century." Late 17th century.
MS.7849 "English Recipe Book." Late 17th century.
MS.7892 "Cookery and Medical Recipe Book." Late 17th century.
MS.7998 "Heppington Receipts Volume 2." Late 17th century to mid 18th century.
MS.7999 "Heppington Receipts Volume 3." Late 17th century to mid 18th century.

Bibliography

British Library, London

Add MS.57944 Glover, Mary. "Cookery and Medical Receipts." 1688.
Sloane 566 "Harrow-Upon-the-Hill. co. Middl. Medical Receipts Collected by an Inhabitant." 17th century
Stowe MS.1077–1078 Temple, Sir Peter of Stanton Barry. "Medical, Cookery and Other Recipes." 17th century.

Primary Sources

Alexander, Sir William. *The Mapp and Description of New England*. London: 1630. STC 342.
AM. *Queen Elizabeths Closset of Physical Secrets*. London: 1656. Wing M5B.
____. *A Rich Closet of Physical Secrets*. London: 1652. Wing M7.
Armin, Robert. *The Two Maids of More-Clacke*. London: 1609. STC 773.
Ayers, Philip. *The Voyages and Adventures of Capt. Barth. Sharp*. London: 1684. Wing A4315.
Barnes, Barnabe. *The Divils Charter*. London: 1607. STC 1466.
Barry, Lording. *Ram-Alley*. London: 1611. STC 1502a.
The Bastard. London: 1652. Wing M548.
Beaumont, Francis. *The Knight of the Burning Pestle*. London: 1679. Wing B1588.
____. *Loves Cure*. London: 1647. Wing B1581.
____. *The Woman-Hater*. London: 1679. Wing B1588.
Behn, Aphra. *The City-Heiress*. London: 1682. Wing B1719.
____. *The Debauchee*. London: 1677. Wing B4869.
____. *Emperor of the Moon*. London: 1687. Wing B1727.
____. *The Feign'd Curtizans*. London: 1679. Wing B1732.
____. *The Luckey Chance*. London: 1687. Wing B1744.
____. *The Revenge*. London: 1680. Wing B2084.
____. *The Rover, Part II*. London: 1681. Wing B1765.
____. *Sir Patient Fancy*. London: 1678. Wing B1766.
____. *The Widdow Ranter*. London: 1690. Wing B1774.
Bellamy, Doctor. *A New and Short Defense of Tabacco*. London: 1602. STC 6468.5.
Betterton, Thomas. *Henry IV, Part I*. London: 1700. Wing S2928.
Blagrave, Joseph. *Supplement or Enlargement to Mr. Nich. Culpepper's The English Physitian*. London: 1674. Wing B3121.
Blome, Richard. *A Description of the Island of Jamaica*. London: 1672. Wing B3208B.
____. *The Present State of His Majesties Isles and Territories in America*. London: 1687. Wing B3215.
Blurt Master-Constable. London: 1602. STC17876.
A Book of Fruits and Flowers. London: 1653. Wing 3708.
Boothby, Richard. *A Breife Discovery or Description of the Most Famous Island of Madagascar or St. Laurence in Asia*. London: 1646. Wing B3743.
Brereton, John. *A Briefe and True Relation of the Discoverie of the North Part of Virginia*. London: 1602. STC 3611.
A Broad-side Against Coffee; or, The Marriage of the Turk. London: 1672. Wing B4830.
Brome, Alexander. *The Cunning Lovers*. London: 1654. Wing B4850.
Brome, Richard. *The City Wit*. London: 1653. Wing B4866.
____. *The Court Begger*. London: 1653. Wing B4867.
____. *The Damoiselle*. London: 1653. Wing B4868.

Bibliography

———. *The English Moor.* London: 1659. STC 3819.
———. *A Joviall Crew.* London: 1652. Wing B4873.
———. *The Late Lancashire Witches.* London: 1634. STC 13373.
———. *Madd Couple Well Matcht.* London: 1653. Wing B4870.
———. *The New Academy.* London: 1659. STC 3819.
———. *The Northern Lasse.* London: 1632. STC 3819.
———. *The Sparagvs Garden.* London: 1640. STC 3820.
———. *The Weeding of the Covent-Garden.* London: 1658. STC 13373.
Brugis, Thomas. *The Marrow of Physicke.* 1640. STC 3931.
———. *Vade Mecum.* London: 1651. Wing B5225.
Bruton, William. *Newes from the East-Indies.* London: 1638. STC 3946.
Budd, Thomas. *Good Order Established in Pennsilvania & New-Jersey in America.* London: 1685. Wing B5358.
Burnaby, William. *The Reform'd Wife.* London: 1700. Wing B5745.
Cartwright, William. *The Lady-Errant.* London: 1651. Wing C710.
———. *The Ordinary.* London: 1651. Wing C714.
———. *The Siedge.* London: 1651. Wing 709.
Cavendish, Margaret. *The Bridals.* London: 1668. Wing N867.
———. *The Humorous Lovers.* London: 1677. Wing N883.
———. *Love's Adventures, Part I.* London: 1662. Wing N868.
———. *Matrimonial Trouble, Part I.* London: 1662. Wing N868.
———. *The Presence.* London: 1668. Wing N867.
———. *The Sociable Companions.* London: 1668. Wing N867.
———. *The Triumphant Widow.* London: 1677. Wing N891.
———. *The Unnatural Tragedie.* London: 1662. Wing N868.
———. *Wits Cabal, Part II.* London: 1662. Wing N868.
Cavendish, William. *The Humorous Lovers.* London: 1677. Wing N883.
———. *The Triumphant Widow.* London: 1677. Wing N891.
Centlivre, Susanna. *The Perjur'd Husband.* London: 1700. Wing C1671.
Chamberlain, Robert. *The Swaggering Damsel.* London: 1640. STC 4946.
Chamberlayne, John. *The Natural History of Coffee, Thee, Chocolate, Tobacco.* London: 1682. Wing C1860.
Chamberlayne, Thomas. *The Compleat Midvvifes Practice.* London: 1653. Wing C1817E.
Chapman, George. *All Fooles.* London: 1605. STC 4963.
———. *Byrons Conspiracie.* London: 1608. STC 4968.
———. *Caesar and Pompey.* London: 1631. STC 4993.
———. *Eastward Hoe.* London: 1605. STC 4973.
———. *May-Day.* London: 1611. STC 4980.
———. *Monsieur D'olive.* London: 1606. STC 4983.
Chardin, Sir John. *The Travels of Sir John Chardin into Persia and the East-Indies the First Volume.* London: 1686. Wing C2043.
Chettle, Henry. *Patient Grissill.* London: 1603. STC 16518.
Child, Josiah. *A Discourse Concerning Trade.* London: 1689. Wing D1590.
———. *A Treatise.* London: 1681. Wing C3866.
Cibber, Colley. *Love's Last Shift.* London: 1696. Wing C4281.
Clark, William. *Marciano.* London: 1663. Wing C4563.
Clarke, Samuel. *The Life and Death of the Valiant and Renowned Sir Francis Drake.* London: 1671. Wing C4533.
———. *A True and Faithful Account of the Four Chiefest Plantations of the English in America.* London: 1670. Wing C4558.

Bibliography

Cock, Thomas. *Kitchin-Physick*. London: 1676. Wing C4792.
____. *Miscelanea Medica*. London: 1675. Wing C4793.
Cokain, Aston. *The Obstinate Lady*. London: 1658. Wing C4894.
____. *Trappolin Suppos'd a Prince*. London: 1658. Wing C4894.
Collins, John. *Salt and Fishery*. London: 1682. Wing C5380B.
Colmenero de Ledesma, Antonio. *Chocolate: or, An Indian Drinke*. London: 1652. Wing C5400.
____. *A Curious Treatise of the Nature and Quality of Chocolate*. London: 1640. STC 5570.
The Compleat Cook. London: 1694. Wing C5638AC.
The Compleat English and French Cook. London: 1690. Wing C5638B.
Congreve, William. *The Double Dealer*. London: 1694. Wing C5847.
____. *Love for Love*. London: 1695. Wing C5851.
____. *The Old Batchelour*. London: 1693. Wing C5867.
____. *The Way of the World*. London: 1700. Wing C5878.
Cooke, Jo. *Greenes Tu Quoque*. London: 1614. STC 6573.
Cooper, Joseph. *The Art of Cookery Refin'd and Augmented*. London: 1654. Wing C6055.
The Cornish Comedy. London: 1696. Wing P3048.
The Court & Kitchin of Elizabeth, Commonly Called Joan Cromwel. London: 1664. Wing C6584D.
The Court of Curiosities. London: 1685. Wing C6588.
Cowley, Abraham. *Cutter of Coleman Street*. London: 1663. Wing C6669.
____. *The Guardian*. London: 1650. Wing C6673.
Crouch, Nathaniel. *The English Empire in America*. London: 1685. Wing B5358.
____. *A View of the English Acquisitions in Guinea and the East-Indies*. London: 1686. Wing C7356.
Crown, John. *City Politiques*. London: 1683. Wing C7378.
____. *The Countrey Wit*. London: 1675. Wing C7380.
____. *The English Frier*. London: 1690. Wing C7387.
____. *The Married Beau*. London: 1694. Wing C7394.
____. *Sir Courtly Nice*. London: 1685. Wing C7404.
C.T. *An Advice How to Plant Tobacco in England*. London: 1615. STC 23612.
Culpeper, Nicholas. *Culpeper's Complete Herbal*. 1653. Reprint, Bedford: Applewood Books.
____. *A Directory for Midvvives*. London: 1651. Wing C7488.
____. *The English Physician*. London: 1652. Wing C7500.
Dalby, Thomas. *An Historical Account of the Rise and Growth of the West-India Collonies* London: 1690. Wing T961.
Dampier, William. *A New Voyage Round the World*. London: 1697. Wing D162.
d'Anghiera, Pietro Martire. *De nouo orbe, or the Historie of the West Indies*. London: 1612. STC 650.
____. *The Decades of the Newe Worlde or West India*. London: 1555. STC 645.
____. *The Famous Historie of the Indies*. London: 1628. STC 652.
____. *The Historie of the VVest Indies*. London: 1625. STC 651.
____. *The History of Trauayle in the VVest and East Indies*. London: 1577. STC 649.
D'avenant, William. *The Distresses*. London: 1673. Wing D320.
____. *The Just Italian*. London: 1630. STC 6303.
____. *The Man's the Master*. London: 1669. Wing D331.
____. *News from Plimouth*. London: 1673. Wing D320.

Bibliography

____. *The Platonick Lovers*. London: 1636. STC 6305.
____. *The Play-House to Be Let*. London: 1673. Wing D320.
____. *The Siege of Rhodes, Part I*. London: 1663. Wing D342.
____. *The Siege*. London: 1673. Wing D320.
____. *The Tempest*. London: 1670. Wing S2944.
____. *The Triumphs of the Prince D'amour*. London: 1635. STC 6308.
____. *The Unfortunate Lovers*. London: 1643. Wing D348.
____. *The Wits*. London: 1636. STC 6309.
Dawson, Thomas. *A Book of Cookery*. London: 1650. Wing B3705.
____. *The Good Husvvifes Iewell*. London: 1610. STC 6393.
____. *The Second Part of The Good Hus-wiues Iewell*. London: 1606. STC 6396.
de Acosta, Jose. *The Natvrall and Morall Historie of the East and West Indies*. London: 1604. STC 94.
de Feyens, Henri. *An Exact and Cvriovs Svrey of All the East Indies*. London: 1615. STC 10840.
Dekker, Thomas. *The Honest Whore, Part I*. London: 1604. STC 6501.
____. *The Honest Whore, Part II*. London: 1630. STC 6506.
____. *If It Be Not Good, the Diuel is in It*. London: 1612. STC 6507.
____. *Match Mee in London*. London: 1631. STC 6529.
____. *The Noble Sovldier*. London: 1634. STC 21416.
____. *The Roaring Girle*. London: 1611. STC 6512.
____. *Satiro-Matix*. London: 1602. STC 6521.
____. *The Shomakers Holiday*. London: 1600. STC 6523.
____. *The Sun's Darling*. London: 1656. Wing F1467.
____. *The Virgin Martir*. London: 1622. STC 17644a.
____. *West-Ward Hoe*. London: 1607. STC 6540.
____. *The Whore of Babylon*. London: 1607. STC 6532.
____. *The Witch o Edmonton*. London: 1658. Wing R2097.
____. *The Wonder of a Kingdome*. London: 1636. STC 6533.
Della, Pietro Valle. *The Travels of Sig. Pietro della Valle, a Noble Roman*. London: 1665. Wing V47.
Dellon, Gabriel. *A Voyage to the East-Indies*. London: 1698. Wing D943A.
Dennis, John. *A Plot and No Plot*. London: 1697. Wing D1038.
A Description of the Excellent Vertues of That Sober and Wholesome Drink, Called Coffee. London: 1674. Wing B4568.
Digby, Kenelm. *Choice and Experimental Receipts in Physick and Chirurgery*. London: 1668. Wing D1424.
____. *The Closet of the Eminently Learned Sir Kenelme Digbie*. London: 1669. Wing D1427.
Dilke, Thomas. *The City Lady*. London: 1697. Wing D1475.
____. *The Lover's Luck*. London: 1696. Wing D1476.
____. *The Pretenders*. London: 1698. Wing D1478.
Dogget, Thomas. *The Country Wake*. London: 1696. Wing D1828.
Drage, William. *A Physical Nosonomy*. London: 1665. Wing D2117.
Drake, Sir Francis. *Sir Francis Drake Revived*. London: 1652. Wing D84.
____. *The World Encompassed*. London: 1628. STC 7161.3.
Dryden, John. *Amboyna*. London: 1673. Wing D2232.
____. *The Assignation*. London: 1673. Wing D2241.
____. *Don Sebastian*. London: 1690. Wing D2262.
____. *An Evening's Love*. London: 1671. Wing D2273.

Bibliography

____. *King Arthur.* London: 1691. Wing D2299.
____. *The Spanish Fryar.* London: 1681. Wing D2368.
____. *Sr Martin Mar-All.* London: 1668. Wing D2359.
____. *Troilus and Cressida.* London: 1679. Wing D2389.
____. *The Wild Gallant.* London: 1669. Wing D2399.
Duffett, Thomas. *The Amorous Old-Woman.* London: 1674. Wing D2443.
____. *The Empress of Morocco.* London: 1674. Wing D2446.
____. *The Mock-Tempest.* London: 1675. Wing D2448.
____. *Psyche Debauch'd.* London: 1678. Wing D2452.
Dufour, Philippe Sylvestre. *The Manner of Making Coffee, Tea, and Chocolate.* London: 1685. Wing D2455.
Du Quesne, Abraham. *A New Voyage to the East-Indies.* London: 1696. Wing D2669.
D'Urfey, Thomas. *The Banditti.* London: 1686. Wing D2700.
____. *The Campaigners.* London: 1698. Wing D2705.
____. *A Common-Wealth of Women.* London: 1686. Wing D2715.
____. *Don Quixote, Part I.* London: 1694. Wing D2712A.
____. *Don Quixote, Part II.* London: 1694. Wing D2713.
____. *Don Quixote, Part III.* London: 1696. Wing D2756.
____. *A Fool's Preferment.* London: 1688. Wing D2729.
____. *The Intrigues at Versailles.* London: 1697. Wing D2736.
____. *Love for Money.* London: 1691. Wing D2740.
____. *Madam Fickle.* London: 1677. Wing D2743.
____. *The Marriage-Hater Match'd.* London: 1692. Wing D2749.
____. *The Richmond Heiress.* London: 1693. Wing D2769.
____. *The Rise and Fall of Massaniello, Part I.* London: 1700. Wing D2722.
____. *The Rise and Fall of Massaniello, Part II.* London: 1700. Wing D2722.
____. *The Royalist.* London: 1682. Wing D2770.
____. *The Siege of Memphis.* London: 1676. Wing D2777.
____. *Sir Barnaby Whigg.* London: 1681. Wing D2778.
____. *Trick for Trick.* London: 1678. Wing D2789.
____. *The Virtuous Wife.* London: 1680. Wing D2790.
The East-India Trade. London: 1693. Wing E101A.
The English Midwife Enlarged. London: 1682. Wing E3104A.
Etherege, George. *The Man of Mode.* London: 1676. Wing E3374.
____. *She Wou'd If She Cou'd.* London: 1671. Wing E3379.
Everie Woman in Her Humor. London: 1609. STC 25948.
Fane, Francis. *Love in the Dark.* London: 1671. Wing F408.
Fanshawe, Richard. *Il Pastor Fido.* London: 1647. Wing G2174.
Farquhar, George. *The Constant Couple.* London: 1700. Wing F517.
____. *Love and a Bottle.* London: 1699. Wing F518.
The Fayre Mayde of the Exchange. London: 1607. STC 13317.
Field, Nathan. *Amends for Ladies.* London: 1618. STC 10851.
____. *The Fatall Dowry.* London: 1632. STC 17646.
____. *The Honest Mans Fortune.* London: 1647. Wing B1581.
____. *A Woman is a Weather-Cocke.* London: 1612. STC 10854.
Fletcher, John. *The Beggars Bush.* London: 1647. Wing B1518.
____. *The Bloody Brother.* London: 1679. STC 11064.
____. *The Captaine.* London: 1647. Wing B1581.
____. *The Chances.* London: 1647. Wing B1581.
____. *The Custome of the Countrey.* London: 1647. Wing B1581.

Bibliography

_____. *The Elder Brother.* London: 1679. Wing B1582.
_____. *The Faire Maide of the Inne.* London: 1647. Wing B1581.
_____. *The Island Princesse.* London: 1647. Wing B1581.
_____. *The Lovers Progress.* London: 1647. Wing B1581.
_____. *The Loyal Subject.* London: 1647. Wing B1581.
_____. *The Maid in the Mill.* London: 1647. Wing B1581.
_____. *Monsieur Thomas.* London: 1679. Wing B1582.
_____. *The Pilgrim.* London: 1647. Wing B1581.
_____. *The Queene of Corinth.* London: 1647. Wing B1581.
_____. *Rule a Wife, and Have a Wife.* London: 1679. Wing B1582.
_____. *The Scornful Ladie.* London: 1616. STC 1686.
_____. *The Sea Voyage.* London: 1647. Wing B1581.
_____. *The Spanish Curat.* London: 1647. Wing B1581.
_____. *The Wild-Goose Chase.* London: 1652. Wing B1616.
_____. *Wit Without Money.* London: 1679. Wing B1582.
Fletcher, Phineas. *Sicelides.* London: 1631. STC 11083.
Ford, John. *The Lovers Melancholy.* London: 1629. STC 11163.
_____. *Perkin Warbeck.* London: 1634. STC 11157.
_____. *The Queen.* London: 1653. Wing Q155.
Fryer, John. *A New Account of East-India and Persia.* London: 1698. F2257.
Gage, Thomas. *The English-American His Travail by Sea and Land.* London: 1648. Wing G109.
Gardiner, Edmund. *The Triall of Tabacco.* London: 1610. STC 11564.
Gardyner, George. *A Description of the New World.* London: 1651. Wing G221.
Garway, Thomas. *An Exact Description of the Growth, Quality, and Vertues of the Leaf Tea.* London: 1660. Wing G282.
The Genteel House-Keepers Pastime. London: 1693. Wing G521.
The Gentlewomans Cabinet Unlocked. London: 1688. Wing G523dA.
The Gentlewomans Delight in Cookery. London: 1690. Wing G523eA.
The Ghost. London: 1653. Wing G641.
G.L. *The Gentleman's New Jockey.* London: 1691. Wing L20aA.
Glanius, W. *A New Account of East-India and Persia.* London: 1682. Wing G793.
Glapthorne, Henry. *The Hollander.* London: 1640. STC 11909.
_____. *Wit in a Constable.* London: 1640. STC 11914.
Goffe, Thomas. *The Careles Shepherdess.* London: 1656. Wing G1005.
Goldsmith, Francis. *Sophompaneas.* London: 1652. Wing 82125.
The Gossips Braule. London: 1655. Wing G1315.
Gould, Robert. *The Rival Sisters.* London: 1696. Wing 81434.
Granville, George. *The She-Gallants.* London: 1696. Wing L423.
Grey, Elizabeth, the Countess of Kent. *A Choice Manual of Rare and Select Secrets in Physick and Chyrurgery.* London: 1653. Wing K310A.
_____. *A True Gentlewomans Delight.* London: 1653. Wing K317A.
Harris, Joseph. *Love's a Lottery.* London: 1699. Wing H864.
Hartman, G. *The True Preserver and Restorer of Health.* London: 1682. Wing H1004.
Hausted, Peter. *The Rivall Friends.* London: 1632. STC 12735.
Hawkins, William. *Apollo Shroving.* London: 1627. STC 12963.
Hemings, William. *The Fatal Contract.* London: 1653. Wing H1422.
Hester, John. *The Secrets of Physick and Philosophy.* London: 1633. STC 19182.
Heywood, Thomas. *The English Traveller.* London: 1633. STC 13315.
_____. *The Fair Maid of the West, Part I.* London: 1631. STC 13320.

Bibliography

____. *If You Know Not Me, You Know No Bodie, Part I*. London: 1605. STC 13328.
____. *A Mayden-Head Well Lost*. London: 1634. STC 13357.
____. *Porta Pietatis*. London: 1638. STC 13359.
____. *The Rape of Lvcrece*. London: 1638. STC 13363.
____. *The Wise-Woman of Hogsdon*. London: 1638. STC 13370.
Higden, Henry. *The Wary Widdow*. London: 1693. Wing H1945.
An Historicall and True Discourse of a Voyage Made by the Admirall Cornelis Matelife the Yonger into the East Indies. London: 1608. STC 1765.
The History of the Tryall of Cheualry. London: 1605. STC 13527.
Holyday, Barten. *Technogamia*. London: 1618. STC 13617.
Hopkins, Charles. *Neglected Virtue*. London: 1696. Wing H2725.
Howard, Edward. *The Man of Newmarket*. London: 1678. Wing H2969.
____. *The Six Days Adventure*. London: 1671. Wing H2974.
Howard, Robert. *The Committee*. London: 1665. Wing H2995.
____. *The Indian-Queen*. London: 1665. Wing H2995.
Hughes, William. *The American Physitian*. London: 1672. Wing H3332.
James I, King of England. *A Counterblaste to Tobacco*. London: 1604. STC 14363.
Jonson, Ben. *The Alchemist*. London: 1616. STC 14751.
____. *Bartholmew Fayre*. London: 1640. STC 14754.
____. *Catiline His Conspiracy*. London: 1616. STC 14751.
____. *Christmas, His Masque*. London: 1640. Wing J1006.
____. *Cynthia's Revels*. London: 1616. STC 14751.
____. *Epicoene*. London: 1616. STC 14751.
____. *The Fortunate Isles, and Their Union*. London: 1640. Wing J1006.
____. *The Gypsies Metamorphos'd*. London: 1640. Wing J1006.
____. *The Magnetick Lady*. London: 1640. Wing J1006.
____. *The Masque of Owles*. London: 1640. Wing J1006.
____. *Mercurie Vindicated from the Alchemists*. London: 1616. STC 14751.
____. *The New Inne*. London: 1631. STC 14780.
____. *Poetaster*. London: 1616. STC 14751.
____. *The Staple of Newes*. London: 1640. STC 14754.
____. *Volpone*. London: 1616. STC 14751.
Jordan, Thomas. *The Walks of Islington*. London: 1657. Wing J1071.
Josselyn, John. *New Englands Rarities Discovered*. London: 1675. Wing J1094.
J.S. *The Accomplished Ladies Rich Closet of Rarities*. London: 1687. Wing S3498A.
Killigrew, Thomas. *The Princesse*. London: 1664. Wing K450.
____. *Thomaso, Part II*. London: 1664. Wing K450.
Kirke, John. *The Seven Champions of Christendome*. London: 1638. STC 15014.
The Knave in Graine, New Vampt. London: 1640. STC 6174.
La Varenne, François Pierre. *The French Cook*. London: 1673. Wing L625A.
Lacy, John. *The Dumb Lady*. London: 1672. Wing L143.
____. *Hercules Buffoon*. London: 1684. Wing L147.
____. *The Old Troop*. London: 1672. Wing L144.
____. *Sauny the Scott*. London: 1698. Wing L146.
____. *Tobacco, A Poem*. London: 1669. Wing L148A.
The Ladies Cabinet Enlarged and Opened. London: 1667. Wing B137.
The Ladies Cabinet Opened. London: 1639. STC 15119.
The Ladies Companion. London: 1653. Wing L152.
Lady. *The Whole Duty of a Woman: or a Guide to the Female Sex*. London: 1696. Wing W2054A.

Bibliography

Lady Alimony. London: 1659. Wing L164A.
Langland, William. *Piers Plowman: A New Translation from the B-Text.* Trans. A.V.C. Schmidt. Oxford: Oxford University Press, 1992.
Leanerd, John. *The Country Innocence.* London: 1677. Wing L795.
Levett, Christopher. *A Voyage Into New England.* London: 1624. STC 15553.5.
Ligon, Richard. *A True & Exact History of the Island of Barbados.* London: 1657. Wing L2075.
L.S. *The Noble Stranger.* London: 1640. STC 22377.
Lust's Dominion. London: 1657. Wing L3504AB.
Manley, Mrs. *The Lost Lover.* London: 1696. Wing M435.
Manuche, Cosmo. *The Just General.* London: 1652. Wing M549.
Markham, Gervase. *The English House-vvife.* London: 1631. STC 17353.
____. *Herod and Antipater.* London: 1622. STC 17402.
Marmion, Shackerley. *The Antiquary.* London: 1641. Wing M703.
____. *A Fine Companion.* London: 1633. STC 17442.
____. *Hollands Leaguer.* London: 1632. STC 17443.5.
Marnettè, Monsieur. *The Perfect Cook.* London: 1656. M706.
The Marriage-Broaker. London: 1662. Wing W84.
Marston, John. *Antonio and Mellida, Part I.* London: 1602. STC 17473.
____. *Antonio's Revenge, Part II.* London: 1602. STC 17474.
____. *The Fawne.* London: 1606. STC 17484.
____. *Iacke Drums Entertainment.* London: 1601. STC 7243.
____. *The Insatiate Countesse.* London: 1613. STC 17476.
____. *The Malcontent.* London: 1604. STC 17479.
____. *What You Will.* London: 1607. STC 17487.
The Maske of Flowers. London: 1614. STC 17624.
Mason, John. *The Turke.* London: 1610. STC 17617.
Massinger, Philip. *The Bond-Man.* London: 1624. STC 17632.
____. *The City-Madam.* London: 1658. Wing M1046.
____. *The Great Duke of Florence.* London: 1636. STC 17637.
____. *The Guardian.* London: 1655. Wing M1050.
____. *A New Way to Pay Old Debts.* London: 1633. STC 17639.
____. *The Pictvre.* London: 1630. STC 17640.5.
____. *A Very Woman.* London: 1655. Wing M1050.
May, Robert. *The Accomplisht Cook.* London: 1678. Wing M1393A.
Mayne, Jasper. *The Amorovs Warre.* London: 1648. Wing M1463.
____. *The Citye Match.* London: 1639. STC 17750.
Mead, Robert. *The Combat of Love and Friendship.* London: 1654. Wing M1564.
Merchant. *A State of the Present Condition of the Island of Barbadoes.* London: 1698. Wing S5323A.
Merchant, West-India. *A Brief Account of the Present Declining State of the West-Indies in Reference to its Trade, and in Particular, That of Barbadoes.* London: 1695. Wing B4514.
Meriton, Thomas. *Love and War.* London: 1658. Wing M1822.
The Merry Devill of Edmonton. London: 1608. STC 7493.
M.H. *The Young Cooks Monitor.* London: 1683. Wing H95.
Middleton, Thomas. *A Chast Mayd in Cheape-Side.* London: 1630. STC 17877.
____. *A Faire Quarrell.* London: 1617. STC 17911.
____. *The Familie of Love.* London: 1608. STC 17879.
____. *A Game at Chess.* London: 1625. STC 17883.

Bibliography

____. *A Mad World, My Masters.* London: 1608. STC 17888.
____. *More Dissemblers Besides.* London: 1657. Wing M1989.
____. *No Wit/Help Like a Womans.* London: 1657. Wing M1985.
____. *The Phoenix.* London: 1607. STC 17892.
____. *The Tryumphs of Honor and Industry.* London: 1617. STC 17899.
____. *The Widdow.* London: 1652. Wing J1015.
The Mistaken Husband. London: 1675. Wing D2318.
Motteux, Peter Anthony. *Europe's Revels for the Peace, and His Majesties Happy Return.* London: 1697. Wing M2948.
____. *Love's a Jest.* London: 1696. Wing M2953.
____. *The Novelty.* London: 1697. Wing M2958.
Mountfort, William. *Greenwich-Park.* London: 1691. Wing M2973.
____. *The Life and Death of Doctor Faustus.* London: 1697. Wing 2975.
____. *The Successfull Straingers.* London: 1690. Wing M2977.
Munday, Anthony. *The Trivmphes of Re-Vnited Britania.* London: 1605. STC 18279.
Murrell, John. *A Daily Exercise for Ladies and Gentlewomen.* London: 1617. STC 18301.
____. *Murrels Two Books of Cookerie and* Carving. London: 1638. STC 18303.
____. *A Nevv Booke of Cookerie.* London: 1615. STC 18299.
Nabbes, Thomas. *The Bride.* London: 1640. STC 18338.
____. *Covent Garden.* London: 1638. STC 18339.
____. *Microcosmus.* London: 1637. STC 18342.
____. *Totenham Court.* London: 1638. STC 18344.
The Nature, Quality, and Most Excellent Vertues of Coffee. London: 1670. Wing V646A.
N.D. *The Vertues of the Coffee.* London: 1663. Wing D72aA.
Ogilby, John. *Asia.* London: 1673. Wing O166.
Oldmixon, John. *Amintas.* London: 1698. Wing T173.
Olivier, Alexandre. *Bucaniers of America.* London: 1684. Wing E3894.
Otway, Thomas. *The Atheist.* London: 1684. Wing O541.
____. *Caius Marius.* London: 1680. Wing O549.
____. *The Souldiers Fortune.* London: 1681. Wing O562.
____. *Venice Preserv'd.* London: 1682. Wing O567.
Ovington, J. *An Essay Upon the Nature and Qualities of Tea.* London: 1699. Wing O700.
Papin, Denis. *A New Digester or Engine for Softning Bones.* London: 1681. Wing P309.
Partridge, John. *The Widdowes Treasure.* London: 1631. STC 19437.
Pathomachia. London: 1630. STC 19462.
Payne, Henry Neville. *The Morning Ramble.* London: 1673. Wing P892.
Pepys, Samuel. *The Diary of Samuel Pepys*, ed. Robert Latham and William Matthews. Vols. I-XI. London : HarperCollins, 2000.
A Perfect Description of Virginia. London: 1648. Wing P1486.
Pix, Mary. *The Beau Defeated.* London: 1700. Wing P2326.
____. *The Innocent Mistress.* London: 1697. Wing P2330.
Plantagenet, Beauchamp. *A Description of the Province of New Albion.* London: 1648. Wing P2378.
Plat, Hugh. *Delightes for Ladies.* London: 1608. STC 19980.
Porter, Thomas. *The Villain.* London: 1663. Wing P2995.
____. *A Witty Combat.* London: 1663. Wing P2998.
Powell, George. *Alphonso.* London: 1691. Wing P3047.

Bibliography

Poyntz, John. *The Present Prospect of the Famous and Fertile Island of Tobago.* London: 1695. Wing P3131.
Price, Samuel. *The Virtues of Coffee, Chocolette, and Thee or Tea, Experimentally Known in this Our* Climate. London: 1690. Wing P3398A.
Prince Giolo Son to the King of Moangis or Gilol. London: 1692. Wing P3484.
The Puritan. London: 1664. STC 17188.
Quarles, Francis. *The Virgin Widow.* London: 1649. Wing Q118.
The Queens Closet Opened. London: 1661. Wing M99A.
The Queens Closet Opened London: 1696. Wing M105.
A Queens Delight. London: 1675. Wing Q157A.
Rabisha, William. *The VVhole Body of Cookery Dissected.* London: 1661. Wing R114.
Randolph, Thomas. *Amyntas.* London: 1638. STC 20694.
____. *Aristippus.* London: 1630. STC 20686.5.
____. *Hey for Honesty, Down with Knavery.* London: 1651. Wing A3685.
____. *The Jealous Lovers.* London: 1632. STC 20692.
____. *The Muses Looking Glasse.* London: 1638. STC 200694.
Ravenscroft, Edward. *The Careless Lovers.* London: 1673. Wing R328.
____. *The Citizen Turn'd Gentleman.* London: 1672. Wing M2383A.
____. *The Italian Husband.* London: 1698. Wing R330.
____. *The London Cuckolds.* London: 1682. Wing R332.
Rawlins, Thomas. *The Rebellion.* London: 1640. STC 20770.
____. *Tunbridge Wells.* London: 1678. Wing R368.
Rebellions Antidote: or a Dialogue Between Coffee and Tea. London: 1685. Wing B131A.
The Returne from Pernassus. London: 1606. STC 19309.
Richards, Nathaniel. *Messallina.* London: 1640. STC 21011.
Rochefort, Charles-Cesar. *The History of the Caribby-Islands.* London: 1666. Wing R1740.
Rowley, William. *A Match at Mid-Night.* London: 1633. STC 21421.
____. *A Woman Never Vext.* London: 1632. STC 21423.
Ruthven, Patrick, the Earl of Forth and Brentford. *The Ladies Cabinet Enlarged and Opened Containing Many Rare Secrets.* London: 1654. Wing B135.
St. Serfe, Thomas. *Tarugo's Wiles.* London: 1668. Wing S6322.
A Satyr Against Coffee. London: 1674. Wing S709.
Scott, Thomas. *The Mock-Marriage.* London: 1696. Wing S2089A.
Sedley, Charles. *Bellamira.* London: 1687. Wing S2397.
____. *The Mulberry-Garden.* London: 1668. Wing S2402.
Settle, Elkanah. *The World in the Moon.* London: 1697. Wing S2730.
Shadwell, Thomas. *Bury-Fair.* London: 1689. Wing S2836.
____. *Epsom Wells.* London: 1673. Wing S2843.
____. *The Lancashire-Witches.* London: 1682. Wing S2853.
____. *The Miser.* London: 1672. Wing S2837.
____. *The Squire of Alsatia.* London: 1688. Wing S2874.
____. *The Sullen Lovers.* London: 1668. Wing S2878.
____. *The Tempest.* London: 1674. Wing S2945.
____. *A True Widow.* London: 1679. Wing S2881.
____. *The Virtuoso.* London: 1676. Wing S2883.
____. *The Volunteers.* London: 1693. Wing S2885.
Shakespeare, William. *The Merry Wiues of Windsor.* London: 1623. STC 22273.
____. *The Tempest.* London: 1623. STC 22273.

Bibliography

____. *Troylus and Cressida*. London: 1609. STC 22332.
____. *Twelfe Night*. London: 1623. STC 22273.
____. *The Two Noble Kinsmen*. London: 1634. STC 11075.
Sharpham, Edward. *Cvpid's Whirligig*. London: 1607. STC 22380.
____. *The Fleire*. London: 1607. STC 22384.
Shirley, James. *The Ball*. London: 1639. STC 4995.
____. *The Brothers*. London: 1652. Wing S3460.
____. *The Constant Maid*. London: 1640. STC 22438.
____. *The Coronation*. London: 1640. STC 22440.
____. *The Gamester*. London: 1637. STC 22443.
____. *Honoria and Mammon*. London: 1658. Wing S3473.
____. *The Hvmorovs Covrtier*. London: 1640. STC 22447.
____. *The Lady of Pleasvre*. London: 1637. STC 22448.
____. *The Royall Master*. London: 1638. STC 22454.
____. *St. Patrick for Ireland*. London: 1640. STC 22455.
____. *The Wedding*. London: 1629. STC 22460.
____. *The Wittie Faire One*. London: 1633. STC 22462.
Smith, John. *A Map of Virginia*. Oxford: 1612. STC 22791.
____. *The True Travels, Adventvres, and Observations of Captaine Iohn Smith*. London: 1608. STC 22796.
Southerne, Thomas. *The Disappointment*. London: 1684. Wing D2334.
____. *The Fatal Marriage*. London: 1694. Wing S4756.
____. *The Maid's Last Prayer*. London: 1693. Wing S4760.
____. *Oroonoko*. London: 1696. Wing S4761.
____. *The Wives Excuse*. London: 1692. Wing S4769.
Strode, William. *The Floating Island*. London: 1655. Wing S5983.
Suckling, John. *Aglaura*. London: 1638. STC 23420.
Tailor, Robert. *The Hogge Hath Lost His Pearle*. London: 1614. STC 23658.
Tavernier, Jean-Baptiste. *Collections of Travel Through Turky into Persia*. London: 1684. Wing T251.
Terry, Edward. *A Voyage to East-India*. London: 1655. Wing T782.
Thomas Lord Cromwell. London: 1664. STC 6991.
Thorny-Abbey. London: 1662. Wing G1580.
Tillinghast, Mary. *Rare and Excellent Receipts*. London: 1690. Wing T1183.
Tomkis, Thomas. *Albumazar*. London: 1615. STC 24101.
____. *Lingva*. London: 1607. STC 24104.
A Treatise of Nevv England. London: 1645. Wing T2092A.
The True Way of Preserving and Candying. London: 1681. Wing T3126A.
Tryon, Thomas. *A Pocket-Companion*. London: 1693. Wing T3192.
Tuke, Samuel. *The Adventures of Five Hours*. London: 1663. Wing T3229.
Turquet de Mayerne, Théodore. *Archimagirus Anglo-Gallicus*. London: 1658. Wing M1427.
The Two Merry Milke-Maids. London: 1620. STC 428.
Two Wise Men and All the Rest Fooles. London: 1619. STC 4991.
Vanbrugh, John. *Aesop*. London: 1697. Wing V53.
____. *The Pilgrim*. London: 1700. Wing F1349.
____. *The Provok'd Wife*. London: 1697. Wing V55.
____. *The Relapse*. London: 1697. Wing V57.
Venner, Tobias. *A Briefe and Accurate Treatise, Concerning, the Taking of the Fume Tobacco*. London: 1621. STC 24642.

Bibliography

The Vertue of the Coffee Drink. London: 1652. Wing V645B.
The Vertue of the Coffee Drink. London: 1660. Wing V646.
The Vertues of Chocolate East India Drink. London: 1660. Wing V648.
The Virtues of Coffee, Chocolette, and Thee or Tea. London: 1690. Wing P3398A.
Webster, John. *The Dutchesse of Malfy.* London: 1623. STC 25176.
____. *The White Divel.* London: 1612. STC 25178.
White, George. *An Account of the Trade to the East Indies Together with the State of the Present.* London: 1691. Wing W1768.
Wild, Robert. *The Benefice.* London: 1689. Wing W2123.
Wilkins, George. *The Miseries of Inforst Mariage.* London: 1607. STC 25635.
Wilson, John. *Belphegor.* London: 1691. Wing W2914.
____. *The Cheats.* London: 1664. Wing W2916.
Wily Beguilde. London: 1606. Wing P2538.
Wine, Beere, and Ale. London: 1629. STC 11542.
The Wisdome of Doctor Dodypoll. London: 1600. STC 6991.
W.M. *The Compleat Cook.* London: 1663. Wing M92A.
Woolley, Hannah. *The Accomplish'd Ladies Delight in Preserving, Physick, Beautifying, and Cookery.* London: 1683. Wing W3270.
____. *The Compleat Servant-Maid.* London: 1683. Wing W3273B.
Wycherley, William. *The Country Wife.* London: 1675. Wing W3738.
____. *The Plain-Dealer.* London: 1677. Wing W3749.
Zouch, Richard. *The Sophister.* London: 1639. STC 26133.

Secondary Sources

Albala, Ken. *The Banquet: Dining in the Great Courts of Late Renaissance Europe.* Urbana: University of Illinois Press, 2007.
____. "Cookbooks as Sources for Food History." In *The Oxford Handbook of Food History,* Edited by Jeffrey Pilcher. Oxford University Press, 2012.
____. *Eating Right in the Renaissance.* Berkeley: University of California Press, 2002.
____. *Food in Early Modern Europe.* Westport: Greenwood Press, 2003.
Amussen, Susan Dwyer. *Caribbean Exchanges: Slavery and the Transformation of English Society 1640–1700.* Chapel Hill: University of North Carolina Press, 2007.
Appelbaum, Robert. *Aguecheek's Beef, Belch's Hiccup, and Other Gastronomic Interjections: Literature, Culture, and Food Among the Early Moderns.* Chicago: The University of Chicago Press, 2006.
Appleby, Joyce. "Consumption in Early Modern Social Thought." In *Consumption and the World of Goods.* Edited by John Brewer and Ray Porter. Routledge: London and New York, 1993.
Ashtor, E. "Profits from Trade with the Levant in the Fifteenth Century." In *Bulletin of the School on Oriental and African Studies, University of London* vol. 38 no. 2 (1975): 250–275.
Baer, Joel H. "Dampier, William (1651–1715)." In *Oxford Dictionary of National Biography.* Oxford: Oxford University Press, 2004.
Bevington, David, et al. *English Renaissance Drama: A Norton Anthology.* New York: W.W. Norton & Company, Inc., 2002.
Bickham, Troy. "Eating the Empire: Intersections of Food, Cookery, and Imperialism in Eighteenth-Century Britain." In *Past and Present* no. 198 (2008): 71–109.

Bibliography

Brewer, John. *The Pleasures of the Imagination: English Culture in the Eighteenth Century.* New York: Farrar, Straus, and Giroux, 1997.
Carr, Archie. *So Excellent a Fish.* New York: Charles Scribner's, 1967.
Clarence-Smith, William Gervase. *Cocoa and Chocolate 1765–1914.* London: Routledge, 2000.
Clarkson, L.A., and E. Margaret Crawford. *Feast and Famine: Food and Nutrition in Ireland 1500–1920.* Oxford: Oxford University Press, 2001.
Colquhoun, Kate. *Taste: The Story of Britain Through Its Cooking.* New York: Bloomsbury, 2007.
Cowan, Brian. *The Social Life of Coffee: The Emergence of the British Coffeehouse.* New Haven: Yale University Press, 2005.
Cressy, David. *Literacy and Social Order: Reading & Writing in Tudor & Stuart England.* Cambridge: Cambridge University Press, 1980.
Crosby, Alfred W., Jr. *The Columbian Exchange: Biological and Cultural Consequences of 1492.* Westport, Connecticut: Praeger, 1973.
_____. *Ecological Imperialism: The Biological Expansion of Europe, 900–1900.* Cambridge: Cambridge University Press, 1986.
Curry, Patrick. "Blagrave, Joseph (b. 1610, d. in or before 1682). In *Oxford Dictionary of National Biography.* Oxford: Oxford University Press, 2004.
_____. "Culpeper, Nicholas (1616–1654)." In *Oxford Dictionary of National Biography.* Oxford: Oxford University Press, 2004.
Dalby, Andrew. *Dangerous Tastes: The Story of Spices.* Berkeley: University of California Press, 2000.
Davidson, Alan. *The Oxford Companion to Food.* Edited by Tom Jaines. Oxford: Oxford University Press, 2006.
DiMeo, Michelle, and Rebecca Laroche. "On Elizabeth Isham's 'Oil of Swallows': Animal Slaughter and Early Modern Women's Medical Recipes." In *Ecofeminist Approaches to Early Modernity,* ed. Jennifer Munroe and Rebecca Laroche. New York: Palgrave Macmillan, 2011.
Elton, G.R. *England Under the Tudors.* London: Routledge, 1955.
Fitzpatrick, Joan. *Food in Shakespeare: Early Modern Dietaries and the Plays.* Burlington: Ashgate, 2007.
Foster, Michael. 'Digby, Sir Kenelm (1603–1665).' In *Oxford Dictionary of National Biography.* Oxford: Oxford University Press, 2004.
Freedman, Paul. *Out of the East: Spices and the Medieval Imagination.* New Haven: Yale University Press, 2008.
Gately, Iain. *Tobacco: A Cultural History of How an Exotic Plant Seduced Civilization.* New York: Grove Press, 2001.
Gilbert, Erik, and Jonathan T. Reynolds. *Trading Tastes: Commodity and Cultural Exchange to 1750.* Upper Saddle River: Pearson Prentice Hall, 2006.
Goffman, Daniel. *The Ottoman Empire and Early Modern Europe.* Cambridge: Cambridge University Press, 2002.
Goodman, Jordan. *Tobacco in History: The Cultures of Dependence.* London: Routledge, 1993.
Goodwin, Gordon. "John Josselyn (c. 1608–1700)." In *Oxford Dictionary of National Biography.* Oxford: Oxford University Press, 2004.
Gurr, Andrew. *Playgoing in Shakespeare's London.* 3rd Edition. Cambridge: Cambridge University Press, 2004.
Hope, Anette. *Londoners' Larder: English Cuisine from Chaucer to the Present.* London: Mainstream Publishing, 2005.

Bibliography

Jones, Adam, ed. *West Africa in the Mid-Seventeenth Century: An Anonymous Dutch Manuscript.* New Brunswick, NJ: African Studies Association Press, 1995.
Keay, John. *The Spice Route: A History.* Berkeley: University of California Press, 2006.
Krondl, Michael. *The Taste of Conquest: The Rise and Fall of Three Great Spice Cities.* New York: Ballentine Books, 2007.
Kupperman, Karen Ordahl. "Ligon, Richard (c. 1588–1662)." In *Oxford Dictionary of National Biography.* Oxford: Oxford University Press, 2004.
Latham, Robert. "The Diary as a History." In *The Diary of Samuel Pepys.* ed. Robert Latham and William Matthews. Berkeley: University of California Press, 2000.
Lehmann, Gilly. *The British Housewife: Cookery Books, Cooking and Society in Eighteenth-Century Britain.* Blackawton: Prospect Books, 2003.
Loveman, Kate. "The Introduction of Chocolate into England: Retailers, Researchers, and Consumers, 1640–1730." *Journal of Social History* vol. 47 no. 1 (2013): 27–46.
McConnell, Anita. "Exotic visitors (act. c. 1500-c. 1855)." In *Oxford Dictionary of National Biography.* Oxford: Oxford University Press, 2004.
McElligott, Jason. "Crouch, Nathaniel [Robert Burton] (c. 1640–1725?)." In *Oxford Dictionary of National Biography.* Oxford: Oxford University Press, 2004.
McWilliams, James E. *A Revolution in Eating: How the Quest for Food Shaped America.* New York: Columbia University Press, 2005.
McWilliams, Mark. "The American Pumpkin." In *Vegetables: Proceedings of the Oxford Symposium on Food and Cookery 2008*, ed. Susan R. Friedland. Blackawton: Prospect Books, 2009.
Mendelson, Sara, and Patricia Crawford, *Women in Early Modern England 1550–1720.* Oxford: Oxford University Press, 1998.
Mintz, Sidney W. "The Changing Roles of Food in the Study of Consumption." In *Consumption and the World of Goods,* Edited by John Brewer and Ray Porter. Routledge: London and New York, 1993.
_____. *Sweetness and Power: The Place of Sugar in the Modern World.* New York: Penguin Books, 1985.
Morrill, John. "Cromwell, Oliver (1599–1658)." In *Oxford Dictionary of National Biography.* Oxford University Press, 2004.
Norton, Marcy. *Sacred Gifts, Profane Pleasures: A History of Tobacco and Chocolate in the Atlantic World.* Ithaca: Cornell University Press, 2008.
Okihiro, Gary. *Pineapple Culture: A History of the Tropical and Temperate Zones* Berkeley and Los Angeles: University of California Press, 2009.
Oldfield, J.R. *Popular Politics and British Anti-Slavery: The Mobilisation of Public Opinion Against the Slave Trade, 1787–1807.* London: Routledge, 1998.
Oliver, Roland, and Anthony Atmore. *The African Middle Ages, 1400–1800.* Cambridge: Cambridge University Press, 1981.
Pagden, Anthony. *Peoples and Empires: A Short History of European Migration, Exploration, and Conquest, from Greece to Present.* New York: The Modern Library, 2001.
Pennell, Sara. *The Birth of the English Kitchen 1600–1850.* London: Bloomsbury Academic, 2016.
Pettigrew, Jane, and Bruce Richardson. *A Social History of Tea: Tea's Influence on Commerce, Culture & Community.* Danville: Benjamin Press, 2014.
Shammas, Carole. *The Pre-Industrial Consumer in England and America.* Oxford: Oxford University Press, 1990.
_____. "The Revolutionary Impact of European Demand for Tropical Goods." In *The*

Bibliography

Early Modern Atlantic Economy, ed. John J. McCusker and Kenneth Morgan. Cambridge: Cambridge University Press, 2000.
Sherman, Arnold A. "Pressures from Leadenhall: The East India Company Lobby, 1660–1678." In *The Business History Review* vol. 50 no. 3 (1976): 329–355.
Sherman, Sandra. "The Pineapple in England." In *Petits Propos Culinaries* no. 81 (2006): 46–67.
Smith, Andrew F. "The Fall and Rise of the Edible Turkey." In *Proceedings of the Oxford Symposium on Food and Cookery 2004: Wild Food*. Blackawton: Prospect Books, 2006.
Stewart, Amy. *The Drunken Botanist: The Plants That Create the World's Great Drinks*. Chapel Hill: Algonquin Books of Chapel Hill, 2013.
Stine, Jennifer K. "Opening Closets: The Discovery of Household Medicine in Early Modern England." PhD diss.: Stanford University, 1996.
Tannahill, Reay. *Food in History*. New York: Three Rivers Press, 1988.
Thirsk, Joan. *Food in Early Modern England: Phases, Fads, Fashions 1500–1760* London: Hambledon Continuum, 2007.
Toussaint-Samat, Maguelonne. *A History of Food*. Oxford: Wiley-Blackwell, 1992.
Turner, Jack. *Spice: The History of Temptation*. New York: Vintage, 2005.
Ukers, William H. *All About Coffee*. 2nd Edition. Mansfield Centre, CT: Martino Publishing, 2011.
Van Den Boogaart, Ernst. "The Trade between Western Africa and the Atlantic World, 1600–90: Estimates of Trends in Composition and Value." In *The Journal of African History* vol. 33 no. 3 (1992): 369–385.
Vester, Katharina. *A Taste of Power: Food and American Identities*. Oakland: University of California Press, 2015.
Vickery, Amanda. *The Gentleman's Daughter: Women's Lives in Gregorian England*. New Haven: Yale University Press, 1998.
Wall, Wendy. *Recipes for Thought: Knowledge and Taste in the Early Modern English Kitchen*. Philadelphia: University of Pennsylvania Press, 2016.
Watt, Tessa. *Cheap Print and Popular Piety, 1550–1640*. Cambridge: Cambridge University Press, 1991.
Wear, Andrew. *Knowledge and Practice in English Medicine, 1550–1680*. Cambridge: Cambridge University Press, 2000.
Willis, John E., Jr. "European Consumption and Asian Production in the 17th and 18th centuries." In *Consumption and the World of Goods*, ed. John Brewer and Roy Porter. London: Routledge, 1993.
Withey, Alun. "Crossing the Boundaries: Domestic Recipe Collections in Early Modern Wales." In *Reading and Writing Recipe Books 1550–1800*, ed. Michelle DiMeo and Sara Pennell. Manchester: Manchester University Press, 2013.

Index

Abbay, Thomas 22–23
ague 103, 108
ague tree 26, 113
Alcorne, Richard 85
ale 82, 105, 112, 122–123, 141, 154–155
Alexander, Sir William 26
almonds 13, 40, 92, 107, 119
amber 69, 80, 105
amber-grease 45, 100
annatto 24–25
anniseed 40, 82, 119
apples 24, 79, 92
apricots 80
aqua mirabilis 102–104, 106
aqua vita 107
Arabia 46–47, 119, 141, 145–146
Argyll, Countess of 126
artichoke 24, 92
avocado 15, 33
Ayers, Phillip 40
Azores 27

banana 34
Barbados 12, 32–33, 38–39, 88
Bay of Panama 33
Beaumont, Francis 15, 53
beer 61, 112–113, 122–123, 141, 154
Behn, Aphra 61
Bellamy, Doctor
Bent, Mary 92–93
Biskar, Hannah 83
Blagrave, Joseph 95–96, 98, 103–108, 111–114, 116–120
Blome, Richard 31, 38, 40
Boothby, Richard 44–45
Bradley, Richard 88

Braganza, Catherine of 125–126
brandy 59, 67
Brazil 38, 139
Brereton, John 27
Brillat-Savarin, Jean Anthelme 152
Brome, Richard 67
Brugis, Thomas 102–105
Brumwich, Anne 110
Burgh, Nicholas 24, 31
butter 7, 10, 33, 82–84, 86, 88, 92–93, 104, 154

Cabot, John 11
cake 29, 79–80, 82–84
Cape of Good Hope 11, 13, 46, 132
Cape St. Anthony 31
capers 23
cardamom 45, 102
Carr, Mrs. 93
Cartwright, William 58
cassado 24
cassia 65–66
castoreum 100
Chamberlayne, John 116, 118–120, 138
Chamberlayne, Thomas 107
Chapman, George 49–50
Chardin, Sir John 47
Charles I (King of England) 12
Charles II (King of England) 13, 55, 90, 125–126
Charles V (King of Spain) 90
cheesecake 82, 90
Child, Josiah 45
Chile (country) 138
chili (pepper) 40, 138
China 44–45, 65, 126, 147–150

213

Index

chocolate 2, 12–13, 17, 40–42, 48, 61, 64–65, 69–71, 93–94, 118–120, 123–124, 126–127, 134–140, 145, 147–149, 151–152, 155–160
chocolate house 64
Cibber, Colley 63
cinnamon 6, 9, 11, 13, 26, 40, 45, 56–57, 64–65, 67, 81–84, 93, 102, 106–108, 119
citron 92
civet 100
Clarke, Samuel 26, 38
Cleveland, Duchess of 90
cloves 6, 9, 13, 15, 44–45, 58–59, 67, 80–84, 93, 102, 105–106, 108, 110, 115, 154
cochineal 12
Cock, Thomas 105
cocoa 2, 15, 40–41, 93, 118–119, 134–135, 138, 152
coconut 45
coffee 2, 13, 17, 46–47, 61, 62, 65, 94, 116, 118–120, 122–127, 137–149, 151–152, 156–158, 160
coffee house 17, 61–62, 64, 120, 124–126, 140, 145, 156–157
Colemenero de Ledesma, Antonio 134–134, 138
Collins, John 85
Colmento, Antonio 40
Columbus, Christopher 10, 30, 90
Congreve, William 58–59, 62–64
Cooper, Joseph 82, 91
Cortés, Hernán 134
cotton 7, 13
Creed, John 155–156
Cromwell, Elizabeth 72–73
Cromwell, Oliver 72–73
Crouch, Nathaniel 22, 27, 29, 44
Crowns, John 62
Cuba 41
cubebs 45, 102
Culpepper, Thomas 95
cumin 13

da Gama, Vasco 11
Dalby, Thomas 38, 40
Dampier, William 15, 19–21, 31–34, 38, 40, 42–48
d'Anghiera, Pietro Martire 30

D'Avenant, William 57
Dawson, Thomas 79, 81, 86, 91, 102
de Acosta, Jose 40
Dekker, Thomas 58, 67
de La Varenne, François Pierre 88
della Valle, Pietro 46
Dellon, Gabriel 45
de Vadesforte, Don Diego 134–135
diamonds 65
Digby, Sir Kenelem 103, 106, 114
Dilke, Thomas 63, 69
Doctor Steven's Water 102–104, 106
Drage, William 113
Drake, Sir Francis 31, 34, 38, 40, 91
Dryden, John 56, 60
Dufour, Philippe Sylvestre 138–139, 145–146, 148–149
Du Quesne, Abraham 45
D'Urfey, Thomas 49–50, 56, 59–63, 67, 69

East India Company (EIC) 13, 22, 45, 124–125, 154
East Indies 20, 34, 42–47, 132
Elizabeth I (Queen of England) 12–13, 23, 103–104, 107, 113–114, 117
Etherege, Sir George 59
Eyton, Amy 83

Fanshawe, Sir Richard 69
Ferdinand II of Aragon 30, 90
Fletcher, John 53–54, 69
Fort St. George 43
Forth and Brentford, Earl of 109–111
frankincense 7, 100
Fryer, John 45–46

Gage, Thomas 38, 40, 42
galangal 13, 45, 102
Galen (Galenic medicine) 10, 50, 66, 68, 98–99
Gardiner, Edmund 130
Garway, Thomas 147–148
Gascocke, Rowland 24, 31
Geoctroyeerde Westindische Compagnie (GWIC) 14
ginger 6, 9, 13, 15, 45, 81–82, 84–85, 102
gingerbread 67, 84
Giolo, Prince 19

214

Index

Glapthorne, Henry 60
Godfrey, Catherine 83, 92
Godfrey, Mary Faussett 92
gold 11, 14, 22, 30, 45, 48, 101, 128
grapefruit 12
green beans 12
Guadeloupe (Island of) 90
guaiacum 6, 68, 111–112, 115
Guam 20
guava 15, 33–34

Harris, Joseph 56
Hartman, G. 85, 102–103, 113
hazelnut 12, 40, 119
Henrietta Maria (Queen of England) 53, 106
Henry VII (King of England) 11
Hester, John 107
Higden, Henry 57–58
Hirst, Elizabeth 110
Hispaniola 30, 41, 72
Holyday, Barten 68
honey 64, 110, 155
Howard, Edward 57
Howard, Sir Robert 57
Hughes, William 32–33, 40–42
Humoral Theory (humors) 5, 10, 26–27, 50, 66, 73, 81, 98–101, 111, 113, 129, 134, 138
Hyde, Bridget 83, 113

India (East India) 3, 11 12, 24, 42–43, 45, 130, 137, 149
Isabella I of Castile 23
ivory 14

Jacob, Elizabeth 113, 117
Jamaica 12, 41
Jamaica pepper 12, 41, 81, 84–86
James I (King of England) 17, 68, 116, 127–130
Jesuits Powder 26
Johnson, Ben 60, 68
Josselyn, John 25–27

Kidder, Catherine 115
Kidder, Edward 115

Lacy, John 132–133
lavender 7

lemons 33, 72, 82–83, 92
Levant Company 13, 124
Levett, Christopher 26
Ligon, Richard 32, 34–36, 38–40
mace 45, 67, 81–85, 92–93, 102–106, 108, 154
maize 12, 24, 29
mallows 7, 80
mangos 43–44
marjoram 7, 115
Markham, Gervase 87, 109
Marnettè, Monsieur 92
marshmallows 80
mead 61, 86, 106
melons 92
metheglin 106, 114
Mexico 41, 138
Middleton, Thomas 53, 57
molasses 38–39
Morton, Robert 142
Motteux, Peter Anthony 58, 61–62
Mountfort, William 56, 58, 64, 68
Murrell, John 79, 91
muscadine 80, 106–107, 111, 114–115
musk 40, 45, 100
myrrh 65

nasturtium 12
Native Americans (Indians) 25–27, 29, 41, 117, 128, 132, 135
New England 22, 25, 29–30
New Spain 41, 138
Newcastle, Duchess of (Margaret Cavendish) 66
Nicaragua 41
nutmeg 6, 9, 11, 13, 15, 44–45, 57–58, 67, 80–86, 88, 92–93, 102–106, 108, 154–155
nutmeg grater 57–58

Ogilby, John 46–47
olive oil 7
olives 82
Olivier, Alexandre 40
omelet 90
opium 63–63
oranges 58–59, 72, 89, 92, 154
Ottoman Empire 13–14
Ovington, J. 150–151

215

Index

pancakes 82, 84
Parker, Jane 83
Parliament 54
Partridges, John 108, 11
peanuts 12
pearls 45, 65
pepper 6, 9, 11, 24, 45, 46, 81–86, 93, 119, 138, 154; chili 42, 138; East Indian 42; long red 40, 119; alaguetta 14
Pepys, Elizabeth 154
Pepys, Samuel 152–157
Peru 20, 49, 129
Philippines 19, 20, 40
pie 34, 49, 78, 80, 83, 87, 91–92, 153
pineapple 2, 11–12, 15, 24, 30, 34–37, 42, 89–92, 158–159
pippin 80, 82, 90
plague 54, 100, 114, 155
plague water 104, 115
plantain 6–7, 15–16, 33–34, 42, 69–70, 108–111, 157
Plymouth 29
Porter, Thomas 62
potato 11–12, 15–16, 23–24, 29, 32–33, 42, 48–50, 56, 69, 89, 91–92, 152, 157, 159
Powhatan 23
Poyntz, John 32, 34, 36
Price, Samuel 139, 146
prickle-Pears 24
pudding 80–82, 91–93, 125
pumpkins 2, 11, 56, 71, 89–90, 92–93

Rabisha, William 90, 115
Raleigh, Sir Walter 12, 90–91, 123, 132–133
Randolph, Thomas 60, 65
Ravenscroft, Edward 69
resin 7, 100
River of Cambodia 43
Roanoke Island 12
Rochefort, Charles-Cesar 31
rose water 90, 92–93, 106–107
Rose, John 90
Rosée, Pasqua 124
rosemary 7, 80, 82, 115
roses 40, 110
Royal African Company 14
rum 29, 39, 94

saffron 13
sage 7, 82
St. Christopher Island 24
Saint John, Johanna 112, 115
St. John's Wart 7
Santo Domingo 35
sarsaparilla 111–115
sassafrass 23, 26, 68, 111–115
scoth collops 82–83, 86
Sedley, Sir Charles 62–63
Shadwell, Thomas 63
Shakespeare, William 2, 49–50, 53, 60, 69
Shirley, James 49
Silk Road 46, 71
Simons, Thomas 24, 31
slavery (slaves) 4, 12, 14, 38–39, 81, 128, 131, 143
Sleigh, Elizabeth 92
smallpox 19, 109
Smith, John 22–26
Southerne, Thomas 63
squash 12
Stubbe, Henry 124
Suckling, Sir John 58
sugar 3, 6, 9–12, 14–16, 29, 32–33, 38–42, 45, 48, 58, 61, 67, 78–82, 90, 92–93, 104, 116–117, 119, 146, 152–154, 156, 159; cakes 79; candy 45, 104, 114, 146; cane 29, 39, 78–79; loaf 58, 67, 154; lump 38–39; works 38
Sumatra 20
sweet potatoes 32–33
syphilis 111–113

tart 82, 90, 92
Tavernier, John-Baptiste 47
tea 13, 17, 44, 61–65, 94, 120, 122–127, 147–152, 160
tea house 64
Terry, Edward 45
Tillinghast, Mary 91
tobacco 6–7, 17, 24, 26–27, 45–48, 59, 68–70, 115–118, 123, 126–133, 151, 155, 159–160
tobacconists 155
tomato 12
tortoise 15–16, 24, 31–32, 59–60, 88–89, 157

216

Index

Townshend Family 80
treacle 67
turkey 2, 11–12, 16, 23, 25, 29, 59–61, 83, 86–86, 89, 153, 156, 159
turpentine 7
turtles 24, 31, 45, 88

vanilla 12, 138–139
Venner, Doctor Tobias 132
Vereenigde Oost-Indische Compagnie (VOC) 13
Virginia 12, 22–23, 26–27, 123
Virginia Company 12

Wadsworth, Capt. James 135
watermelon 26

Webster, John 53, 57
West Indies 20, 30, 34, 40, 42, 72, 130, 134
White, George 45
Whitfield, Felicia 92
Wilson, John 56
wine 24, 29, 46, 63, 66–67, 102, 104, 106, 115–116, 122–123, 141, 145, 154, 157; claret 61, 66, 80, 82, 105, 145; malmsey 104; sack 93, 105, 136; sherry 67, 145; white 83, 85, 93, 106–107, 110
woundwort 7

yam 15, 32–33
Yucatan 138

www.ingramcontent.com/pod-product-compliance
Ingram Content Group UK Ltd.
Pitfield, Milton Keynes, MK11 3LW, UK
UKHW041955140426
5217IPUK00015B/809